Christian Education on the Plains of Texas:

A History of the School of Religious Education at Southwestern Baptist Theological Seminary, 1915-2015

Jack D. Terry, Jr.

SEMINARY HILL
PRESS

Christian Education on the Plains of Texas: A History of the School of Religious Education at Southwestern Baptist Theological Seminary, 1915-2015
By Jack D. Terry, Jr.
Copyright © 2018 by Seminary Hill Press

Seminary Hill Press (SHP) is the publishing arm of Southwestern Baptist Theological Seminary, 2001 West Seminary Drive, Fort Worth, Texas 76115.

All rights reserved. No part of this book may be used or reproduced in any manner whatsoever without written permission from SHP except in the case of brief quotations embodied in critical articles and reviews. For more information, visit seminaryhillpress.com/licensing/permissions.

All Scripture quotations, unless otherwise indicated, are from the New American Standard Bible® (NASB), Copyright © 1960, 1962, 1963, 1968, 1971, 1972, 1973, 1975, 1977, 1995 by The Lockman Foundation. Used by permission. (www.Lockman.org)

Hardback
ISBN-10: 0-9994119-3-4
ISBN-13: 978-0-9994119-3-3

Paperback
ISBN-10: 0-9994119-4-2
ISBN-13: 978-0-9994119-4-0

DEDICATION

To Barbara, my loving, devoted, encouraging wife for over 62 years. You have been my strength, my stability, my compass, and my finest loving critic. Without your tenacity and steadfastness in the Word of God and constancy in prayer, I would be just another minister and seminary professor doing good things but not doing the very best things that you challenged me to attempt and accomplish. Your patience and lovingkindness through these long months of research, your willingness to spend many hours alone while I sat just a room away at the computer, and your gentle touch that told me you understood what needed to be done can never be repaid in a lifetime. I thank God from the depth of my soul for giving you to me as the perfect companion in life and ministry.

Thank you, my loving wife and best friend. You completely fulfill the injunction in Proverbs 31:30—"Charm is deceitful and beauty is vain, but a woman who fears the Lord, she shall be praised."

Table of Contents

PREFACE	7
CHAPTER 1 SCHOOL OF RELIGIOUS PEDAGOGY ON THE PLAINS OF TEXAS	11
CHAPTER 2 THE CALLED—WILL THEY CONTINUE TO COME?	47
CHAPTER 3 UNPRECEDENTED GROWTH CONTINUES	119
CHAPTER 4 MAJOR CHANGES IN PRESIDENTIAL LEADERSHIP	187
CHAPTER 5 THE SCHOOL OF EDUCATIONAL MINISTRIES IN THE 21ST CENTURY	247
CHAPTER 6 THE EVOLUTION OF A SCHOOL	317
AFTERWORD	357
INDEX	359

Preface

In the spring of 2013, President Paige Patterson asked me to write a 100-year history of the department of religious education founded by J.M. Price in 1915. The task was to research and write a history of the school from its inception as a department in 1915 to its present nomenclature as the Jack D. Terry, Jr. School of Church and Family Ministries in 2015. The request was at first intimidating because of the lack of published information about the school and at best overwhelming in its imagined scope. Where were published materials about the school, if any, and where would they reside in published form? The challenge was awe-inspiring but something that needed to be done. I accepted the assignment with fear and trepidation, knowing somewhere printed materials would be available, but where and in what form?

The first line of inquiry would be the trustee minutes, general faculty minutes, and faculty minutes from the department of religious education and then the school of religious education. Each set of minutes was extremely helpful and provided a wealth of insightful information about the historical activities involved in each of the years. A personal thanks to President Patterson for making the trustee minutes from his administration available for investigation and historical reporting. J.M. Price wrote one small paper on the history of the school from its beginning to 1942 that was most helpful, as did Joe Davis Heacock in preparation for his Founder's Day address on J.M. Price. Bits and pieces floated together from campus activities, such as the Southwestern Baptist Religious Education Association (SWBREA) meeting minutes. The SWBREA was organized by J.M. Price in the late 1920s and continued meeting annually on the campus until the late 1980s. Robert Baker's *Tell the Generations Following*, although a history of the seminary per se, contained excerpts from each of the schools' activities and became a helpful source of information.

Southwestern News, the seminary's magazine (since 1943), became a major source for stories about the activities and educational institutes and workshops going on during the years. The development of Youth Ministry Lab in 1968 became a regular feature reported in each of its 47 years. Reading through over 50 years of Southwestern News (some years six editions, and others four) jogged my memory with many interesting stories, activities, happenings, and undertakings that had been forgotten but were brought back to shed light on major activities of the school. Other ancillary documents—such as The Baptist Standard of Texas, The Fort Worth Star-Telegram, and other convention state papers—reported interesting insights about happenings on the campus as well. I am grateful to many of my colleagues and friends who have shared their recollections of events and activities that formed the fabric of the education school during the ensuing years.

I am grateful to Drew Dowden, a Ph.D. graduate in the Terry School who became my research assistant for a six-month period while waiting for a teaching position at a Christian educational institution. He was my "search engine," reading through and photocopying 50 years of articles from Southwestern News magazines pertaining to the school of religious education and its personnel. His yeoman work saved untold hours that would have been spent in the archivist and special collections section of Roberts Library. In the same breath, I am indebted to Jill Botticelli, archivist/special collections librarian in Roberts Library, and her staff for assisting in securing photocopies of reams of historical material and digitizing historical photos for inclusion in the history.

I want to thank my dear friend of seminary years, Dr. Jimmy Draper (a member of my Sunday School class), who read the portion of the history that included the Conservative Resurgence movement. As a former president of the Southern Baptist Convention, past chairman of Southwestern Seminary's board of trustees, and former president of LifeWay, he had insights about the resurgence and its influence on the boards of our SBC agencies far beyond my feeble understanding. He agreed my references to the resurgence and its impact on Southwestern Seminary and other agencies were well-taken and right on target.

Preface

I am most indebted to Eddie Gifford, my wonderful computer guru friend (also in my Sunday School class). What I know about a computer, Eddie forgot a long time ago. On many occasions, while I was bogged down in computer problems and frustrated that my computer would not do what I wanted it to do, Eddie, a phone call away, would come to my assistance day or night and, with the stroke of a key or two, solve my problem, once again making me feel like the "computer dummy" I am. He saved me from so many computer traps that I will never be able to thank him enough.

I am most appreciative to Dr. Sarah Spring, professor of English in the Scarborough College at Southwestern. Dr. Spring served as the proofreader of my manuscript, assisting in correcting errors in grammar, spelling, and sentence structure. Her expertise is exceptional, and if any errors remain, they are strictly mine and not the fault of Dr. Spring.

Last, and by no means least, I want to thank Dr. Dorothy Patterson, who agreed to assist in the editing and publishing of this history. Her expertise in editing and publishing various kinds of books and articles is unequaled in every quarter. I am most grateful she was willing to assist me in this momentous endeavor. Thank you, Miss Dorothy.

I am certain I have in no way adequately covered the happenings in the education school over this period of 100 years. Collating quotations, recalling hundreds of specific dates from other decades, remembering school events and activities, naming specific personalities and making foregone conclusions can be skewed. If you find some, please accept my apology. It was a pleasant opportunity to remember the faces of faculty friends and students gone on, to admire every one of them who impacted my life in any way, and to have full assurance that all of us will one day enjoy that fellowship once again in the Kingdom of our Lord and His Christ.

Jack D. Terry, Jr.

Chapter 1

School of Religious Pedagogy on the Plains of Texas
1899-1969

In The Beginning... (1899-1914)

B.H. Carroll, the founder of Southwestern Baptist Theological Seminary, knew that theological education would not be complete until every facet of theological life was impacted by courses offered at the new seminary set on the hill six miles south of Fort Worth, Texas. Carroll understood the necessity of a training curriculum for Sunday School leadership, for youth and children's ministry, and missionary training needs that focused on an ever-expanding world horizon. He must have discussed this dream with L.R. Scarborough in the early years of the fledging school on the banks of the Brazos in Waco, Texas, because the need for Christian pedagogy was deeply entrenched in the mind of Scarborough as well.

A theological department was established at Baylor University under the leadership of B.H. Carroll and Oscar Cooper, Baylor's new president, who followed Rufus C. Burleson in 1899. With the full support of Cooper, Carroll announced in 1901 that ministerial instruction at Baylor would now be known as the Theological Department of Baylor University.[1] Carroll had his vision of a theological school during a memorable train ride to the panhandle of Texas. The vision caused him to press on with full intention to establish a complete School of Theology on the Baylor campus. L.R. Scarborough, the young evangelistic pastor of the First Baptist Church in Abilene, Texas, was listening at the Southern Baptist Convention in 1906 to the reports about a Chair of Evangelism for the new seminary in Waco, Texas. Later, he would fill the first Chair of Evangelism ("the Chair of Fire") at this or any other seminary.[2]

The Baptist General Convention of Texas unanimously approved the founding of the seminary with its own charter and board of trustees in 1907. Immediately, Carroll began thinking about his passion, a Chair of Evangelism, for the seminary. After two years of persistent persuading, Scarborough agreed to join Carroll as professor of evangelism. Southwestern Baptist Theological Seminary was founded and chartered on March 14, 1908, but would remain in Waco until a new location and funding were secured. During 1909, Fort Worth, Texas, presented a formal invitation for a permanent location for the seminary. Baptist pastors, community leaders, and city officials offered the fledgling school $100,000, tracts of land south of downtown, and major support for the new educational institution. The money was used to move the seminary to Fort Worth and build its first building, Fort Worth Hall, in honor of the city.[3]

In the spring of 1910, Southwestern had its final graduation in Waco, marking a first in the brief history of the seminary. William T. Rouse received the first Doctor of Theology degree.[4] At the cost of $175,000 and after four years of construction, parts of Fort Worth Hall were usable. When classes began in 1910, only the first floor had been completed. Later, Fort Worth Hall would house the entire seminary including classrooms, administration offices, faculty offices, an auditorium, residences for married couples, residence rooms for single men and single women, a library of 3,000 books, and a food services cafeteria.

As early as 1909, B.H. Carroll's failing health prompted him to ask the trustees to name L.R. Scarborough as an assistant to the president until his health could improve. Improved health was not to be, and just before his death, Carroll called Scarborough to his bedside and gave him these final words, "Lee, keep the seminary lashed to the cross." These words became the inspiration that set the stage for Scarborough's future presidency.[5] B.H. Carroll died on November 11, 1914.

Birth of the School of Religious Education (1914-1940)

Before the seminary was moved to Fort Worth and as early as 1906, there were courses offered in religious pedagogy by Frederick Eby while the seminary was still a part of the Bible Department of

Baylor University.[6] In fact, before the school moved from Waco to Fort Worth, B.H. Carroll was greatly interested in seeing the development of a department of religious pedagogy. In addition to a course or two offered periodically, every Friday was given over to open discussions of missions, evangelism, and Sunday School work by the faculty and other invited guests. Soon after the school was moved to Fort Worth in 1910, one course was offered covering the history, psychology, pedagogy, organization, curriculum, and administration of religious education in the church and home—a rather broad offering for one course.

That same year, special lectures were given on Sunday School and young people's work by Sunday School Board field secretaries Harvey Beaucamp and E.E. Lee. Also, the principal of the Woman's Missionary Training School gave special lectures in kindergarten methods while the professor of Sunday School pedagogy gave lectures on Sunday School problems. On the faculty page of the catalogue that year, the "Professor of Sunday School Pedagogy" was listed but no name given.[7]

The 1913 catalogue showed that C.B. Williams, professor of New Testament, was scheduled to give two courses: Pedagogy A, the psychology and pedagogy of the Sunday School; and Pedagogy B, the history, organization, and administration of the Sunday School. The next year's catalogue (1914) showed that W.W. Barnes, professor of church history, was listed to offer these courses again. Additional courses, C and D, were added in three special phases: psychology, child study, and Sunday School development. A study of kindergarten methods for Sunday School and missionary workers was still in the curriculum of the Woman's Missionary Training School.

In 1914, J.B. Gambrell, then state superintendent of missions for Texas, asked Harvey Beaucamp to suggest to Texas Baptists that a Sunday School program be established as a permanent feature at Southwestern Seminary or Baylor University. The course of study would lead to degrees such as Bachelor, Master, and Doctor of Religious Pedagogy. Such a school would draw students from all parts of the United States and elicit the support of the denomination in a most remarkable way.[8]

So the stage was set for the initiation of the Department of Religious Education by Scarborough, faculty, and trustees at their trustee meeting,

March 11, 1915. This idea was in line with the founder, B.H. Carroll, who had said in the beginning, "Not being restricted to preachers, it [the seminary] will aid in the training of Sunday School teachers of both sexes."[9] The very next day, March 12, 1915, Scarborough wrote J.M. Price, then a student at the Southern Baptist Theological Seminary in Louisville, Kentucky, offering him one of two professorships being proposed. In the three-page letter written to Price, Scarborough outlined several interesting educational axioms:

> (1) We will be teaching young, scholarly, spiritual, wise and growing men how to do educational work in the church.
> (2) This center will build along the lines of practical up-to-date strengths in all the churches and kingdom movements.
> (3) An extension division will be inaugurated to carry the courses to the people who cannot come to the lecture halls.
> (4) We will focus special courses on country churches and their problems in order to send men equipped to meet the special needs of the country church.
> (5) This will greatly enlarge our Training School for Women by offering courses of study along lines needful for missionaries at home and on the foreign fields.
> (6) A special emphasis will be placed on evangelism, and every student taking a degree will have two courses in evangelism and the art of winning men to Christ.
> (7) It is our purpose to establish a school of Christian pedagogy, as a department of this seminary, to touch the lives not only of the special educational students who will come to study Sunday School work but also the lives of all the students who come to study here along with the Missionary Training School.[10]

Price was, at that time, finishing work for a Th.M. degree. Previously, he had taught for two years in the public schools of Kentucky and served two years as the principal of the Marlow Indian Territory High School in Marlow, Oklahoma. He also had pastoral experience in Texas, Kentucky, and Rhode Island. His friends urged him to come to Fort Worth and teach in the new seminary. Price came to Seminary Hill in August of 1915, and he did "come by the way of the throne of God," as Scarborough had requested, because he had just been elected as the Sunday School secretary for the state of Kentucky but was led to come to Fort Worth instead.[11]

Growth on the Plains of Texas

The Department of Religious Pedagogy had a fast start, with Price offering five hours of study as part of a theological curriculum in 1915. The following year, he developed a curriculum for a diploma in religious education, and by 1919, the faculty approved the offering of a Bachelor in Religious Education degree. The first graduate, Miss Lou Ella Austin, graduated in May 1917 with the diploma of Religious Education.

In 1919, two additional pioneering steps were taken. One was the structuring of age-group studies including courses in elementary, adolescent, and adult religious education. Another, first coming in March 1919, was the admission of students in religious education to apply for the Doctor of Theology degree with a major in religious education.[12]

The year 1919 was a banner one for new courses offered in the department. The introduction of a course in age-group studies, in elementary religious education, and an additional course in adult work were offered. It was also the year in which courses leading to the degree Bachelor of Religious Education, which required an additional year beyond the Diploma of Religious Education, was offered as well. The first Bachelor of Religious Education was awarded to J.W. Davis in 1920. N.R. Drummond and Bertha Mitchell were added to the faculty, with 12 courses offered in order to expand the two-year course to a three-year study leading to the degree Master of Religious Education for college graduates. Seventy-two students were enrolled in the Bachelor and Master of Religious Education degree programs. The department was rapidly taking on the form of a school, with many young people becoming interested in the new opportunity of educational ministry in the local church.

A definite turning point was reached in 1921, when the work was formally set up as a separate school, which it had theoretically been for some time.[13] The kindergarten was transferred from the Woman's Missionary Training School to the School of Religious Education, with two additional courses added in elementary religious education. Additional courses were developed in secondary religious education, with a course in social recreation offered for credit as the first of its kind in any seminary. That semester, there were 121 students enrolled from 16 states across the convention. With the inclusion of the new course in social recreation, T.B. Maston was added to the faculty primarily in the field of adolescent religious education with an emphasis in social recreation.

In 1922, the first Master of Religious Education degree was conferred on C.T. Davis. The degree program was moving quickly, and in 1924, the Doctor of Religious Education degree was outlined. A new department of religious journalism was established with the director of seminary publicity, Lewis A. Myers, as the instructor.

While Price was giving direction to the rapid growth of the school, he knew he had to make Baptists conscious of the need of such a school and of the fruit that would come from it. He began what later would be called the State Sunday School Convention of Texas. He invited Sunday School workers from across the state to help strengthen the work of the churches. It was a very informal conference and was in connection with the State Training Union conference, but no permanent organization grew from this conference.

Price wrote personal letters to a few vocational workers and some recent graduates now serving in churches as ministers of education to inquire about supporting a more permanent organization that would meet annually. Enthusiasm ran high, and the organization had its definite beginning at the Southwestern Conference on Vocational Sunday School and Baptist Young People's Union held on Seminary Hill, April 15, 1921.[14] During the next few years, the organization met sporadically. In 1926, the name was changed to the Texas Baptist Religious Education Association. At the meeting, which included many religious educators from other states, the organization voted to change the name to the Southwestern Baptist Religious Education Association (SWBREA).

Faculty of the School of Religious Education Baptist Seminary Term 1923

The organization met annually on the campus at Southwestern for 84 years. In the mid-1990s, because of some strong feelings among the religious educators from more moderate theological persuasion states, the name was once again changed to the Baptist Religious Education Association of the Southwest (BREAS).

Beginning with the fall semester in 1925, the School of Religious Education was departmentalized into seven departments: principles, administration, adolescent, elementary, kindergarten, journalism, and sociology of religious education. That year, T.B. Maston, already on the faculty, received the first Doctor of Religious Education degree.[15] Prior to the financial crash of 1928, enrollment had reached 142, with 42 in the graduating class. Additional courses were added to the curriculum in craft work, chalk illustration, and religious dramatics.

Difficult Years Ahead

During the Depression, Price found reduction of the staff and consequently the course offerings, as well, to be expedient. The decline in giving throughout the Southern Baptist Convention made it necessary for the seminary to slash the salaries of the faculty in half during this difficult period, and even then, the seminary was unable to pay those reduced amounts. With grim courage and sacrifice, many of the faculty stayed in their places. Several received calls to churches that could have paid them many times the amount they were promised at the seminary. Some left to take other positions, but many others did not turn aside to another ministry task. They remained faithful to the educational task at hand, even though the final outcome looked bleak.

The list of the faithful in the department of religious education included J.M. Price, T.B. Maston, W.L. Howse, and Floy Barnard. These pioneer educators had a tenacious spirit, a can-do attitude, and a solid belief in what God was doing at Southwestern Seminary. They would go on to serve with distinction in the ministry of their calling as noteworthy Southern Baptist educators at Southwestern Seminary and in other areas of denominational activities in the Southern Baptist Convention.

Floy Barnard was an unusually bright young woman who knew she had been called to the educational ministry of the church as a young teenager. She twice graduated from Southwestern, first with an M.R.E. in 1929 and then with a D.R.E. in 1939.[16] While in seminary, she served several churches in Fort Worth as an educational director, and she became a faculty member in the department of religious education at Southwestern in 1933. She later became the dean of women in 1942, continuing to serve in that capacity until 1960.

Barnard came to the Southwestern faculty in the heart of the Depression. There was a need for diversity in course offerings because of the reduction in teachers at that time. Barnard combined several course offerings and continued to teach them during those trying years. Later, she developed courses in religious dramatics, which gave that discipline a major place in future curriculum development in the department of religious education.

Perhaps Barnard's most distinctive contribution was her contact and influence with several hundred young women in her capacity as dean of women. As the director of the women's dormitory, she served as counselor, friend, house mother, confidant, and older sister to many of the young women in her care. She projected her life into the lives of these young women to such an extent that the trustees named the women's dormitory the Floy Barnard Hall in 1960, which is still the official residence for women on the Southwestern campus.

Another pioneer during the Depression era when the department of religious education had to reduce its faculty was William L. (Bill) Howse, Jr. Howse was born in Fayetteville, Tennessee, in 1905, and he graduated from Union University in 1926. After a visit with J.M. Price on the Union University campus during his junior year, Howse felt he needed to dedicate his life to work in the church in the field of religious education and affirmed the conference with Price as the turning point in his ministry decision. He completed his M.R.E. in 1934 and the D.R.E. in 1937 at Southwestern, where he served on the faculty before even completing his first degree.[17]

Howse's service in local Southern Baptist churches as minister of education provided him a rich background for his classroom lectures in the area of education administration and church administration. Over the years, he became the consummate spokesperson on church and educational administration. Undoubtedly, the major contribution made to Southern Baptist student ministers during his 21-year tenure (1933-1954) was the practical knowledge he shared with his classes about educational administration in the church. Howse brought to his classes a rich background of consecration, training, and experience in the local Southern Baptist churches, which was his first love. He informed, counseled, inspired, and encouraged thousands of religious education students to devote their lives and commitment to the local church and to its growth.

Both of these educational giants—Barnard and Howse, along with Thomas Buford (T.B.) Maston—withstood the onslaught of the depression and came out the other side as shining lights of moral and spiritual stability. In 1925, T.B. Maston was the first graduate of the School of Religious Education with the Doctor of Religious Education degree, which had been approved by the faculty on May 11, 1924.[18] He had been a member of the faculty of the School of Religious Education since 1922 while completing his doctoral work in church recreation and social work.

Maston had shown great interest both in religious education and theology, and in 1937, he was teaching in the School of Religious Education and also in the School of Theology. He would transfer completely to the School of Theology in 1944.

By 1955, under the leadership of Maston and several faculty members, the last institutional remnant of racial discrimination was erased. Black students had been admitted to regular classes in 1950, with the first two graduating in the spring of 1955. However, dormitories of the school continued to be segregated. The trustees had been discussing the desegregation of the dormitories both in 1954 and 1956, and the faculty, under the quiet leadership of Maston, strongly favored this action by the trustees. As a result of Maston's leadership, the vestige of racial discrimination was eliminated from all boarding facilities of the seminary.

On May 31, 1963, Maston announced his retirement from the position of professor of Christian ethics. He was honored at a faculty-staff-student banquet on June 2, 1963. The T.B. Maston Scholarship

Fund was begun by students the same year, and he was named a distinguished alumnus in June 1965.[19]

In 1934, by a vote of the faculty council, the Woman's Missionary Training School instruction and degree programs were integrated into the regular seminary curriculum. Upon the suggestion of Scarborough, the faculty made a thorough study of the matter and recommended to the advisory board of the Woman's Missionary Union of the South that the curriculum of the women's training school would be absorbed principally into the department of administration in the School of Religious Education. The reason for the change was that the degrees in missions were not recognized by the regional accreditation agencies of the United States, while other seminary degrees were recognized. The new curriculum and a standard accredited degree would be more valuable than an unrecognized missions degree.[20]

A Growing Faculty (1940-1960)

L.R. Scarborough helped the seminary endure the lean years of the Depression, setting them on a course to financial security. With the help of the SBC's Hundred Thousand Club campaign, Southwestern eventually paid off all its debts shortly after the end of his presidency. Advanced age encouraged Scarborough to resign his position as president in 1942. For 34 years, his fiery passion for evangelism and training preachers, evangelists, and missionaries fueled the heartbeat of the institution, securing the foundation of its future.[21]

Coming out of the depression into the early 1940s, better days for the School of Religious Education lay ahead. The board of trustees turned to E.D. Head, pastor of the First Baptist Church in Houston, Texas, to be the third president of Southwestern. The world had changed drastically since the presidential days of B.H. Carroll and L.R. Scarborough. The conclusion of World War II provided a renewed sense of national pride, economic security, and a strong feeling of peace in the world. The seminary became a benefactor of this new sense of missionary zeal. Young men and women, who had served with distinction during the war and were moved by the Spirit of God to take the Gospel to the world, made their way to Southwestern and other Southern Baptist seminaries. The call of God on their lives and their desire for seminary education brought growth to the seminary both in enrollment and finances during the next decade.

The School of Religious Education benefited from this surge in enrollment as well. In 1945, 345 were enrolled with a graduating class of 65. However, that number was not enough to meet the growing need for educational ministry positions expressed by the churches. It was past time to secure additional faculty and to add additional courses to the curriculum.

Several internal moves gave added impetus to the expressed need for additional faculty. T.B. Maston transferred totally to the School of Theology. Floy Barnard was forced to drop some of her courses to assume the deanship of the Woman's Training School. To strengthen the curriculum and meet the needs of the churches, several new faculty members were added during the next ten years. Ralph Churchill (1944) was invited to fill the faculty position in religious publicity and journalism, and Joe Davis Heacock (1944), an outstanding minister of education in several large churches in the convention, was brought to the faculty to teach principles and adolescent education.[22]

In 1945, Ann Bradford was elected to teach elementary education and to direct the work of the kindergarten. During 1945, Alpha Melton was elected to direct the social work department. In 1947, Othal Feather, an army chaplain during World War II, was added as director of field education work and clinical training, which also included some courses in Baptist Student Union ministry and administration. Gracie Knowlton was enlisted as a part-time instructor that same year and would teach secretarial service.

In 1949, Phillip Harris was elected to teach adolescent education. A. Donald Bell was elected to teach psychology and counseling in 1951, and James Daniel joined the faculty in elementary education administration in 1953.[23] This large number of new faculty acquisitions breathed new life into the very small department of religious education.

The background of the new faculty members brought a plethora of religious education expertise and experience to the School of Religious Education. Price was pleased with the background of each of the new acquisitions for the training of men and women in the work of educational ministry in the churches.

The churches were calling for educational ministers of all kinds: ministers of education, ministers of youth education, ministers of elementary education, ministers of preschool and kindergarten education, ministers of publicity and journalism, ministers of social work, and ministers of Christian counseling to name a few. Price and the School of Religious Education were determined to provide as many ministers of education as the churches in the convention would need as quickly as possible. As each of these new faculty members began a teaching career, there came with them a background of educational preparation, experience in church ministry, and a heart filled with love and appreciation for the young people who would be given to them to develop into ministers of education in local churches.

Ralph D. Churchill was born in Murray, Kentucky, in 1905. He graduated from Southwestern Seminary with both a B.S.M. and M.R.E. in 1946, and then a D.R.E. in 1956. Churchill was elected to the faculty of the School of Religious Education in religious publicity and journalism. The emphasis of his courses was to train students to become more effective in written communication in the church, general public communication pieces, and denominational publications, as well as in personal writing styles for human interest stories, news stories, and editorials. He wanted each graduate to be proficient in writing for church publications.

Churchill served as the seminary's public relations officer and mass communication representative to the various publics both church and secular. A small quarterly called Southwestern News began in 1943, with T.B. Maston as editor. In October 1947, the quarterly was expanded and published monthly under the editorship of Churchill.

R. Othal Feather was born in Comanche, Oklahoma, in 1903. He graduated from Southwestern with an M.R.E. in 1947 and a D.R.E. in 1956. Feather served as an army chaplain with the rank of major during World War II with the 139th General Hospital in Belgium.

Feather developed a field education program for the School of Religious Education that attempted to put every student in a ministry situation with a church or parachurch organization as an intern, part-time, or paid staff member during enrollment at the seminary. Feather also taught all of the military chaplaincy courses in the seminary for 18 years. During his ministry at Southwestern, he was used extensively by other Southern Baptist agencies because of his expertise in military chaplaincy, but mainly because of his expertise in educational evangelism.

Philip B. Harris was born in Creal Springs, Illinois, on June 9, 1912. Harris graduated from Southwestern with his M.R.E. in 1947 and his D.R.E. 1954. He was elected to the faculty in adolescent education and taught from 1949-1959.

During his tenure at Southwestern, Harris continued to serve in the churches as minister of education for Lakewood Baptist Church, Dallas, Texas, and as youth director at Broadway Baptist Church, Fort Worth, Texas. He was also the president of the State Sunday School Convention of Texas. His life revolved around the Training Union organization in the churches as well as in the state. He served as a young people's department director and intermediate leader, general director in a local church, and as an associational director in the Texas Baptist Training Union. Harris' students remembered his wonderful sense of humor, his ability to lead others, and his knowledge of organizational administration in Young People Training Union departments and in Sunday School work.

A. Donald Bell was born in Vancouver, Washington, in 1920. He graduated from Southwestern Seminary with an M.R.E. in 1945 and the D.R.E. in 1949. Bell served as professor of psychology and counseling and director of graduate studies in religious education at Southwestern in 1951 and again from 1963-72.

Along with the men elected to the religious education faculty during this time of great growth, there were three female professors added as well: Ann Bradford, Alpha Melton, and Gracie Knowlton. Each of these women contributed to the educational experiences of the students in the School of Religious Education from their own diversified educational expertise: Ann Bradford from her experience in elementary education, especially kindergarten studies; Alpha Melton as she developed and enlarged the ministry of social work so admirably established by

T.B. Maston; and Gracie Knowlton, from her extensive experience as a church and educational secretary in local churches and her vast work in developing and maintaining libraries in churches as well as on mission fields.

Ann Bradford was born in Glasgow, Kentucky. She completed her B.R.E. (1930), M.R.E. (1933), and D.R.E. (1956) at Southwestern. In 1945, she was elected to the faculty of the School of Religious Education to reorganize the department of elementary education, including kindergarten work. She was brought to the faculty by J.M. Price and followed in the steps of her mentor, Orabelle Cross Jones.

During her tenure, Bradford had a once-in-a-lifetime opportunity. She had been on the faculty four years when funds were available for the construction of the most unique building in all the Southern Baptist Convention, a building that would be dedicated explicitly for the instruction of religious education. The construction of this building provided her with the opportunity to be a design consultant for "a charming model kindergarten."[24]

The design was unique, featuring an indoor model of a house opening into a backyard play area, which was the kindergarten classrooms. The house façade provided rooms for observation through two-way glass windows. This kindergarten area provided the laboratory for childhood and kindergarten education until the construction of the Naylor Children's Center. In the spring 1989 meeting of the trustees, a recommendation was made and passed that the foyer of the Naylor Children's Center be named the "Ann Bradford Foyer." To commemorate this trustee action, the 75th anniversary committee of the School of Religious Education chose April 4, 1990, as "Ann Bradford Day" and had the official dedication of the Ann Bradford Foyer in the Naylor's Children Center. A portrait of Bradford and a plaque now hang in the foyer of the Naylor Children's Center.[25]

Alpha Melton was born in Laurel, Mississippi, in 1906. She developed the first complete social work program offered by the School of Religious Education and for 10 years was the director of the Tarrant Baptist Good Will Center. Along with her teaching, her writing, the Good Will Center, and speaking engagements, she encouraged Southern

Baptists to become conscious of the value of assisting those who are less fortunate and need the Gospel as much as those who have plenty. Her work in the Good Will Center was more like ministering on a foreign mission field than in the beautiful cities of America. Along the way, she inspired and trained an army of workers now stationed around the world who caught something of the spirit of her work and have deployed throughout the world to assist the underprivileged. Only heaven will reveal how much good she did and inspired others to do also.[26]

Gracie Knowlton was born in 1908 in Santa Anna, Texas, not far from Waxahachie in Ellis County. Her distinctive service was in the area of secretarial science and church library development at Southwestern Seminary, where she created an outstanding department in this field. She taught secretarial work; church office management; and routines, office machines, church library, and crafts. Many student wives took her secretarial courses in order to assist their husbands when they were called to churches in the future. She sent out many capable workers prepared to do church secretarial ministry and to establish and maintain church libraries.

She also developed significant courses in arts and crafts and inspired many to enroll in her classes through her annual exhibits. Each year, her arts and craft classes had an exhibition of the various kinds of items that can be made for Vacation Bible School; senior adult arts and crafts classes; and various community organizations such as the boy and girl scouts, Royal Ambassadors, and Girls in Action. One year the exhibit featured the use of plastic bottles to make piggy banks, flower vases, and a dozen other storage items. Knowlton was quoted as saying about one of the exhibits:

> There will be visitors from many different denominations that will have Vacation Bible Schools and Senior Adult ministries who will do arts and crafts in their churches this year. Many will come from other states and many churches in Texas, Louisiana, Oklahoma and New Mexico will attend. This year we will specialize in plastics with all of the items made from waste materials. Plastic bottles take

unexpected turns and can be turned into everything from candle holders, flower vases, piggy banks and pot-bellied stoves. Most of the items are made from plastic, scrap wood, paper, cardboard, felt, cloth, metal, glass and other materials.[27]

During the last years of Head's administration, the seminary paid off its long-held debt. The faculty nearly doubled, and the enrollment moved from 734 in 1942 to 2,160 in 1953. The campus was improved during his administration with the renovation of several buildings. The construction of the B.H. Carroll Memorial Building and the George W. Truett Chapel was begun, as was J.M. Price Hall. All of this building renovation and construction was taken on without adding any additional debt.

Price Hall

Using the momentum of the construction of the Memorial Building, J.M. Price, the director of the School of Religious Education, seized the opportunity to raise funds for a specialized building for the teaching of religious education. The first reference to this building was in April 1945, when Price and the religious education faculty had a conference

with E.D. Head; J. Howard Williams, chairman of the executive committee of the Southern Baptist Convention; W.R. White, chairman of the special gifts committee for the B.H. Carroll Memorial Building; and Mrs. B.A. Copass, president of the Woman's Missionary Union of Texas.[28] All agreed that an effort should be made to raise funds for the religious education building, not with an all-out campaign, but with allotments and special gifts.

A brief note in the November 1945 edition of Southwestern News stated that L.R. Scarborough had made plans for this building as early as 1927. The earliest reference to such a building appeared in the trustee minutes on February 17, 1946, when they approved a report about it to the Southern Baptist Convention. A groundbreaking ceremony was held on October 6, 1948, with T.L. Holcomb, Mrs. B.A. Copass, President Head, and J.M. Price handling the shovels.

This building was the first of its kind to be constructed in the United States. The two-story structure with a basement was designed specifically for the teaching of all aspects of religious education. It contained, in addition to classrooms, faculty offices, a chapel, a charming demonstration kindergarten, a demonstration church library, and other facilities for specialized educational study and activities.[29]

On March 9, 1949, upon recommendation of the faculty, the trustees named the building J.M. Price Hall, a worthy memorial to the pioneer religious educator from Kentucky. Price continued to lead the School of Religious Education to additional heights. In 1945, the school was accredited by the American Association of Schools of Religious Education, the first school of religious education among Southern Baptists to receive the distinction. During this period of time, the School of Religious Education enrolled over 600 students from practically every state in the United States and from several foreign countries. It graduated 146 that year, sending them out to the ends of the earth in local churches, on foreign mission fields, and in colleges and seminaries.

Continuing Faculty Growth

In 1952, Head experienced a heart attack that prompted him to consider resignation from his position as president. In 1953, the board

SCHOOL OF RELIGIOUS PEDAGOGY ON THE PLAINS OF TEXAS

of trustees turned to the executive director of the Baptist General Convention of Texas, J. Howard Williams, to become the fourth president. During his administration, the School of Religious Education grew expeditiously, adding such notable professors as John Drakeford, who had served in the Australian army during the World War II, in psychology and counseling (1954); Lee H. McCoy in church administration (1955); Monte McMachon in Vacation Bible School and Woman's Missionary Work (1955); Leon Marsh, who was a teaching fellow for J.M. Price during his doctoral studies, in principles of education (1956); and Harvey Hatcher in education arts and dramatics (1958).[30] This extensive faculty growth was coupled with major faculty loss. In 1956, W.L. Howse, professor of administration and religious education, accepted a position as the director of the new educational division of the Southern Baptist Sunday School Board.

In the year of Price's retirement, the seminary catalog listed a number of "firsts" initiated by Price in the School of Religious Education:

- The first school in America to confer religious education diplomas and degrees (1917).
- The first school among Baptists to offer a doctor's degree with a major in religious education (1919).
- The first school to lead Baptists in requiring supervised field work (observation, practice, and clinical work) as a requirement for graduation (1920).
- The first school to initiate a Sunday School superintendent's conference (the forerunner of state Sunday School conventions) in the South (1920).
- The first school to offer a vocational conference on religious education (1921), now the Southwestern Baptist Religious Education Association.
- The first school to originate a demonstration and practice kindergarten in a Southern Baptist seminary (1921).
- The first school to lead a movement among Southern Baptist seminaries for requiring academic prerequisites for seminary degrees (1922).
- The first school to provide separate special courses for seminary students without college training (1922).
- The first school to sponsor a Vacation Bible School conference west of the Mississippi and the oldest existing one in the South among Southern Baptists (1922).
- The first school in America to construct a building designed exclusively for teaching and practice for all activities of religious education (1950).
- The first school of religious education among Southern Baptists to be accredited (1951).
- The first school to offer complete credit courses among Baptists in age-group work (1919), recreational leadership (1921), vacation and weekday schools (1921), secretarial training (1922), religious publicity (1922), church finances (1923), Baptist Student Union work (1923), arts and crafts (1923), religious dramatics (1924), visual aids (1926), religious counseling (1933), and church library work (1948).

- The first school of religious education to sponsor a workshop for ministers of education in the Southern Baptist Convention (1957).[31]

Only the pioneering heart of J.M. Price and his tenacious mind could have brought together all these educational innovations in one place during a period of over 40 years.

In 1956, two directors, Price in the School of Religious Education and Jeff D. Ray in the School of Sacred Music, resigned from their positions. The need to fill these positions as quickly as possible with quality individuals was the trustee's first order of business. The trustees named Joe Davis Heacock to lead the School of Religious Education and James C. McKinney to lead the School of Sacred Music. In the same meeting, they requested that Jesse Northcutt remain the director of the School of Theology. However, on February 26, 1957, the trustees voted to change the title "director" for all three of these men to "dean."[32]

Sorrow on the Plains of Texas (1950-1958)

J. Howard Williams had a grand vision to raise $10 million for the seminary, with $5 million going toward endowment and the rest of the money going to enlarge the faculty, complete renovations to existing buildings, and construct buildings as needed. However, he would not live to see these magnificent dreams become reality (though this vision would set the wheels in motion for his successors to reach new heights).

After suffering a severe heart attack, Williams' presidency was cut short by his sudden death on April 20, 1958. His death occurred in the middle of Southwestern's 50th Anniversary Celebration. All festivities were put on hold while the seminary and the Southern Baptist Convention mourned the loss of this great leader and Christian statesman.

During Williams' administration, the faculty of the School of Theology was increased by 18, the School of Religious Education faculty by eight, and the School of Sacred Music faculty by 11, for a total of 37 new faculty acquisitions.[33] Along with these faculty acquisitions, other financial benefits for the faculty and staff were made possible by the foresighted leadership of President Williams. The faculty and staff had the opportunity to have expenses paid to attend the Southern Baptist Convention or a professional meeting of their choice each year, a retirement plan with the Relief and Annuity Board of the Southern Baptist Convention (now GuideStone) was put in place, and an assistance plan to encourage young professors to purchase a home with the help of the seminary and local banks was also established.

Another major benefit was an assistance program that would encourage faculty to write and publish. Upon request, each of the faculty members would be allowed to reduce their teaching load by two to four hours and be given secretarial assistance in completing a writing project. These benefits, among many other provisions, were the legacy handiwork of the J. Howard Williams presidency.

A New Horizon (1958-1970)

In an attempt to keep the momentum of the dream that was in the mind of J. Howard Williams, the trustees moved quickly to elect a president to lead the seminary into the next several decades. Robert E. Naylor, pastor of the Travis Avenue Baptist Church, Fort Worth, Texas, and chairman of the board of trustees at the seminary, was elected to step into the void left by the death of Williams. Naylor indelibly inscribed in the hearts of Southwestern students the necessity of a world mission outreach. His own daughter, Dr. Rebekah Naylor, M.D., became a missionary doctor to the lost multitudes in India, serving as a surgeon and chief of staff for the Baptist hospital in Bangalore, India. Evangelism, missions, and the Gospel were the main theme of Naylor's entire presidency, and it was articulated as a pivotal premise of his inaugural address in 1958. Depicting it as the main business of the Kingdom, he said,

> Evangelism is to be the main business of the Kingdom of God. To the degree that this seminary is based on evangelism, bathed in evangelism, committed to evangelism, rooted in evangelism, the institution is a quickening flame and an all-embracing arm of love around the whole world.[34]

Not only did Naylor bind the seminary to the Gospel, but he provided the stability that would be needed during a time of drastic social change and denominational controversy. Among some of the world problems affecting Naylor's administration were the Vietnam War, the Cold War, tensions in the civil rights movement, and denominational controversy over the inspiration and reliability of Scripture. During his presidency, the seminary adopted the 1963 Baptist Faith and Message as its confession pointing to the seminary's position on the primacy and inspiration of Scripture.

Naylor improved the seminary's faculty structure, programs, and facilities during his administration. When he became president, the faculty numbered 53 teaching over 2,000 students for a ratio of 1 to 45 students per faculty member. At the close of his administration in 1978, the student/teacher ratio had been reduced to 1 to 28 students per faculty member.

Naylor felt the need for a better academic recognition for the seminary. He served as a member of the executive committee of the Association of Theological Schools (ATS), which accredited theological schools in the United States and Canada. This committee appointment opened his eyes to the necessity of securing such outstanding accreditation for Southwestern. Under his leadership, the School of Church Music became the first school of church music in any seminary to receive accreditation in the National Association of Schools of Music (NASM). In 1970, ATS and the Southern Association of Colleges and Schools (SACS) granted accreditation to all three schools at Southwestern.

Naylor saw the need for endowed academic chairs to provide additional funds for the budget. During his administration, several endowed chairs and endowed fellowships were established. Two academic chairs were already in place and occupied by theology faculty members. The L.R. Scarborough Chair of Evangelism ("the Chair of Fire") was so named because of Scarborough's intense love for evangelism and reaching the lost with the Gospel of Christ. This chair was partially endowed from gifts of individuals who had great love and appreciation for Scarborough. After his death, the chair was fully endowed with interest income from a trust established by William Fleming. In 1924,

Mrs. George W. Bottoms provided a gift of $100,000 to endow a chair in missions. Later, a chair would be named the George W. Bottoms Chair of Missions. Cal Guy, prominent Southern Baptist missionary and professor of missions, was named to the chair in 1948.[35]

Following the establishment of these two chairs, there were none others established until the administration of Naylor. On November 23, 1965, trustees approved the J. Wesley Harrison Chair of New Testament in recognition of a generous gift. In 1976, the trustees voted to initiate the George W. Truett Chair of Ministry. A. Webb Roberts, of Dallas, contributed $150,000 for the establishment of this chair with the proviso that the seminary would raise an additional $600,000 before December 1977. The challenge gift was met, and the chair was established. The last chair was the result of an offer from the Baptist Sunday School Board of the Southern Baptist Convention early in 1977 to fund a chair for teaching the principles set out by the board. The chair was to provide additional instruction in the programs designed and developed for religious education in the local churches fostered by the Sunday School Board. It was approved by the trustees on November 22, 1977, and Charles A. Tidwell was named to the chair.[36]

During Naylor's administration, the unity of the schools was a matter of concern. Each semester, all graduating students were invited to a graduate luncheon. At each of these luncheons, the vice president for academic affairs or one of the deans of the individual schools was the speaker. The title given to each of these speeches was "One Seminary." Each speaker made a valiant effort to demonstrate the necessity of unity on a church staff or in a denominational position. As sterling as these speeches might have been, it was a difficult situation to conjure up the importance of unity beyond seminary while brick and mortar separated one school from the other, and pastor from minister of education or minister of music. The division, though efficient, played havoc with a true sense of ministerial unity that was going to be vitally necessary on the staff of a local church or denominational organization.

The required self-study by the accrediting agencies brought together the faculties into a single committee. This provided an opportunity for the faculties to work harmoniously with one another, fostering better communication and dialogue among the faculty members. The common accreditation of the three schools by ATS and SACS provided a better understanding of the work being done by the separate faculties. Standing committees, such as the curriculum council and the advanced studies council, integrated the expertise of the faculties into a seminary work in progress. A preschool retreat, which had been the exclusive activity of the theological faculty, was modified to include the entire faculty. The new approach of the faculty retreat was organized in such a way as to appeal to the interest and concerns of the entire seminary faculty. This small activity brought a great deal of unity to the faculty. It was a breath of fresh air to be able to talk to one another on common ground for a change.

Along with the accrediting agency achievements, Naylor moved vigorously to complete William's dream of additional buildings on the campus. Faculty offices and classrooms for the School of Theology were moved from Cowden Hall to the now completed Scarborough wing of the Memorial Building. This move constituted the necessity of a major renovation of Cowden Hall for the School of Church Music, a new roof for J.M. Price Hall, and extensive renovations to the women's dormitory.[37] Plans for four new buildings were prepared, and construction began on a couple of them. Just a few weeks after Williams' death, the first apartments in the Student Village had been completed, and trustees voted to name these new student apartments the J. Howard Williams Student Village. Construction for the Student Center began in 1965 and was completed in 1968. On February 27, 1968, trustees voted to name this building the Robert E. and Goldia Naylor Student Center. The third building planned was a medical center to replace the medical services that had been in the basement of the Memorial Building. The medical center was named the F. Howard Walsh Medical Center in honor of a major donor and trustee. Preliminary studies for the new official home for the president were developed in 1969 with the completion of the new home in the spring of 1971.[38]

The faculty of the School of Religious Education benefitted from the Naylor administration, as did the other three schools. Added to the faculty of the religious education school was Harvey B. Hatcher in communication arts (1958); Harold T. Dill in youth education (1959); A. Donald Bell in psychology and human relations (1951-60, returning in 1963); James D. Williams in adult education (1964); Jeroline Baker in childhood education (1964); Charles A. Tidwell in church administration (1965); LeRoy Ford in foundations of education (1966); and the last faculty member elected before the turn of the 1970s, Jack D. Terry, Jr., in philosophy and history of education (1969).

The religious education faculty suffered the loss of several tenured professors by death and retirement. Many who had been teaching in the school during the administration of J.M. Price were near retirement. The untimely death of Lee H. McCoy (July 5, 1965), who taught in the field of church administration, removed an effective and beloved professor, author, and classroom giant after 10 years of service.

During the latter part of the 1960s, several senior faculty members retired. Floy Barnard, professor of missionary education since 1933 and dean of women since 1942, retired after the spring graduation in 1960. The educational faculty presented a request to the trustees to name the women's dormitory Floy Barnard Hall. The trustees agreed and did so at their 1960 spring meeting.[39]

R. Othal Feather, professor of education administration since 1947, retired after the spring term in 1970. He simply changed his base of operation, because he had been very active in the churches teaching, writing, lecturing, and leading clinics as well as other military chaplain ministries.

Ann Bradford had directed the early childhood program using the unique kindergarten teaching area in Price Hall. The establishment of kindergarten education as a ministry operation in local churches had been the dream of J.M. Price and Ann Bradford. Bradford, who had taught effectively in the area of kindergarten and childhood education since 1945, chose to retire in 1970.

Ralph D. Churchill, the first professor of communication arts and religious journalism (since 1944), chose 1970 as his retirement year as well. Churchill, who was the editor of Southwestern News for several years, worked diligently to get the story of Southwestern Seminary into the local newspapers, radio broadcasts, and eventually television broadcasts. Alpha Melton, who had taught social work since 1945, retired in 1971, as did Gracie Knowlton, who had taught educational arts, secretarial work, and church library science since 1945.

In the true pioneering spirit of J.M. Price, Joe Davis Heacock and the faculty of the School of Religious Education continued to pile up "firsts" as new academic programs, departmental conferences and workshops, and technological innovations were introduced in the school. The "first" Youth Ministry Lab was organized by Harold Dill, professor of youth education, along with a committee of students in youth ministry. Youth Ministry Lab invited youth ministers, students, and lay men and women interested in youth ministry to come to the campus for a three-day workshop. The first of these was in May of 1968, with more than 200 in attendance from 35 colleges and universities and many youth leaders of local Southern Baptist churches.

During this same period, more advanced technology (televisions and television recorders) was purchased to enhance the work of the educational professors in principles of teaching (videotape teaching presentations); psychology and counseling (John Drakeford introduced a new Rogerian process of intake interviews via television with prospective psychology clients); and Jeroline Baker introduced the process of preparing videotape presentations of kindergarten teaching sessions that could be used in local churches for training kindergarten and elementary education leadership. Under the leadership of Bradford, Baker, and Hazel Morris, plans for a demonstration children's building were being developed. The building would have a dual purpose: (1) provide care for the preschool children of the student body; and (2) have a children and preschool demonstration program (birth through 5 years of age) going on daily for church, association, and state leaders who work with children to visit and observe. Each of the teaching rooms of the building would have an observation room in which visitors could watch, analyze, and evaluate preschool education programs in action. This building would be the first of its kind on any Baptist campus and would set the gold standard for preschool education in the local church.

Academically, the School of Religious Education continued to improve the quality of its degree programs. The program known as the Associate in Religious Education was changed in 1962 to become the Diploma in Religious Education. The Master of Religious Education degree was improved and substantially strengthened. The social work program was expanded in 1964. The enhanced program provided social work students an opportunity to major in this discipline, thereby preparing them to receive credit on a Master of Social Work degree in nearby universities and colleges. The unusual progress being made in the programs for preschool children in the Children's Building placed childhood education at the vanguard of the School of Religious Education.

Under the capable leadership of R. Othal Feather, the field education program was identified as one of the best seminary internship programs among Southern Baptist seminaries. Every student was required to do two semesters of field education. One option was for the student employed in a church to use that church while in seminary as a field experience; or, if the student was not employed in a church, he could choose to work alongside a seasoned educational minister or age-group specialist in a church—watching, evaluating, and leading where feasible.

A new degree, Graduate Specialist in Religious Education, a "first" in seminary education, was developed for students and on-the-job church practitioners who wanted to specialize in a more specific area of educational ministry. Courses were offered in the summer sessions, I Terms, and other creative educational modules. The Graduate Specialist degree was well-received by ministers in local churches who desired additional studies in a specific field of religious education but did not want to pursue a doctorate in the field.

In 1965, Leon Marsh, chairman of the doctoral committee in the School of Religious Education, led in a study to the replace the older Doctor of Religious Education (D.R.E.) degree developed in 1924 with a new degree, Doctor of Education (Ed.D.). Marsh, aided by Heacock, did a comprehensive study in 1964-1965 of the direction that advanced studies committees in other seminaries were moving as well as a complete review of the needs of the School of Religious Education's doctoral program. A set of major requirements were added to the structure of the new degree. Entrance examinations and a portion of the Graduate Record Examination were included, and a grade point average of A- on the Master of Religious Education degree[40] became the prerequisite along with a demonstration of professional competence as an educational minister. The curriculum was increased from 8 to 20 courses, which included courses in research and statistics as a language requirement for the degree. Written and oral examinations were required at the end of the course of study, as was a defense of the prospectus for the dissertation. The final step in the degree plan was an oral defense of the dissertation.

A historic curriculum workshop was organized by the School of Religious Education to revitalize the curricular offerings of the school. Joe Davis Heacock and the faculty spent weeks in preparation for the workshop that was held on April 6-8, 1970. An invitation was sent to religious educators across the nation to join with the faculty and selected students to discuss the new concept of a performance-oriented curriculum. As a result of this conference, several faculty study committees were organized. A major change in curriculum design, bringing new flexibility for students in the School of Religious Education, was being developed. New students coming to Southwestern from Southern Baptist colleges or universities where the seminary's doctoral graduates had become professors of religious education or religious studies began to question the necessity of taking specific courses in a prescribed curriculum for the Master of Religious Education degree at Southwestern. The information they brought to the table was that the content of the prescribed core courses and the outlines of the courses of study in the School of Religious Education were either exact or similar to the outline and content of like-named courses that the professors were teaching at their college or university. It was discovered that doctoral graduates who had been elected in religious education departments in Baptist colleges or universities in the Southern Baptist Convention were teaching the exact or a similar course content that they had received when they were students at Southwestern.

It was imperative that the School of Religious Education faculty take a serious look at the required prescribed core and determine if there might be an opportunity to introduce advanced courses that could be taken in lieu of the prescribed course requirement. Faculty committees were organized to evaluate each of the courses in the prescribed curriculum to determine if an advanced course in the same discipline could be offered to allow the student an opportunity to enhance learning rather than repeat information that had already been taught. This path to new flexibility in the curriculum design doubled the number of elective courses in all the core disciplines. The faculty felt that it moved the School of Religious Education into a curriculum that was educative rather than prescribed, and that it expanded and enhanced the learning opportunities for the students.

An added benefit of the curriculum study was the change of nomenclature for the first educational discipline brought to the department of religious education by J.M. Price in 1915—principles and psychology of teaching. The department was renamed the Department of the Foundations of Education. This department would encompass all of the five courses taught by J.M. Price in 1915—psychological principles of religious education, aims and methods of biblical teaching, psychology of religion, organization of the Sunday School, and survey of religious education.[41]

Jack Terry led the School of Religious Education to pay more careful attention to its student orientation program in the use of the more student-friendly elective curriculum instead of a restrictive prescribed one. This more modern educative rather than prescribed curriculum had been carefully constructed to allow students from Baptist colleges and universities to elect the courses listed in the curriculum that would be most beneficial to their ministry calling, determined by the religious education courses they had taken in their college curriculum. The School of Religious Education had developed an elective curriculum and organized the faculty to give maximum counseling to the students as each began studies for effective ministry.

Eventually, this new elective curriculum would be published in a curriculum guide, with each department's curricular offerings explained in achievable terms. The goals and objectives of each course would be listed so the student would be able to search each of the offerings from each of the departments to determine which of the courses offered would fulfill ministry dreams. The faculty felt this was a major step toward eliminating unnecessary repetition from courses taken at the college or university level. Not only was the new elective curriculum beneficial to the student, but it was beneficial to the faculty member, who could more carefully construct each course offering to provide maximum instruction while at the same time achieving necessary goals and objectives for more effective teaching. Former alumni expressed approval of the new elective curriculum structure because it gave the student an opportunity to reach beyond the college courses in religious education and provided the faculty members an opportunity to expand their course offerings into advanced studies of many subjects.

It would be very difficult to describe the numerous innovative ideas and programs that were developed during the Naylor administration. Each school felt free to explore, examine, and embrace new innovative criteria for classroom teaching effectiveness. With the advent of television and video recording, instructors were provided an opportunity to introduce these technological devices into the classroom teaching and learning experiences. Television and video recording provided an opportunity for instant recall of a teaching, preaching, counseling, or other classroom procedure. Evaluation, critique, and enhanced instruction accompanied the video recording session.

Under the leadership of John Drakeford, the School of Religious Education established a Marriage and Family Counseling Center. The need for such a center was recognized the first year when 229 students, local residents, and others attended the center for 362 counseling sessions.[42] Most of the sessions were devoted to marriage problems, personal problems, premarital counseling, parent-child relationships, grief counseling, and vocational counseling. Video recording became a major instructional activity in the Marriage and Family Counseling program. The videotaped "in-take interview," when the counselor could ask questions and receive answers and reactions, provided the key to future investigations. Video recording of these sessions with the opportunity of reviewing them later with a trained counselor allowed students in the program to observe the skills of the leader-counselor and make important inferences to the attitudes and feelings of the clients. John Drakeford purchased the first television recording machine for use in the School of Religious Education's Marriage and Family Counseling program.

Desiring to assist the wives of seminary students to achieve as much educational training as possible, the School of Religious Education developed a cooperative arrangement with Dallas Baptist University. This arrangement would allow the student or student wife to take classes at both institutions. The end product was securing a Texas Teaching Certificate as they earned their seminary master's degree.

A teaching certification would be an enhancement for a minister and especially for his wife if they were called to pioneer areas where they may need to become bi-vocational. The teaching certificate would provide a job for the minister or his wife to supplement the salary of the small growing church in pioneer areas. Many student wives took advantage of this opportunity as they prepared to do ministry with their husbands in other states. The teaching certificate would assist the student or student-wife to find a position in a public, private, or Christian school. Eventually, some of the teaching certification departments of several of the states began recognizing the Master of Religious Education degree from Southwestern Seminary as a qualified master's degree and would honor the degree with additional master's pay.

"The Called"—Will they continue to come?

The enrollment at the seminary during the first 14 years of President Naylor's administration showed an unexpected decline. This was not just a problem at Southwestern Seminary but at all seminaries, including other Southern Baptist seminaries that were part and parcel to declining enrollment as well. Whatever the cause of this decline may have been, seminaries, along with many other educational institutions, experienced the same kind of decline in enrollment. Southwestern demonstrated a cumulative enrollment drop in 1958-1959 to 2,395. The low point was reached in 1966-1967, when the naysayers were predicting the death of theological education when the enrollment was at 1,859.[43]

The reason for the decline was never completely identified, but the annual cumulative enrollment never reached the 1958-1959 figures of 2,395 again until the 1972-1973 sessions, when the enrollment increased to 2,406. The decline was most drastic in the School of Theology and the School of Religious Education, with only a small drop in the School of Church Music. In the midst of the downturn, a turnaround was on the horizon, and everyone could feel the spirit of the growth spurt beginning to rumble in the halls of the Kingdom. God was once again going to send "the called" to prepare for ministry to reach the lost in a dying world, and the seminary would once again ring with the voices of men and women "called to the ministry of Christ."

Notes

1 Carroll, B.H., *Standard*, 16 November, 1905, p. 2.
2 *Proceedings*, B.G.C.T., 1906, pp. 45-46.
3 *Celebrating 100 Years, Est. 1908*, Southwestern Baptist Theological Seminary, 2008, p. 20.
4 Ibid., p. 20.
5 Ibid., p. 20.
6 Price, J.M., *School of Education*, Unpublished Paper by J.M. Price, p. 1.
7 Ibid., p. 2.
8 Ibid., p, 3.
9 Ibid., p. 3.
10 *Invitation Letter from L.R. Scarborough to J.M. Price*, March 12, 1915.
11 Ibid., *Price*, p. 4.
12 Baker, R.A., *Tell the Generations Following* (Nashville: Broadman Press, 1983), p. 206.
13 Ibid., Price, p. 5.
14 Joe Davis Heacock, *A Historical Sketch, 1921-1989, SWBREA*, April, 1921, p. 2.
15 Ibid., p. 6.
16 Operational Baptist Biographical Data Form for Living Person, Southwestern Baptist Theological Seminary, Fort Worth, Texas, 1933.
17 *The Scroll*, Southwestern Baptist Theological Seminary, Vol. 3, No. 5, Fort Worth, Texas, 1946.

18 Baker, R.A., *Tell the Generations Following*, (Nashville: Broadman Press, 1983), p. 220.
19 Ibid., p. 398.
20 Faculty Minutes, 3 March and 11 March, 1932.
21 *Celebrating, 2008*, p. 39.
22 Ibid., Price, p. 7.
23 Ibid., Baker, p. 335.
24 Terry, Jack, Dedication of the Ann Bradford Foyer, Robert and Goldia Naylor Children's Center, Unpublished Document, 4 April, 1990, p. 1.
25 Ibid., p. 2.
26 Price, J.M., Unpublished document, 1945.
27 The Fort Worth Press, "Bible School Leaders to See Arts and Crafts," Friday, April 26, 1963, p. 20.
28 Ibid., Baker, p. 293.
29 Baker, R.A., *Tell the Generations Following*, (Nashville: Broadman Press, 1958, p. 220.
30 Ibid., p. 335
31 Ibid., p. 336-337.
32 Ibid.
33 Ibid., p. 338.
34 *Celebrating 100 Years, Est. 1908*, Southwestern Baptist Theological Seminary, 2008, p. 85.
35 Ibid., Baker, p. 380
36 Trustee Minutes, 22 November 1977.
37 Ibid., p. 390.
38 Ibid., pp. 391-392.
39 Ibid., p. 401.
40 Ibid., p. 408.
41 Ibid., Price, p. 4.
42 Ibid., Baker, p. 410.
43 Ibid., 417.

Photos
Page 10– Portrait of J.M. Price.

Page 17– Religious Education faculty circa 1923. **Front** (from left): J.M. Price, Anne Laseter, L.R. Scarborough, Bertha Mitchell, N.R. Drummond. **Back**: T.C. Gardner, T.B. Maston, Forbes Yarborough.

Page 20 – T.B. Maston's social recreation class, 1945.

Page 27 – J.M. Price addressing spectators at the groundbreaking for Price Hall, 1949.

Page 29 – Students of the School of Religious Education, 1949-1950.

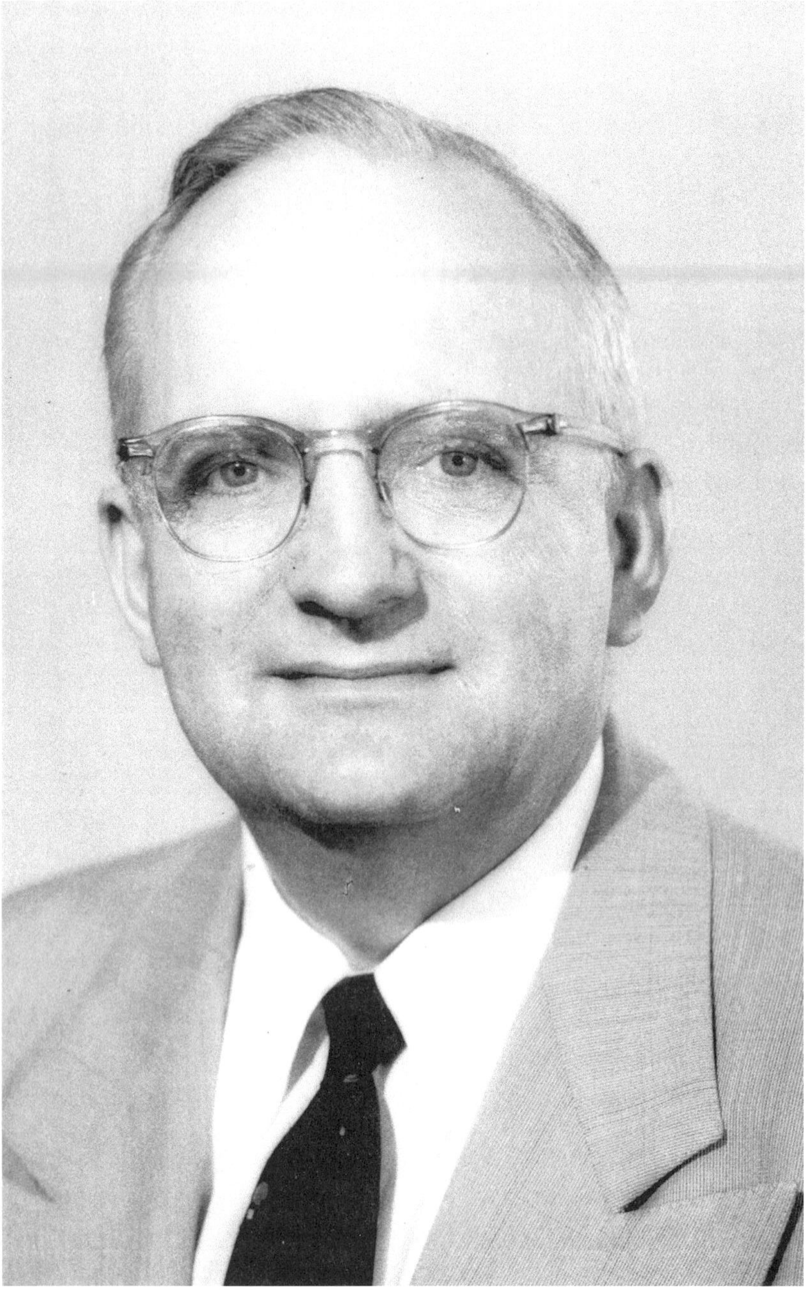

Chapter 2

The Called—
Will They Continue to Come?
1970-1979

The School of Religious Education Begins to Grow

The enrollment turnaround was not immediate between the late 1960s to the mid-1970s but more of a gradual movement of the Spirit of God working in the hearts and lives of men and women identifying opportunity for ministry in churches and convention organizations. The needs of the churches were moving far beyond the traditional tasks of ministers of education, youth, and children, which had been the norm. In a more broad sense, ministry positions that could only have been imagined a decade before were beginning to appear in churches. Many churches recognized the need for highly specialized educational ministers who could do more than organize a Sunday School or establish an evangelistic outreach program; they could reach out into a vast, growing plethora of educational experiences and bring to the church the new exciting opportunities for educational initiatives needed in these church programs. President Naylor saw the growing needs and encouraged Joe Davis Heacock, dean of the School of Religious Education, to look beyond the parameters of the present educational programs in the church, to evaluate what kind of educational leadership roles would be needed in the decades to come, and to secure qualified faculty to teach to these growing educational leadership roles now being discovered in the church.

Academic Growth Begins with the Faculty

Joe Davis Heacock was the man to get the job done. He was a "gentle giant" and an outstanding administrator. Heacock led the great Olivet Baptist Church, Oklahoma City, Oklahoma, for seven years as minister of education and served with the Southern Baptist Sunday School

R.E. Faculty - 1965

Heacock's heart was in the church, and he knew its educational needs as well as the need for educational leadership in the denomination. Heacock had served with distinction in both arenas and knew what kind of educational ministers would be needed in the years to come. Who, then, was better to evaluate the teaching ministry of the School of Religious Education and to recommend faculty acquisitions to meet those needs than Heacock?

The School of Religious Education had experienced a number of faculty retirements with such notables as T.B. Maston, R. Othal Feather, Gracie Knowlton, Ann Bradford, Ralph Churchill, and A. Donald Bell. To replace these faculty stalwarts would be a task in itself, but to replace them with well-trained practicing churchmen and women who could lead the students to the next level of educational leadership growth was a challenging task.

Faculties attract students, and this was the reason Heacock matriculated at Southwestern in 1935. His greatest desire was to study principles of teaching at the feet of master teacher J.M. Price and education administration with W.L. Howse, the consummate administrator. In 1944, Heacock was elected to the faculty in the department of religious education administration and was a colleague with W.L. Howse until Howse moved to the Baptist Sunday School Board in 1954.

During the 1960s, Heacock discovered and recommended seven new prospective faculty members, and all were elected: Harvey B. Hatcher from Carson-Newman College, Jefferson City, Missouri, in communication arts and drama; Harold T. Dill in youth education; A. Donald Bell to psychology and human relations; James D. Williams as assistant professor of adult education; Jeroline Baker as assistant professor of childhood education; Charles Tidwell as assistant professor of education administration; and Jack D. Terry, Jr., as assistant professor of history and philosophy of education.

Enrollment Begins to Climb

The timing of the acquisition of these seven new faculty members coincided with the beginning of a new student growth in all three schools. The enrollment in the 1970 spring semester was 1,679, the largest spring enrollment in 10 years. There were 1,089 in the School of Theology, 425 in religious education, and 116 in church music. A composite report of the 1969-1970 annual enrollments indicated a growth of 60 students more than in 1968-1969, for a total enrollment of 2,069 students.[1] Naylor reported to the board of trustees at their spring meeting, March 3-4, 1970, that there were 1,314 enrolled in the theology school, 570 in religious education, and 212 in church music (its largest enrollment ever). More than 600 new students began their instructional programs at this time.[2]

SACS Accreditation Received

The newly acquired accreditation by the Southern Association of Colleges and Schools (SACS) may have prompted this increase in enrollment. The SACS accreditation followed the re-accreditation of Southwestern Seminary by the Association of Theological Schools (ATS). ATS is the major accrediting agency for theological schools in America. This re-accreditation came after a 10-year self-study. Southwestern received its full SACS accreditation during its business session at the regional accrediting agency's annual convention in Dallas, December

3, 1969.³ Heacock had served as chairman of the faculty committee that had worked for several years toward achieving the accreditation. The seminary was now recognized as equal in its accreditation to any major university or school in the United States.

Felix Gresham, dean of students, noted, "This accreditation will make easier the transfer of credit between the seminary and other graduate schools of other colleges and universities. Although courses may be transferred from one school to another, requirements of each individual school will still have to be met in respect to definite courses that will transfer."⁴

Students completing academic work at other institutions had the opportunity to transfer course work to Southwestern as it applied to the degree program sought. The new accreditation may be one of many factors for the enrollment increase.

Children's Building and Price Hall

The board of trustees was very active during its 1970 March and November meetings, discussing the much-needed renovation of Price Hall, the construction of a new children's building, and the need for a new home for the president. The trustees had broached the subject of a new official residence for the president but not without confrontation. J.L. Burke, who represented a minority report from the building and grounds committee, acknowledged the problems the seminary would face concerning the official residence because of a denominational controversy (use of Cooperative Program funds not specified for construction) that had arisen. In a congenial spirit, he declared himself to be in favor of continuing the official residence on its original schedule in the development of the campus plan.⁵ The continuation of land negotiation for the location of the children's building was reported to the executive committee as well as the resumption of plans for the renovation of Price Hall following the removal of the kindergarten room from that building.⁶

The curriculum committee of the trustees recalled a motion made in 1965 about a change in nomenclature of the doctor's degree offered by the School of Religious Education from Doctor of Religious Education

(D.R.E) to the Doctor of Education (Ed.D.). There had been substantial alumni inquiry about exchanging the D.R.E. for the Ed.D. This interest resulted in a recommendation from the committee on advanced studies of the School of Religious Education and with the approval of the president and deans of the schools:

> That all Southwestern graduates who desire to exchange the D.R.E. for the Ed.D. Degree be required to take two seminars or four semester hours of regularly scheduled doctoral courses in Religious Education preferably in the area of their major.[7]

The motion carried, and several who had inquired about the change of nomenclature of their D.R.E. to an Ed.D. degree made requests to the committee on advanced studies of the School of Religious Education. A plan to complete the leveling work to change the nomenclature of the degree would be discussed with the appropriate committee.

In the November 24, 1970, trustee meeting, the curriculum committee of the trustees approved a new addition to an already generous sabbatical leave program, which provided a one-year sabbatical after seven years of continuous service. Attached to this provision was a stipulation that all faculty members would serve for as many as two years following a sabbatical leave and that no sabbatical leave would be granted within the three years prior to retirement age.

A new course in the School of Religious Education, Modern Philosophies of Education, was advanced for approval. With the coming of Terry in history and philosophy of education, there was a need for a second course to investigate modern educational philosophies. The one philosophy course offered was primarily focused on the study of the five classical historical philosophical schools of thought: Idea-ism, Realism, Thomism or Scholasticism, Pragmatism, and Existentialism. The new courses would explore the emerging philosophies of education such as: Progressivism, Essentialism, Perennialism, Reconstructionism, Language Analysis, and Postmodernism and the impact on the 20th century educational movement.[8]

The new children's building was an important topic during this November 1970 trustee meeting, following up on references made from the May 5, 1970, meeting of the executive committee. The negotiation for the land needed for the construction of the children's building was discussed along with the importance of planning for the renovation of Price Hall after the removal of the kindergarten from that building.[9] Price Hall renovation became more significant during this meeting because there had been an evaporative condensing component that had failed in that building, and the trustees approved the acquisition of air-cooled condensing equipment with installation before the next air-conditioning season.[10] F. Howard Walsh reviewed the preliminary planning toward the construction of the children's building and the renovation of Price Hall as the next immediate capital projects.[11]

Heacock, in a special edition of Southwestern News on the School of Religious Education (November 1970), emphasized the growing need for specialized ministries in the field of religious education. He noted, "Last year we received 600 inquiries from local churches and the denomination for personnel for 18 different educational vocations, not including the pastoral and music fields." He continued, "We get calls for social workers, day school directors, campus student workers, religious journalists and curriculum writers. This is a healthy trend. Although church staffs may not be increased numerically in the local church the scope of the staff member's work may be altered." Heacock said, "I think the men and women we have prepared have helped break down the false conception that there is an 'education program' versus a 'pastoral program,' and each part complements the other."[12]

Price Hall renovation called for major changes to be made in the building. The plan called for a learning center that would be a resource center for future curriculum writers. A video library—with videotapes of various kinds of teaching situations that could be viewed, critiqued, and evaluated—was part of the plan. The tapes would be of classroom teaching experiences, counseling sessions, soul-winning situations, and leadership enlistment demonstrations. The curriculum required every student to have an individual learning situation similar to those that are presently used in major universities and colleges. Programmed instruction, a newly developing concept under the direction of LeRoy Ford, would assist students to learn at their own pace.

Charles Tidwell, chairman of the School of Religious Education's curriculum committee, supported Heacock's proposal for more diversified training for the educational minister. Tidwell said, "The movement toward a more individualized curriculum for each student is the future goal. Presently each religious education student is taking 36 hours in the School of Religious Education, 22 in the School of Theology and two in the School of Church Music with 8 hours of free electives taken in any of the schools."[13]

Learning a way of teaching that allowed a student to progress at his own pace was part of the required curriculum for religious education students. The concept of programmed instruction, a method of teaching and learning, was developed over the last several years by LeRoy Ford, professor of programmed instruction and principles of teaching. This concept of self-paced instruction squared beautifully with the emerging concepts expressed by the curriculum committee for more individualized instruction. Ford, who came to Southwestern from the adult division of the Sunday School Department of the Baptist Sunday School Board (LifeWay), had been working on this teaching methodology for several years. Ford said,

> Programmed Instruction involves the use of 'program holders'—materials designed to hold information to be assimilated by the student at his own speed. The holders may be specially designed textbooks, filmstrips, audio or video tapes. Programmed Instruction forces the teacher to be specific in sating the learning objectives. Each program

begins with a statement of what the student is expected to learn by the time he finishes the course.[14]

Students who used programmed instruction listened to the materials again and again until they grasped the material. Before the end of the 1970s, a new curriculum in the School of Religious Education would emerge with goals and objectives guiding the entire learning process for every course listed. A course description manual would be developed so each student could search the content of every course to determine if that course would be valuable to him as he prepared to choose the ministry path that he planned to follow. It would be an exciting adventure as each student and faculty member worked in tandem to see that the student would receive the necessary information and skills needed for performing ministry in the local church as well as in many positions in the denomination.

M.R.E./M.S.W. Degree Available

As the 1970s rolled toward the holidays and the end of the fall semester, another "first" took place in the School of Religious Education. Gary and Shelia McInnis, a new breed of Baptist churchmen, were enrolled in the department of social work in the School of Religious Education, where they studied and did clinical work under the direction of Alpha Melton, professor of social work. Gary combined studies in the education school with others in the music school while Shelia worked on a combination degree plan that would give her degrees in religious education and social work. They both combined their seminary study with field work in the Baptist Goodwill Center in Fort Worth.

Southwestern had a cooperative arrangement with the University of Texas at Arlington that allowed students to receive the Master of Social Work degree at the same time they received the Master of Religious Education degree. Gary used his music background with the children at the Baptist Goodwill Center while Shelia used her studies to work with the social and spiritual needs of the people who came to the center. Both expected to work in a local Southern Baptist church in their respective fields. Gary said, "We view what we do as a complement to the ministry of preaching and teaching, as a valid part of the ministry of the church in reaching people where they are and helping them. Our ultimate aim is vitally connected with evangelism."[15]

The Master of Religious Education/Master of Social Work (M.R.E./M.S.W.) degree was a new degree offered by the School of Religious Education for those who desired to do social ministries in churches or in the denomination. Furthermore, an advanced degree, Graduate Specialist in Religious Education (GSRE), was planned for those who desired to specialize in a specific area of religious education. A thesis or its equivalent in approved research or clinical work setting would suffice. With the change of nomenclature in 1965, the Doctor of Education degree was offered to prepare men and women for advanced service in the field of religious education in colleges, universities, seminaries, or denominational agencies.

ATS Grants Awarded

Toward the end of the year, two faculty members were awarded grants from the American Association of Theological Schools (AATS). The faculty fellowships were used during their sabbatical leaves the next year, 1971.

John J. Kiwiett, professor of historical theology, studied the theme "Faith and Good Works: A study of 'Christian Voluntarism' in Dutch Theology (1459-1650)." Born in the Netherlands, Kiwiett did most of his research at the library of the University of Leiden and the Royal Dutch Library of the Hague.

James D. Williams, associate professor of adult education, did research on several patterns of adult education and hospice care intervention in Great Britain. He was a participant-observer in several "lay institutes" in England and on the continent. Williams was the "first" faculty member from the School of Religious Education to receive such a grant.

Naylor said, "It is unusual for AATS to provide two such grants to a single institution. The $4,000.00 grants are awarded only to professors whose sabbatical programs of study and writing are approved by AATS and are made possible from foundation funds."[16]

Enrollments Continue to Grow

The spring and fall enrollments continued to show a steady increase in the number of students preparing for ministry. The enrollment for the spring of 1971 was 1,775 compared to 1,669 a year ago—an increase of 88. This figure included 154 students enrolling for the first time compared to 116 the previous year.[17] In a similar manner, the fall enrollment was 1,920—the largest fall enrollment in the last 11 years.[18] The School of Theology recorded 1,282, the School of Religious Education reported 454, and the School of Church Music enrolled 184, "the highest enrollment for any single semester in the history of the school."[19]

This was the fifth consecutive year in which the enrollment at Southwestern had increased when the trend in theological education had been declining in enrollment. There were 505 students enrolling for the first time. President Naylor's report to the trustees at their November 22, 1971, meeting was a final accumulative enrollment of 2,171—1,384 in the School of Theology, 577 in the School of Religious Education, and 210 in the School of Church Music. First-time students numbered 724.[20]

As Heacock declared, students came to study where an excellent faculty resides in any school, and the continuing growth was indicative of this prediction. During the 1971 academic year, five professors were elected to the School of Religious Education by the trustees. In an effort to increase the staff in the social work program, two social work professors were chosen along with two adjuncts. William L. Crews was elected as associate professor of social work after serving as assistant secretary in the department of Christian social ministries of the Home Mission Board (now the North American Mission Board, or NAMB). Clark Dean was appointed as instructor in social work. He had served under appointment of the Foreign Mission Board (now International Mission Board, or IMB) as a social worker in Hong Kong. He was also a social worker with the Detroit Public Welfare Department. Dean taught courses in child welfare, human growth and development, and theoretical dimensions of social work.

Also teaching in the department as an adjunct was Tom Foster, on juvenile delinquency and problems and tasks in social work. Dr. Gordon

Maddox, seminary physician and director of the Walsh Medical Center, taught in the field of medical information.

Alva G. Parks was invited to serve as an instructor in education administration. Parks had served the First Baptist Church, Montgomery, Alabama, for the past 13 years as minister of education. He was later elected to the faculty as associate professor of administration in 1973. Phil Briggs was elected associate professor of education administration. He completed his M.R.E. (1957) and D.R.E. (1964) at Southwestern Seminary. While a student at Southwestern, he was a graduate fellow in the School of Religious Education. He served as an associate pastor, youth director, and minister of education in various churches in Oklahoma and Texas.

The last of the five elected and/or appointed in 1971 was Hazel Morris. Morris was elected as assistant professor of childhood education. Her background included five years of teaching experience in the public schools of Ohio. She also served as the director of a day nursery program in Louisville, Kentucky. Prior to her appointment at the seminary, she served as director of children's work at First Baptist Church, Jackson, Mississippi, from 1968-1971.

Gift Makes Children's Building a Reality

The largest single gift in the history of the seminary at the time was made by a friend of the institution. The reported gift of the Fleming Church Loan Trust with the Baptist Foundation of Texas was designed first "to provide the cost of constructing and equipping a children's building to be known as the Goldia and Robert E. Naylor Children's Building, following which the income from the principal shall continue to be paid to the Seminary as unrestricted endowment income."[21] The gift of $750,000 to the seminary's endowment fund was announced by Naylor during the semi-annual meeting of the board of trustees, November 22, 1971.[22] Preston Geren Architects finalized the plans for the new building.

The estimated cost of the building was $500,000, and construction was anticipated to begin in early 1972. The building provided nursery facilities, day school, and kindergarten programs for preschool children of seminary families. A laboratory for students as a clinical and research training center in childhood religious education was a major function of the building. The completion of the building provided churches, educational institutions, and other educational agencies an invitation to visit the building and to see how preschool departments for church-related activities (i.e., Sunday School, church training, missions education, preschool children's choirs, musical instrument instruction, and kindergarten instruction from birth to 5 years of age) need to be constructed and furnished.

The furnishings in the building were the most modern, up-to-date preschool furniture designed with the preschool child in mind. Each of the learning centers for small group activities (home-living, art, books, puzzles, music, nature) plus the use of the larger portion of the room for the big-group teaching and worship activities would have the finest educational furnishings for preschool education available.

Visiting institutions were invited to observe each of the classes in action from special observation rooms in each of the classrooms. The two-way glass allowed the visitors to observe the activities being done in the classroom without interrupting the class. The observation rooms would be used for classes in preschool education in the School of Religious Education to come and observe the teaching methodologies, teaching activities, and leader administration to be used in their class work. This building was designed to be the most correct preschool building for the implementation and study of preschool education in the nation.

As a closing part of the building and grounds committee presentation to the trustees, March 2, 1971, it was recommended that the planning for the renovation of Price Hall be put in place as rapidly as possible after the construction of the children's building, to which the kindergarten operation, now in Price Hall, would be transferred. The chairman, F. Howard Walsh, went on to state that the recommendation of the building and grounds committee that:

> the administration, the Chairman of the Building and Grounds Committee, and the Chairman of the Finance

Committee be given power to act in arranging to begin construction on the Children's Building and the renovation of Price Hall, and to borrow funds for these projects, to enable the improvements to be made without waiting for receipt of capital needs income from the Southern Baptist Convention.[23]

Walsh announced that the plans for the official residence for the president were near completion and that contract negotiations were in the making. The trustees expressed pleasure with the outlook for an early beginning of construction for the official residence, which would be completed by the end of 1972.

The motion by Walsh was realized in early 1972. The official residence construction began in 1971 and completed in January 1972.

In the president's annual report to the trustees, he identified what Heacock and others had been predicting; that is, the number of students, the quality of their commitment to ministry, and the effectiveness of their service had finally become the measure of the institution. The accumulative enrollment of 2,171 and the continuous movement upward were the criteria the president wanted to show the trustees, and this year, it could be shown.

Echoing Walsh, Naylor said, "There will continue to be building needs. The Children's Building, so long hoped for, is now a reality. The Physical Fitness Building seems near at hand. Certainly, the time for the renovation of Price Hall waits only upon the removal of the kindergarten from that building."[24]

Faculty Recognized and Honored

During the year, several members of the religious education faculty were active in institutes, workshops, and conferences on and beyond the campus. The Southwestern alumni luncheon held in conjunction with the June Southern Baptist Convention annual meeting in St. Louis, Missouri, honored several outstanding alumni. Joe Davis Heacock, dean of the School of Religious Education, was one of three honored at the annual meeting. Heacock had been on the faculty since 1944 and had been dean since 1956.

Three School of Religious Education faculty members—Charles Tidwell, James Williams, and Jeroline Baker—were recognized for outstanding achievement and professionalism during their sabbatical studies. Tidwell, professor of church administration, studied at The American University in Washington, D.C. His studies were in church program development and church family financial planning. In addition to his studies, he also planned to author a textbook for use in church administration curriculum.

James Williams, associate professor of adult education, studied at the University of London. He was invited to be a guest lecturer at Spurgeon's College during the second and third terms. His lectures included "The Church's Educational Program and Evangelism" and "The Church's Opportunity in Adult Education." Williams was at the University of London studying and researching various patterns of adult education in Great Britain, including the British hospice movement. Williams returned with a hospice program that was implemented in St. Joseph's Hospital, a large Catholic hospital in Fort Worth. That hospice program is still actively engaged in Fort Worth hospital communities at this writing.

Jeroline Baker returned to North Texas State University to complete her residency on her Ed.D. Baker planned to graduate with her doctorate before the completion of the new children's building. She would serve as the professor/director of the Goldia and Robert E. Naylor Children's Building when it opened.

Two prolific writers on the religious education faculty published books during this academic year. John W. Drakeford, director of the Marriage and Family Counseling Center and professor of psychology and counseling, wrote a new book entitled *Games Husbands and Wives Play*. The book was published by Broadman Press and was described as a unique approach to some of the common problems encountered in marriage, including resentment, hurt, sexual antics, spying, and other troubling marital situations. His seventh book, *The Awesome Power of the Listening Ear*, published by Word, was his best seller.

LeRoy Ford, professor of programmed instruction and principles of teaching was another prolific author on the faculty. He wrote the fourth in a series of *Using the ... in Teaching and Training* books. His first book in the series, *Using the Lecture in Teaching and Training*, took on the format of a multi-media publication. Each book blended text and cartoons to give instruction to teachers and leaders of large groups to use when employing the lecture as a teaching/learning activity. Each book was available in book, filmstrip, and chart-set format.

Ford's new series of programmed instruction manuals gave rise to the religious education emphasis *Using Video Tapes in Teaching and Training* and was the emphasis for the School of Religious Education on the Southwestern campus in April 1971. All who attended received practice in the operation of television equipment provided by major manufacturers and participated in demonstrations of such teaching and training techniques as "microteach." Microteaching involves the use of videotapes to replay short segments of a teaching-learning situation for the purpose of developing specific skills in teaching and training. Each participant learned to use videotape as a diagnostic tool.

The use of television in the individualization of instruction also received attention from the teaching authorities. Outstanding authorities in the field of education and programmed instruction and instruction using microteach led to Southwestern hosting a conference on these subjects. Co-chairmen for the conference were Southwestern professors LeRoy Ford and Jack Terry. The television equipment made available for this teaching/learning conference was part of the new technology emphasis under the leadership of President Naylor. During his administration, the seminary began to use more advanced technology to improve education.

Enrollment Growth Continues

As 1972 came blustering in with a vicious Texas "Blue Northerner" winter storm, so did the need for the completion of additional buildings on the campus at Southwestern. The official home for the president was in the forefront, with preliminary studies completed as early as 1968 with approval for residence completion by the spring of 1971.

The major thrust for a building for the care and instruction of children had been a high priority of the trustees for many years. With the gracious gift of $750,000 by Mrs. Bessie Fleming, the building would be built and endowed.

Even as early as 1963, the last of the major building projects, the physical fitness center, had held high priority as a major project for many years. The possibility of this center was brought up again in late 1971 at both trustee meetings.

The construction of these new major buildings changed the appearance of the campus. Differing from the Memorial Building architectural style, the new student center faced the south side of the original campus, with the president's new residence immediately across the street to the south of the old campus. This new arrangement gave credence to the plans of the trustees to extend the campus to the south.[25]

The need for the new buildings and additional space was highlighted by the spring enrollment, because the 1972 spring enrollment was the largest enrollment in the 64-year history of the seminary. The enrollment of 1,840 was an increase of 83 over the 1971 enrollment figures. The accumulative enrollment of 2,295 represented the highest total enrollment in 14 years.[26] The School of Religious Education increased from 430 to 436 students.

Trustees Move Quickly to Construct and Renovate

The trustee spring and mid-year meetings, March and July, were important to the continuing leadership of the School of Religious Education. Dean Heacock would reach retirement age at the end of the 1971-1972 academic year, but because of the emphasis on the children's building and the renovation of Price Hall, trustees felt it necessary for him to continue his responsibilities as dean through 1973. Jack Terry, who had completed three years of service, was given tenure, and Jeroline Baker was recognized for completing her Ed.D. degree at North Texas State University. Baker, along with Hazel Morris, assistant professor of childhood education, would play key roles in the development and planning of the children's building. Their expertise and knowledge of childhood equipment and usage would become an invaluable commodity when the selection and purchase of equipment would be made.

Several key components of the children's building and the renovation of Price Hall were introduced at this mid-year meeting. As soon as the architects and engineers had the plans for the children's building ready, professional consultants were engaged for the immediate planning, remodeling, and renovation of Price Hall after the kindergarten was moved from the building. Naylor reported on the prospect of a designated gift to provide facilities for a Learning Resources Center to be located in Price Hall, room 117.[27] This facility would be utilized by the entire seminary when cassette tapes, videotapes, and other visual materials of the lectures of the professors were made available. The Learning Resource Center was an enhancement to the continuing development of programmed instruction and instructional television.

Revolutionary Curriculum Changes in the School of Religious Education

A workshop held in April 1970 brought together religious educators from across the nation to discuss the importance of performance-oriented curriculum. Out of this conference came additional study committees that led to a major revolutionary change in the School of Religious Education curriculum. Unless there was some educational need to know what was happening to the curriculum design of the School of Religious Education, the great revolutionary changes that were being made would have slipped by. Surveys of churches, foreign and home mission boards, denominational organizations, state conventions, local Baptist associations, and multiple denominations that had ministers of education who attended Southwestern were conducted. When the surveys were completed by the curriculum committee, the move to determine exactly what kind of "educational ministers" were needed to do the task of educational ministry in the church began to come to light.

The curriculum design in the past had been a "tightly structured" curriculum requiring all students to progress in lockstep educational studies that were important to the churches and agencies. That curriculum was a "prescribed curriculum" that students took no matter what they had taken at their college/university or had in church experiences. The new approach was to move to a totally "elective curriculum" based on the student's past learning and experience. James Williams, chairman of the curriculum committee of the School of Religious Education, said,

> The program is designed to enable students to tailor a program according to their needs and interests. In order to provide comprehensiveness and balance to the program, a student will be required to take a certain number of hours in major discipline areas. In the past the student was required to take an over-abundance of 'survey-type' courses. We were not putting our best foot forward by offering such a curriculum. But, now, we can assist the student in selecting courses primarily related to his needs and interests.[28]

A curriculum syllabus, prepared by the faculty, was made available to each student who enrolled under the new program. It contained a complete description of every course in the curriculum. Such items as course objectives, units of study, descriptions and examples of tests, a sample assignment sheet, and a working bibliography were included.

The new curriculum program was developed by the religious education faculty based on a study that asked the question, "What do churches and agencies expect of our graduates?" Recognizing this was a baby step in the development of a comprehensive curriculum plan, this intermediate step toward a more performance-oriented curriculum was designed to relate to the student's present situation more effectively.

Ted Ward Directs Instructional Television Workshop

A major outgrowth of the introduction of programmed instruction in the School of Religious Education was the use of television as an instructional tool in the educational ministry of the church. Television can be used as a major teaching tool with any programmed instruction format. The content input provided by a television clip is followed by probing questions and inquiries. The student is asked to practice with the information and listen to the feedback from the information given in the television clip. The feedback directs the learner toward the correct learning outcomes.

During the spring of 1972, a major instructional television workshop was provided by the School of Religious Education. The workshop was designed to help church leaders understand the role and use of television in the church's educational program. The keynote speaker for the workshop was Ted Ward, director of international education at Michigan State University. Ward was known for his contributions in the field of programmed learning techniques. As an educational consultant in the field of programmed instruction via television, Ward had been utilized by such organizations as the Committee to Assist Mission Education Overseas, the Ford Foundation, the British Broadcasting Company, and the U.S. Office of Education. Instructional television and programmed instruction took a leap forward after the conference.

Fifth Annual Youth Lab – "Breakthru"

In the spring of 1972, following the Instructional Television Workshop, was the fifth annual Youth Lab with the theme "Breakthru," which took over the campus. The first Youth Lab (1968) invited youth ministers and those who wanted to become youth ministers to come to the campus and attend a youth ministry conference. In this fifth year, the intent was to introduce activities that generally take place away from the church campus, such as indoor and outdoor recreation, social recreation, camps, retreats, mission outreach activities like a "Coffee House" house, etc.

A new youth course, "Minister to Youth," which dealt with the specific aspects of youth ministry like qualifications of a youth minister, job description, problems that confront youth ministers, developing relationships with parents, grandparents, and the youth's circle of friends was introduced to the conferees for the first time. This course was specifically aimed at the professional preparation of youth ministers. The lab attracted a large group of youth ministers as well as would-be youth ministers and a large group of adult youth leadership who desired more training for working with youth.

The Growth of Theological Education by Extension (TEE)

In 1968, there were no Brazilian laymen enrolled in any type of theological educational extension program. Two years later, more than 1,500 laymen in Brazil had been enrolled in various seminary extension courses. By 1972, more than 4,800 laymen in Latin America were taking courses in theological education by extension (TEE). LeRoy Ford said, "Most mission areas are highly dependent upon the local layman. However, bringing these natives to a central point for theological training proves impractical. The only answer was to take the school to the pupil and programmed instruction made this possible."

In January of 1970, Ford was invited to lead a programmed instruction seminar for missionaries from 15 foreign mission societies and boards. In summer 1971, CAMEO (Committee to Assist Mission Education Overseas) sent Ford to Brazil to conduct two one-week seminars. These were designed to train mission personnel how to prepare curriculum for individualized instruction.[29]

Ford led workshops in programmed instruction for Southern Baptist missionaries in Indonesia on the campus of the Baptist Theological Seminary, Semarang. The campus expanded to include additional branch centers for programmed instruction around Indonesia. This approach to theological training, education by extension, was essential for the larger growth of seminary education for Christian leadership and Christian lay-leadership overseas and around the world.

Change Is in the Air

At the suggestion of Naylor, the trustees appointed a committee on November 20, 1972, to study the possibility of restructuring the administrative organization of the school. This committee recommended on March 2, 1973, that the trustees name four vice-presidents: for administrative affairs, for academic affairs, for business affairs and for student affairs. The vice president for administrative affairs would supervise the work of development, public relations, and alumni activities. The vice president for academic affairs was charged with overseeing the academic program of the school, the work of the three deans, the director of admissions, the registrar, the director of libraries, and the continuing education program. The vice president for business affairs involved leadership in business management, the controller, the director of computer services, and the director of the medical center. The function of the vice president of student affairs gave direction to the school chaplain, the director of student aid, the dean of men and the dean of women, the director of student housing, the director of student activities, and the director of recreation and physical fitness center. President Naylor was pleased with the results of this administrative overhaul.[30]

An additional change in the air was the campus rumor mill discussing who would be the new dean of the School of Religious Education. Joe Davis Heacock had been given a year beyond his normal retirement date to oversee the construction of the children's center and the renovation of Price Hall. Both of these major building activities were well underway and would be completed within the next year. Heacock had played an important role in bridging the difficult gap and providing continuing leadership when J.M. Price, the founder of the school, retired in 1956. Robert Baker said of Heacock:

> In his relations with his faculty and the other two schools of the seminary, Dean Heacock fostered a new unity that reflected his gracious ministry. As will be noted, he broke new ground in building on the foundations laid by J.M. Price. He had the ability to seek out creative men and women for his faculty and utilize their talents completely. He was a popular administrator, teacher, writer and speaker before his retirement and has continued on to be effective in these areas since that time. Honored by the trustees and faculties of the three schools when he retired, he was named to be dean emeritus of the School of Religious Education on November 22, 1977.[31]

Outstanding Faculty Additions

Heacock sought out four bright young professors to join the ranks of the faculty of the educational school. Even though they knew his retirement was near and would have enjoyed close colleagueship with him, they chose to join the faculty of the School of Religious Education, placing their future ministry with Southwestern Seminary. These elected faculty included Phillip H. Briggs, an outstanding youth minister and professor of educational ministries and youth ministries at Mid-America Baptist Theological Seminary, Kansas City, Missouri (1971); Hazel Morris, who had been an adjunct teacher at the seminary and assisted Jeroline Baker in the planning, development, and construction of the children's building (1971); Theodore Dowell, 20-year missionary in Korea and an outstanding psychologist (1973); and Alva G. Parks, a graduate of Southern Seminary and an outstanding minister of education from Birmingham, Alabama, who was working on his Ed.D. and teaching adjunctively for a couple of years at Southwestern Seminary before being elected to the faculty as instructor in educational administration (1973).

The Goldia and Robert E. Naylor Children's Center

In January 1973, ground was broken for the construction of the children's building. Joe Davis Heacock, dean of the School of Religious Education, reminded the crowd, "We have an obligation to provide the best religious education training for the more than 700 preschool children of our students and indirectly the multiplied thousands of children across the convention."[32]

The facility is a learning and clinical training center for seminary students studying in the field of childhood education. Located next to the Walsh Medical Center, the 27,000-square-foot building is designed for flexibility and efficiency. There are two rooms for each age level, from 6 months to 5 years of age. As the needs increase or decrease in any age-level rooms, the rooms are equipped with movable walls to handle that problem. Every two rooms have adjoining restroom facilities and storage space. Each room is equipped with ample counter space with adult- and child-size sinks.

A large inner court for the center of the building serves to accommodate additional classes (i.e., music clinics, specific exercise activities for special students who need additional exercise outside their learning environment, etc.). The large room doubles as a playground (with in-door movable playground equipment) in inclement weather.

A spacious outdoor playground wraps completely around the building and is available for daily play (weather permitting) for the children from many exits of the building. Jeroline Baker said, "Blocks of time will be devoted to Bible teaching, planned activities, music activities and playtime."[33]

Enrollment Surges to a New Record Level

Southwestern Seminary, already the world's largest theological seminary at the time, registered a 10 percent enrollment gain in the fall 1972 semester as the seminary experienced its largest single semester enrollment increase in its 66-year history. The final registration was 2,227—208 over the previous record of 1972—with a total of 592 new students. The School of Theology enrolled 1,390; the School of Religious Education, 597; and the School of Church Music, 240.

Jesse Northcutt, vice president for academic affairs, believed three reasons contributed to the enrollment increase: (1) a revival among American youth; (2) a large increase in the number of young people in Southern Baptist colleges and universities committed to vocational Christian work; and (3) a major part of the youth revival movement with a return to a more evangelistic conservative outlook. Prospective students were looking for an evangelistic, biblically conservative seminary. The accumulative enrolment for 1972-1973 was 2,406.

Changes in the School of Religious Education

The talk was buzzing around the campus as the trustees came in March 1973 about who would be the new dean of the School of Religious Education. Many names were batted about, but until the trustees met in their March meeting, no one would know for sure. Everyone knew Joe Davis Heacock would retire in December, and there had to be a new dean in place who could work with him for at least six months before the mantle was passed on. As part of the academic committee's report to the trustees was made, in it was the name of the person who would become dean. The motion by Jim Coggin was "that Jack Terry be elected Dean of the School of Religious Education to succeed Joe Davis Heacock at his retirement at the end of this fiscal year." Dr. Coggin's motion had a second by Joe Burnette. President Naylor presented data relating to experience, training, and response to exploration made concerning the prospect of Dr. Terry's service in this area. The motion was carried unanimously.[34]

There were other elections and promotions made at the same meeting. These were James D. Williams, raised to the rank of professor of adult education; Clark Dean, elected assistant professor of social work; Ted Dowell, elected assistant professor of psychology and counseling; Alva G. Parks, elected assistant professor in education administration; Derrel R. Watkins, elected assistant professor in social work; and George R. Wilson, elected professor of administration and principles.

Though unknown at the time, the School of Religious Education was poised to become the largest in the world. Enrollments and additional faculty added in the next six years provided the impetus that would put the School of Religious Education at the forefront of religious education worldwide. It was a proven fact that students came to study with the finest professors in the field of Christian education, and the School of Religious Education would have those fields of study available within the next five to seven years.

Not long after his election, Terry was interviewed in Southwestern News about his vision for the future of the School of Religious Education. In the interview, Terry laid out his vision for the students who would be coming to study and the courses they would take. Working with LeRoy Ford at the beginning of the development of the new self-paced programmed curriculum, Terry deemed it important for the school to become more aware of the performance of the graduates when they went to a church or place of service. There was a need to put in the churches competent people who were skilled in education leadership and had experience in the educational ministry of the local church. The self-paced curriculum that was in the process of development would determine what students were offered and how thoroughly they would be trained in the performance of the ministry of education.

Terry gave glowing accolades to the leadership of Joe Davis Heacock. He had observed that Heacock encouraged the faculty to put more emphasis on accountability in performance. His openness allowed many of professors to go far beyond the limits of a prescribed curriculum and explore the possibility of performance-based instruction as the guide to a more elective experience infused in the curriculum. Heacock was a great educator and leader. This was demonstrated in his leadership of participatory activity rather than top-to-bottom directed management. He allowed his faculty to range far and wide and to bring to the table different kinds of educational sequencing that would determine how they would make the students more competent and skilled in the work of ministry. The School of Religious Education had turned out competent people, but what needed to be added was a curriculum that would provide an evaluation of their ministry skills before they graduated and left the school.

The course curriculum guide would set goals and objectives and was being worked on every day with the intent that all departments and disciplines would write their course syllabi in achievable goals and objective statements that could be accomplished. There would be an increased use of videotape in the classroom, especially in principles of teaching courses that did microteaching and psychology and counseling, which would allow students to evaluate their own teaching or counseling performance with the opportunity to critique the teaching/counseling experience immediately. There was a plan to expand the use of videotape beyond microteaching into the other disciplines so simulations of educational processes could be used for future instruction with classes. There was a need to use case studies, via videotape, from various disciplines in the classroom that encouraged additional studies in the field of study.

One of the most important needs was the development of a comprehensive internship program. Students beginning in the fall 1973 semester would take two semesters of field education. The first term was to acquaint the student with the numerous professional fields of ministry available to a person trained in religious education. At one time, it was minister of education and youth minister, but now, possibilities included recreation leaders, children's leaders, preschool leaders, kindergarten leaders, social workers, psychologists and counselors, and missions both at home and abroad. Most came with one idea of the educational ministry, and the task was to take them beyond this one idea and lead them to the ministry for which they were best trained. The final semester would include an internship in a church with an educational minister in his discipline in order to be in the center of that ministry work.

An important provision of this new approach to curriculum design and the new goals and objectives associated with each course would allow the faculty to take students to the professionalism they desired in their chosen field of service. The basic desire was increased evaluation of performance as well as academic knowledge. The catalog said the School of Religious Education is a graduate and professional school; that was true. The plan was to fulfill that major objective given the school by the trustees and the Southern Baptist Convention.

Who is this New Dean?

Jack Terry came to Southwestern in 1969 after 10 years in local churches as minister of education and music and four years as associate professor of Bible and religious education at Hardin-Simmons University, Abilene, Texas. He first came to Southwestern as a student in August 1956, earning his Master of Religious Education (1962), Doctor of Education (1967), and later his Ph.D. (1994). During that time, he served at churches in such Texas towns as Fort Worth, Baytown, Lake Jackson, and North Richland Hills.

In the late spring of 1969, President Naylor invited Terry to join the Southwestern faculty as assistant professor of philosophy and history of education, principles of teaching, and history of Jewish education. He has remained at Southwestern, serving in both faculty and administrative roles, ever since.

Car Trouble Brings Blessings

Southwestern News magazines from 1950 to 2015 contain many interesting articles and human interest stories that happened on and beyond the seminary campus during those 65 years that feeble minds have forgotten. Anyone can leaf through the copies of Southwestern News and find thrilling stories in every issue, every year, every decade that have impacted the School of Religious Education and the seminary. To put closure on the year 1973 is the amazing God-directed intervention story about LeRoy Ford's spiritual experience on a vacation to Mexico.

Ford had led conferences, institutes, and workshops in Latin American countries using the newly developing programmed instruction model and developing goals and objectives for instruction. The vacation was to be a tour through Mexico ending in Acapulco. Just a few miles from Mexico City, his transmission went out. He was towed into the city to a garage, and for four days, he waited for his car to be repaired.

The National Autonomous University of Mexico was just adjacent to the garage where Ford's transmission was being repaired. This story that transpired was so impressive that Robert Baker in *Tell the Generations Following* writes about the God-directed broken transmission and the chance meetings that followed. There was no doubt it was a God thing, and He was in each aspect of activities in Mexico and the next seven years. Baker recounted,

> Ford of the School of Religious Education happened to have his car near the campus of the National Autonomous University of Mexico in Mexico City. While waiting for repairs, he visited the Center of Didactics to observe what they were doing in teacher training, since he was involved in instructional technology involving programmed instruction. He conversed with *Inge Alphonso Bernal Sahagun* at the center, who had become so interested in Ford's work that they talked for two hours, and the American teacher promised that he would return to assist the faculty in Mexico in mastering the principles they discussed.[35]

Ford returned to Mexico City to fulfill his promise. He was asked by the university to develop a system of teacher training for use by its faculty. During the time he assisted the professors in Mexico, he developed a system of training for Sunday School teachers of the Southern Baptist Convention to improve their teaching as well.

The National University of Mexico was so impressed by the thoroughness and effectiveness of the program that at the end of 1973, a group of their teachers, mainly scientists, was sponsored by the Mexican government for a visit to Southwestern's campus to study the techniques involved in the program.[36] The group returned in succeeding years, and in 1974, a conference was developed on the Southwestern campus to train these friends from Mexico. There were eight universities of Mexico represented at this conference.

During the next five years, invitations to visit the National University of Mexico in Mexico City were extended to several religious education and theology faculty members. This international fellowship of scholars was fruitful for each party involved.

God Bless the Children

The spring meeting of the seminary trustees had, among other things, three major reports from the building and grounds committee. A final inspection for the children's center with the architect, contractor, project manager, and seminary representatives was held at the end of the trustee meeting, March 1, 1974. The inspection showed the building was ready for opening on Founder's Day, March 14, 1974.

The second report highlighted the renovation and remodeling of Price Hall, to begin immediately following the removal of the kindergarten from Price Hall to the children's center. It was noted in the minutes that the faculty committee of the School of Religious Education had decided upon the space utilization that would best provide additional classrooms and faculty office space to be shared, as needed, by the members of the teaching staffs of the other instructional divisions of the seminary.

The third report was about a recent conference with Robert Naylor, Harold Dill, Jesse Northcutt, John Seelig, Jack Terry, and J.R. Leitch to adopt the faculty plan for space utilization for immediate adaptation by the architects and engineers for structural and mechanical plans to carry out the design determined by the faculty. The three-pronged report was enthusiastically received by the trustees. Later, at the July 2, 1974, trustee meeting, Naylor reported the progress of the renovation of Price Hall for the School of Religious Education and that the building renovation itself would be completed in time for the fall semester.

During that trustee meeting, Jeroline Baker was recognized for her leadership in the planning and construction of the Naylor Children's Center, named director of the Goldia and Robert E. Naylor's Children Center, and given a merit raise for work well done. Hazel Morris, assistant professor of childhood education, who worked diligently alongside Baker, was given academic tenure. Harold Dill was moved from the youth education department in the School of Religious Education to become professor of field education. His minimal load would be six hours of field education classes on campus and four hours of work as director of field education experiences in local churches. Phillip Briggs was moved to the youth education department to assume the youth education responsibilities formerly carried by Dill. Briggs was promoted to associate professor of youth education, teaching courses in communication arts, church publicity, and church public relations.

Goldia and Robert E. Naylor Children's Center

The Goldia and Robert E. Naylor Children's Center was dedicated following chapel on a beautiful, chilly spring Founder's Day, March 14, 1974. The chapel program was a tribute to J.M. Price, "Trailblazer in Religious Education." Joe Davis Heacock, recently retired dean of the School of Religious Education, traced the historical activities that brought Price to this day. He recalled how Price received a letter from L.R. Scarborough inviting him to establish a "School of Christian Pedagogy" at the new Southwestern Seminary. Scarborough wrote, "I think we have hold of the small end of a *larger proposition*. We will have to do pioneer work and break ground."[37] Price became synonymous with religious education among Southern Baptists, and by the time he retired in 1956, the school he founded was offering more than

129 courses, had enrolled more than 6,000 students and graduated 2,250, and had become the model of a school of religious education for similar institutions.

The School of Religious Education building was the first educational building in America exclusively designed for teaching religious education and offering bachelor's, master's, and doctoral degrees. Throughout his career, Price used his writing to enlarge his ministry. His best-known book, *Jesus the Teacher*, has sold more than 250,000 copies and has been printed in four languages. Heacock concluded, "Scarborough had been right. The task at Southwestern had proved to be a *big proposition*."[38]

At the conclusion of chapel, all were invited to meet at the children's center just across the street from Price Hall. President and Mrs. Naylor led in vows of dedication for the 27,000-square-foot structure, which would accommodate more than 200 preschool children of seminary students, staff, faculty, and the Fort Worth community. The center was made possible by an anonymous $750,000 contribution. The donor stipulated that the building be named the Goldia and Robert E. Naylor Children's Center in honor of the fifth president of the Fort Worth seminary, which he had served since 1958.[39] A spacious inner court offered such creative playthings as an oversized turtle, blocks large enough to crawl through, and a flexible caterpillar-like tunnel, all in bright colors that children like best.

As part of the dedicatory program, seminary student Olin D. Collins expressed appreciation on behalf of families like his in which the wife must work while the husband attends seminary. Conner concluded his remarks by saying, "I predict that the new building will pay 'future dividends for God's work.'"[40]

The Called Are Coming in Droves

For the fifth consecutive semester, Southwestern Seminary continued to set enrollment records. This spring's total of 2,109 was a new high for a spring registration, and it pushed the cumulative total for the 1973-1974 academic year to a record 2,662. The previous cumulative record was 2,471 in 1957-1958. This outstanding spring enrollment of 2,109 included the School of Theology with 1,315, the School of

Religious Education with 574, and the School of Church Music with 220. Assisting in reaching this record cumulative enrollment was a large summer school enrolment. A total of 892 students enrolled for two summer sessions, including 121 new students. There were 515 in theology, 253 in religious education, and 124 in church music. Registrar L.L. Collins reported that the increase in enrollment had followed a trend begun in the summer of 1971. Since that time, a new enrollment record had been established each fall, spring, and summer.

In response to the continuing growth and the need for a more intensified field education program, the faculty of the School of Religious Education had been in the planning process for over a year of developing a program and organizing a strategy to introduce a new innovative design for field education at the seminary level. Harold Dill had been professor of youth education since 1959. However, Dill was the perfect faculty person to fill the role of professor of field experience. His exceptional educational experience in the local church prepared him to lead the new field education program by using his church ministry expertise as the model for the development of the new intensified field education course experience. This move allowed the faculty to expand its offerings in youth education. A large number of prospective students desiring to become youth ministers were matriculating at Southwestern.

Phil Briggs was no stranger to the field of youth education either. He had six years of youth education teaching experience at Midwestern Seminary. He gained additional experience from participating in numerous conferences and workshops with special emphasis on youth culture. Although Southwestern Seminary had been the pioneer in the youth education field, the new re-emphasis was the result of several conditions. An increasing number of churches were searching for trained youth ministers or combination people who could do youth work and some other phase of ministry (i.e., music, recreation, social missions, etc.). The other emphasis was the growing awareness that the call to youth ministry is a lifelong vocation and not a stepping stone to some other position on the church staff. Major changes in the curriculum were expected to include the development of several additional courses in youth education. Also expected was the expanded use of resource persons, such as established youth workers and denominational personnel, who could provide input into the development of the special youth emphasis courses.

The Renovation of Price Hall

The religious education students who came to the campus for the 1974 academic year were greeted with the new Naylor Children's Center and the renovation of Price Hall in progress. The renovation necessitated that all faculty and classes be moved to other parts of campus because the whole of the building was under renovation. As a result, classes were being held on the stage in Truett Auditorium, various rooms in the student center, and in some of the School of Theology classrooms that were not in use that semester.

All of the religious education faculty offices were temporarily established in the missions room next to Truett Auditorium. The entire room was retrofitted with standing partitions, giving each department in the school a particular part of the room. Upon entering the room, one would see signs identifying where each department group and respective faculty cubicles were located. Each department had a small open area where students could meet with the professors. Secretaries were scattered all over the room convenient to the individual professors, and each professor had a cubicle where materials and books were kept for classroom instruction. The dean's office was at the entrance to the room, with a cubicle for Dorothy Pulley, administrative assistant to the dean; a small area for the printer, supplies, and on-campus mailbox; and a cubicle for the dean.

Despite the minor inconvenience, there was a great spirit of cooperation among the students, and colleagueship among the faculty. A major problem for the professor was carrying all the books, papers, and other materials that needed to be used in the classroom. The "camp-out" experience, in the long run, proved to be a fun fellowship activity. The renovation of Price Hall was completed November 1, 1974.

The newly renovated Price Hall may have looked like the same building from the outside (with the exception of the Astroturf runners at the four entrances), but on the inside, the interior was not what it used to be. The 25-year-old structure was under renovation for six months, and the result was new flexible spaces that would meet the training needs of religious educators for the next 25 years. Classroom space had been changed from seven large classrooms to eleven smaller classrooms. Each of the new classrooms was equipped with an overhead projector and screen as well as chalkboards, bulletin boards, and large tablet stands with large writing tablets. The large tablet pages could be pasted around the room for multiple learning activities such as recall, brainstorming, problem-solving, paraphrasing, and other learning activities. Movie projectors, tape recorders, and other electronic equipment were available from the learning resource center. In the near future, video cameras and recorders would be available for classes to produce learning activity sequences in the classroom.

The largest of the seven multi-purpose rooms was divided into five different teaching areas where smaller learning activities could take place within the context of the larger learning activity of the professor for that day. The kindergarten area was replaced by an experimental learning center equipped with the latest video and audio-visual materials. New office space was added, with seminar rooms for graduate doctoral seminars located in close proximity to that discipline's department area and near the professor's office suite.

An extensive area was prepared for the school's pioneer psychology program, The Southwestern Baptist Marriage and Family Counseling Center. The area in the building was expanded and had a permanent location. An added feature was several in-take interview rooms, which would be used to meet with the clients who came for counseling and to do private and class evaluation of video-recorded counseling sessions and for evaluation by the professors and the graduate students in psychology and counseling.

A new elevator was added to the building. Former students remember how many times they carried classmates, who were in wheelchairs, to the second floor so they could attend class. The elevator would be a benefit to faculty members who needed to transport heavy loads from their offices to the classrooms.

LeRoy Ford was instrumental in the development of the Learning Resource Center in Price Hall. The room was developed with the faculty in mind as they prepared and developed audio and video learning materials for their classes. The demand for the availability of video and audio tape equipment, in a central location for professors who developed non-print learning activities for class, was the major impetus for such a room. Naylor suggested the facility be placed in a central location on the campus so faculty and students from all three schools could use it. The center would be located on the northwest section of the first floor. Although the committee felt the space was not what they needed, plans went on to get what was available with the hope that more space could be carved out later.

Ford said the development of the center would "no doubt open up new dimensions in teaching approaches. The ultimate aim of the center is to enable professors to develop a personalized system of instruction and a programmed instruction system of instruction for the students."[41]

The School of Religious Education was going to continue with the "firsts" that Price had established. The renovated Price Hall would provide the first opportunity for a student in religious education to study the development of programmed instruction for church ministry, and that opportunity was readily available in the renovated building that offered faculty and students opportunities to explore an expanded method of study that happens in and beyond the classroom. Dean Jack Terry said, "Flexibility is the key word for the newly renovated Price Hall for the School of Religious Education."[42]

Teacher Certification for Religious Education Students

A statement of agreement between Southwestern Seminary and Dallas Baptist College (DBC) was approved for students to receive teacher certification while studying at the seminary. This agreement would make it possible for seminary wives to obtain teaching certificates as well. With these credentials, the religious educators or pastors' wives could qualify for a teaching job to supplement the family income, especially in pioneer areas where pastor salaries may be meager.

Dean Jack Terry announced that the School of Religious Education and J.R. Osborne, director of teacher education at DBC, enabled DBC graduates to obtain up to 16 hours of advanced standing toward a master's degree in religious education. The agreement was expected to eliminate duplication in course content in the two schools' degree programs and encourage more education majors to select religious education as a career.

By encouraging more students to consider religious education as a ministry, the new arrangement would help meet the increasing demand for qualified persons in churches and the denomination. In a typical year, Southwestern received over 600 requests for recommendations for various vocational positions in religious education. However, the School of Religious Education only graduated 125 to 150 persons with degrees in this area. The new agreement took effect immediately, and the first students to benefit from it could begin their program in the spring semester of 1974.

Unprecedented Enrollment in 1975

Both the spring and fall enrollments established unprecedented benchmarks for enrollment growth. Registrar L.L. Collins reported that 2,343 students had enrolled for the spring 1975 semester, with 248 new students. Collins also noted that there usually was a significant decrease in enrollment from fall to spring, but this year that trend was reversed. Another record-breaking statistic was an all-time high cumulative enrollment of 2,858. The count by schools for the spring semester was School of Theology, 1,448; School of Religious Education, 631; School of Church Music, 264. Collins noted, "We are seeing more students remain in the seminary to complete their training rather than leave after a year or two. These young people are tired of the false values of society which have been highlighted by recent national events."[43]

Following the unprecedented growth of the spring semester, there was a growth-shattering record in the fall enrollment. All previous records were broken with an unprecedented 2,892 signed up for fall classes. This total shows a 20 percent increase over the previous fall's record-breaking enrollment of 2,394. Included in these new figures were 921 new students. This represented a 45 percent increase in new student enrollment. Of this number, 108 students had enrolled at the seminary's branch program in Houston. The program, called Southwestern Seminary in Southeast Texas (SET), offered graduate-level courses in the Houston and Galveston area. Jessie Northcutt, vice president for academic affairs, pointed out that the seminary had already reached the projected student enrollment for 1981:

More students seem to be committing themselves to Christian ministry.... Our work here closely parallels with the number of church work volunteers in Southern Baptist colleges and universities. Much of this interest can be attributed to the recent revivals in the youth culture that have caused students to turn toward a more conservative faith and to Southwestern Seminary. There is also an immeasurable spiritual factor involved in the enrollment upswing.[44]

Northcutt and the three deans had nothing but praise for the increased enrollment. Huber L. Drumwright, dean of the School of Theology, said, "The increased enrollment will make demands on us to continue doing a first-rate teaching job."[45] James McKinney, dean of the School of Church Music, observed that, since 1967, "we have more than doubled our enrollment. The church music field is an area which is fairly new and is experiencing growth throughout the Southern Baptist convention."[46]

The School of Religious Education experienced the greatest percentage of growth among the three schools. Commenting on the 23.5 percent enrollment increase, Jack Terry, dean of the School of Religious Education, said, "The enrollment increase is due in part to the increasing awareness of the 'multi-faceted opportunities in ministry that religious education offers.'"[47]

The count for the 1975 fall enrollment by schools was School of Theology, 1,760; School of Religious Education, 821; School of Church Music, 311. The ever-increasing enrollment made it necessary for Naylor and the trustees to consider additional faculty acquisitions for each of the three schools.

Trustees Praise Completed Construction

Five years of trustee involvement in selecting property for new construction, making determinations of buildings to be constructed and/or renovated, developing architectural drawings and schematics, receiving unusual blessed gifts from major ministry partners to fund the desired construction needs, and breaking ground for construction of the children's center and the president's residence had, at last, ended in a flurry of construction and renovation. The trustees could sit back, take a deep breath, and get on with the business of running the largest theological seminary in the world.

The regular mundane business of overseeing the institution became the emphasis of the 1975 trustee meetings. An evaluation of the operating funds from the Southern Baptist Convention for the year 1976-1977 was reported. Obligations of expenses retired from the Cooperative Program, capital needs income designated for the Barnard Hall project, and other items were important subjects discussed along with other denominational necessities and responsibilities.

The report of the academic affairs committee to the trustees reviewed the unprecedented enrollment in the spring and fall semesters, noting that the enrollment increase was 20.8 percent. Northcutt reported on the success of the Houston Extension (SET) located on the Houston

Baptist College campus and that other areas such as San Antonio and Oklahoma City had expressed a desire to explore the possibility of an extension program similar to the Houston plan. He also gave a comprehensive explanation of the support pledged for the southeast Texas program by nine associations in the Houston-Beaumont-Galveston area.

A major nomenclature change was made for two academic committees in the School of Theology: "The name of the Advanced Studies Committee changed to the Committee for the Doctor of Philosophy Degree; the name of the Professional Studies Committee changed to the Committee for the Doctor of Ministries Degree."[48] Each of the two other schools changed the names of their doctoral committees within the next year.

Derrel R. Watkins was elected as assistant professor of social work. Watkins came with a social work background with practice as a research assistant, training consultant, and director of the Good Will Center, Fort Worth, Texas.

George R. Wilson was elected as professor of education administration in the School of Religious Education. Wilson was appointed by the Foreign Mission Board of the Southern Baptist Convention in 1956 as a career missionary to Hong Kong. He served Hong Kong Baptist College as professor of religious education, acting president, and dean of academic affairs. Trustees approved two new doctoral courses—administration by objectives and research in administration—to fit Wilson's administrative expertise.

Scholarships Named for School of Religious Education

The School of Religious Education became the recipient of endowed scholarships that recognized worthy and outstanding students of religious education while recognizing honored religious education faculty members:

The *Joe Davis Heacock Scholarship Fund* was established by the Southwestern Religious Education Association in honor of the retired dean of the School of Religious Education. It was to be given to an outstanding first-year M.R.E. student and provided funds for two semesters of school. The recipient of this scholarship would be decided on by a vote of the religious education faculty. The scholarship was awarded annually.

The *Albert G. Marsh Memorial Scholarship Fund* was established by Dr. Glenn Marsh, a Kentucky physician and brother of Leon Marsh, professor of principles and philosophy of religious education, in memory of their father. The award would be made every three years and benefited an outstanding Doctor of Education student selected by the committee for advanced studies in the School of Religious Education on the basis of scholarship, experience, and potential for leadership.

The *R. Othal Feather Scholarship Fund* was given to a first-year doctoral student majoring in administration and doing research in educational evangelism. This fund was set up by Bob Feather to honor his father, who served as a professor of educational administration at Southwestern Seminary for 23 years before he retired. The dean of the School of Religious Education, the professor of educational evangelism, and one other member of the religious education faculty selected the recipient of this scholarship.

The *George W. Stuart Memorial Scholarship Fund* was established by Mrs. Ferne Stuart in memory of her husband. This fund provided a scholarship for one year of academic work for a person 30 years of age or older who had answered the call to full-time religious education service.

Terry pointed out,

> In order to insure an on-going recognition of these outstanding religious education students, former students who studied with and were closely involved with these faculty personalities for whom these endowed scholarships are named, are going to be encouraged to make additional contributions to these funds to be certain that each fund will have sufficient resources to make the awards each time they are given.[49]

Bookshelf Contributions in 1975

The normal faculty theme around most academics institutions is "publish or perish." Southwestern does not hold as tenaciously to this academic requirement as most institutions of higher education; however, the trustees and administration do expect the faculty to be researching and publishing scholarly works on a regular basis.

John Drakeford, the most prodigious author on the religious education faculty, continued to produce new volumes during the year. He published *How to Manipulate Your Mate* (1974) and *Do You Hear Me, Honey?* (1975). These were Drakeford's eighteenth and nineteenth publications. His works have gave Drakeford such notoriety that he was invited to be one of the featured speakers at the Continental Congress on the Family that met in St. Louis in October 1975. More than 3,000 church leaders and family-life specialists were invited to participate in the national symposium. The purpose of the four-day meeting was to clarify and re-define the church's biblical mission to the family and to consider ways to deal with contemporary issues facing American families. Drakeford's address was titled "Strengthening the Pastor's Family Counseling Skills." '

Another religious education faculty member publishing materials during the year was James Williams, professor of adult education. He wrote "Personal Learning Activities" for the 1976 January Bible Study week in *Hosea: Prophet of Reconciliation*.

Charles Tidwell, professor of church administration, co-authored *Creative Church Administration* with Lyle E. Schallar, regional church planning officer for a non-denominational agency representing 14 denominations in the Akron-Cleveland-Lorain region of Ohio. This was a book of ideas and insights that offered churches innovative ideas on increasing membership, decision-making, and finances.

Eighth Annual Youth Lab

The eighth annual Youth Lab's theme for 1975 was "Faith, Footprints and Foolishness." Phil Briggs, newly elected professor of youth education and coordinator for this year's lab, noted that the year's theme came out of three major considerations concerning the ministry of youth education. "Faith" represented the spiritual elements that are major players in any dynamic youth educational program; "footprints" were the suggested guidelines needed to produce a well-balanced program of youth education; and "foolishness" covered the fun and recreational aspect of all youth programs.

The lab attendees were: practicing ministers of youth education from around the convention, lay-leaders who worked with youth in the church, and members of youth groups from churches locally and across the state. Enrollment exceeded 250 for this year's lab.

R.E. FACULTY – 1957

Death of J.M. Price, Pioneer Educator

The most important lead story from the School of Religious Education in 1976 was the death of its founder, J.M. Price. Price died January 12, 1976, at a local hospital after a brief illness.

For a man of small physical stature, Price cast a lengthy educational shadow over the religious educational world of the Southern Baptist Convention, the nation, and the world. Price stood only 5 feet, 8 inches tall and weighed just 150 pounds, but he was a *big man* when it came to religious education. He was much like his fellow Kentuckian, Daniel Boone, for he, too, was a "trailblazer" who crossed the mountains to pioneer countless opportunities for advances in religious education in the West.

During his lifetime, Price had the privilege of seeing his religious education books translated into four languages. His greatest book, *Jesus the Teacher*, became a standard study course book among the Southern Baptist Convention Sunday School training course study programs.

Price earned six degrees, two of them doctorates as well as two honorary doctorate degrees. Over his 41 years as director and professor in the School of Religious Education, Price touched the lives of thousands of students. He laid the foundation for future advances in religious education. His personal work in the churches touched and inspired Sunday School workers all over America.

When Price retired in 1956, the school was offering 129 different courses and had enrolled over 6,000 students in the preceding four decades.[50] At his death, Southwestern News reported,

> While Price was busy establishing the School of Religious Education his objective was to establish a biblical basis for such an education. He stressed the teaching aspect of ministry and laid the groundwork for the various teaching ministries which would follow in the years to come. It was his keen understanding of new trends that made it possible for the School of Religious Education to have students ready when new vocations opened up. Courses were offered at Southwestern that had never been offered anywhere before. Price also worked for coordinating and establishing church organizations and vocations. He had the idea of a complete church where all the parts were working together. Under Price's leadership the School of Religious Education became the first religious education school in the nation to be accredited by the American Association of Theological Schools.[51]

The Called—Will They Continue to Come?

Faculty colleagues recalled personal memories of their student days and faculty association with Price. Joe Davis Heacock, retired dean of the School of Religious Education, noted his concept of the total place religious education has in God's plan for the redemption of man and his ability to think far ahead of his day, always reaching out for new ideas.

T.B. Maston, retired professor of Christian ethics: "He was one of the best teachers I ever had. He was alert to new developments and very creative. He was very meticulous and his desk was always covered with stacks of papers, but they were systematic stacks."

Leon Marsh, professor of foundations of education: "Price was a fighter, he had to be trying to build the School of Religious Education and establish it as a reputable field of Christian learning. I never once saw him angry. He had the uncanny ability to look ahead and form ideas for a school that would meet the educational ministry needs of local churches in the future."

John Drakeford, distinguished professor of psychology and counseling, came from Australia and took some religious education courses with Price. He said he owes a debt of gratitude to Price for taking him in, offering financial assistance, and most of all trusting him to teach a course or two while he worked on his doctorate.

Phil Briggs, professor of youth education, wrote his doctoral dissertation on the religious education of Price. He said, "[Price] always used humor to get his point across and never hurt anyone with it."

Before the funeral, Price lay in state in Price Hall. There could have been no better chapel, no finer monument, no greater honor.

Price was small in stature, but he lived large, and the shadow cast by his untiring career at Southwestern Seminary will touch generations of religious education students for years to come. Humor, determination, innovation—J.M. Price was many things to many people, but there was one thing they would all agree on: "He was clearly, priceless Price."[52]

The Students Just Keep Coming

1976 was a banner year for an increased enrollment of over 3,200 students. The figures demonstrated that Southwestern doubled its enrollment in the last 10 years. The fall total for 1976 was 11 percent over the previous fall's record-breaking enrollment of 2,892. This record doubled the enrollment of 1,560 in the fall of 1966. The seminary had experienced a record high enrollment every fall semester since 1966. All three schools had record enrollments: School of Theology, 1,915; School of Religious Education, 968; School of Church Music, 319. In addition, the Houston SET program enrolled 113, and the Oklahoma program, in its first year, enrolled 51.

J.M. Price would have loved to see the high enrollment in the School of Religious Education, having known the school began with two students and five courses. However, this was not the end of the enrollment growth. God was going to bring additional students to Southwestern to study in the three schools and at the extension centers in Houston and Oklahoma.

Trustees Hail Opening of Extension Center in Oklahoma

The Houston SET extension proved to be an important opportunity for students in the Houston and surrounding area to have seminary education in their own backyards. As of fall 1976, this would be true for prospective students in Oklahoma City and its surrounding areas, as well. Southwestern Seminary opened a branch center offering fully accredited training in the Oklahoma City area during the fall 1976 semester. This program was a joint endeavor with the Baptist General Convention of Oklahoma that underwrote the program along with the seminary. Oklahoma Baptist University provided the classroom space and support activities. The initial opening day of classes was August 30.

All the courses were expected to be taught on the OBU campus at Shawnee, with the full resources of the Mabee Learning Center to be made available to seminary and new students. Professors from Southwestern flew to Oklahoma each week to conduct the various courses. According to Jesse Northcutt, vice president for academic affairs,

> The opening of the second branch reflects a growing movement in theological education throughout the country. As a part of this movement more seminaries are taking their resources to the minister rather than have the minister

come to the seminary. Extension centers of this nature are especially needed among Southern Baptist churches where less than half of all pastors have little if any seminary training. We are encouraged by the response of pastor and church staff personnel to our two extension center programs.[53]

With such an enrollment increase and the need for professors to teach in Houston as well as Oklahoma, the trustees recognized the need for additional faculty in all three schools. William G. Caldwell was elected assistant professor in educational administration and became director of the Church Business Administration Certification Center at Southwestern in 1980. Mrs. Hal (Paula) Brooks was elected as instructor in communication arts. She taught church public relations and drama in the church. Phil Briggs, professor of youth education, introduced a new course, The Church's Ministry with College and University Students, which was approved by the trustees.[54]

The trustees made a motion to adopt an appropriate resolution recognizing the outstanding service rendered through Southwestern Baptist Theological Seminary by the late J.M. Price and to put an appropriate plaque in the rotunda of Price Hall to honor the occasion. Another motion was made to honor the family of the late J.K. Winston, Jr., who gave the initial land on which the seminary is located. The appropriate plaque was placed in the entrance foyer of Fort Worth Hall to honor the family's generous gift. The executive committee made a suggestion that the president and staff explore the location of a plaque in the rotunda of Price Hall in the School of Religious Education appropriate to the identification of its founder, after whom the building was named.[55]

Naylor Announces His Retirement

One final action at the November meeting was the announcement by President Naylor about his plans to retire. The announcement came during the opening session of the meeting. His retirement would become effective in August 1978. The retirement date would culminate 20 years as president and 50 years since he entered the seminary as a student.

Judge Oswin Chrisman, chairman of the board of trustees, said, "The announcement of Naylor's retirement as president of Southwestern Seminary comes at a significant time in the life of this great institution and in his life as well. Naylor's 20-year anniversary and retirement will climax a 50-year relationship with Southwestern, which spans almost two thirds of its history."[56]

Course Description for the Master's Programs

An educational process that had been fermenting since LeRoy Ford introduced programmed instruction to the faculty was the development of each course in the master's programs in competency terms. The religious education faculty voted and had a workshop on March 8, 1976, to continue working on the Course Description Manual, asking each faculty member to realistically set a challenging goal of completing in his discipline "X" number of courses that needed to be written in competency goals, objectives, student outcomes, learning indicators, etc., by the time of the workshop in March.

At this point, 48 percent of the courses had been expressed in competency terms in the present syllabus. Looking ahead to the workshop, the curriculum committee made these provisions for the coming publication of the Course Description Manual:

> That the following principles be followed in the preparation for the book form of the Manual rather than in Syllabus form: Copy ready materials be in the printer's hands four weeks before release date, to allow for one week at the bindery. Last year, 1975, 421 Syllabus were printed and 10 copies are left in syllabus form; Forty-five of ninety-two courses are in competency terms for this year's Manual; Goal for next year to increase the number of courses in competency terms to seventy five to eighty per cent of the ninety-two course offerings.[57]

The workshop was successful, and the Course Description Manual was completed on schedule and sent to the printer. Finally, the Course

Description Manual was in bound-book form and not in a loose-leaf notebook. The manual was updated annually to keep improving the quality of the descriptions so every student could examine the course syllabus in the manual and determine the competencies that were available to be learned during the course of the study. Eventually, the manual became a great tool for course selection and degree completion in the School of Religious Education.

Faculty Members Publish

Communications and devotions in the family were the theme of the new book written by John Drakeford, professor of psychology and counseling. *A Proverb a Day Keeps the Troubles Away* was a book designed for family devotions. There were 90 different proverbs from the Bible listed here. Each had a devotional passage for use with it. There was a section on how to have "table grace." Drakeford felt that the book of Proverbs in the Bible is a marriage and family counselor's handbook. He believed that the proverbs deal with many of the current issues concerning the family. This was Drakeford's 20th published work, and he prayed the book would assist families in developing a better home life, devotional life, and church life.

Charles Tidwell, professor of church administration, co-authored a book called *Creative Church Administration*. Tidwell wrote chapters on subjects such as motivation, enlisting and developing volunteer leaders, developing a church ministries plan, and financial capital improvements. The book was designed primarily for practicing church ministers, no matter what position they may hold in the church: pastor, minister of education, business administrator, executive administrator, etc. Tidwell confessed that these were the very subjects that plagued him during his time as a minister of education in a local Baptist church and wanted to help the young ministers avoid some of the mistakes most often made in the church administration.

Presidential Search Committee Appointed

A presidential search committee was named by Oswin Chrisman, chairman of the board of trustees, at the spring 1977 meeting. The nine-member committee comprised seven trustees, a faculty member, and a student representative. The task assigned them was to recommend a successor for current president Robert Naylor, who had announced plans to retire in 1978. Trustees named to the search committee were James Carter, Lynn Clayton, Dan Cooper, William Cumbie, Louis Gibson, J.T. Luther, and Robert Potts. The faculty representative was William B. Tolar, and the student representative was Mary Lois Summers.[58]

The search committee spent several months seeking a man whose background and stature had prepared him to take up the task of leading the world's largest seminary in a challenging era. On November 22, 1977, James Carter, chairman of the search committee, brought the recommendation to the trustees that Russell H. Dilday, pastor of the Second-Ponce de Leon Baptist Church, Atlanta, Georgia, be named the sixth president of Southwestern Baptist Theological Seminary. Dilday was presented to the trustees for nomination and to the seminary as a whole at the conclusion of his election.

Dilday was invited to address the board for the first time and outlined a three-point vision for the seminary at a strategic time in the life of the denomination, when the bold mission thrust was on the horizon. The three-point vision included:

- "a strong spirit for the relationship which must exist between the seminary's three schools, the local association, the state convention, and other Southern Baptist agencies. I seek a new relationship between trustees, administration, faculty, and students."
- a strong faculty "committed to faith in Jesus Christ and committed to the local church." Dilday noted the importance of faculty having academic excellence and reputation and being adequately compensated.
- a strong curriculum with specialized studies for the diversified interests of student preparing for ministry. "It is my commitment for a biblically based curriculum with the Bible

on every reading list. It is also my hope that our training can be practicalized."[59]

The trustees were pleased with the vision statement and named Dilday as the sixth president of Southwestern Seminary, to begin his tenure in 1978.

A major item from the three trustee meetings in 1977 was a request for additional faculty because of the increased enrollment in the three schools. Tommy L. Bridges was elected as assistant professor of administration. Bridges had served as minister of education at several churches in Texas and Arkansas, and he served as director of special mission ministries for the Arkansas Baptist State Convention from 1972-1977. Charles W. Ashby was elected as instructor in foundations of education. Charles A. Tidwell was named to fill the newly endowed Chair of Denominational Relations established by the Baptist Sunday School Board of the Southern Baptist Convention (LifeWay). The inauguration of this chair provided for additional instruction in all the programs fostered by the Sunday School Board.

The School of Religious Education had such growth in the past two years that several adjunct professors were appointed to teach additional courses: W.F. Howard, adult Education; William (Budd) Smith, foundations of education; Bill McKinney, foundations of education (research and statistics); Mel Brown, social work; and Joe Davis Heacock (retired dean), education administration.[60]

One last item on the academic agenda was a motion by Joe Burnett, trustee from North Carolina, that the board of trustees name Joe Davis Heacock dean emeritus of the School of Religious Education.[61] The motion passed.

During the mid-year meeting, June 15, 1977, the trustees voted on a severance package for President Naylor and bestowed on him the title "president emeritus." The package contained seven items that would assist Dr. and Mrs. Naylor in their retirement years. A list of these severance items are in the June 15, 1977, trustee minutes.[62]

The business affairs committee announced that the trustees accepted a bid from the Walker Construction Company for the construction of the physical fitness building. The contract was approved, and ground was broken for the construction of the building in April 1977. Construction officially began in September 1977, with the awarded contract of $1.6 million for the multi-purpose recreation and physical fitness center.

The 40,000-square-foot building would be the focal point for a 6.5-acre space, with activity fields planned to the south. The one-level building was expected to be completed by summer 1978 and would feature a gymnasium with jogging track, a junior Olympic-size swimming pool, four below-ground handball/racquetball courts, a large game-activities room, and a conversation pit. Also included would be an exercise area with professional strength training equipment, separate men and women's locker areas with a separate sauna and whirlpool, a classroom seating up to 100 students, and a building control area.

Plans were made to expand the School of Religious Education's curriculum with courses of instruction to train church recreation and youth ministers. Additional courses in health care and a well-rounded physical fitness program would also be offered.

The center was to be patterned after the Dallas-based Cooper Aerobics Center. Dr. Kenneth Cooper, founder of the Aerobics Center, served as a consultant to the seminary on the physical fitness center. Although the center was funded by the Slover family of South Texas, the center has accepted the name "Recreation and Aerobics Center" and is better known to the students as "the RAC."

The trustees also approved two recommendations to establish memorials in the new physical fitness center then under construction. The gymnasium was named in honor of W. Marvin Watson, who served as the chairman for the "Eight by Eighty" campaign fund drive. A baseball field adjacent to the new center would be called Berry Field in honor of Kendal Berry of Arkansas and Alan Berry of Tennessee. Kendal Berry is a former executive officer of the Southern Baptist Foundation, and Alan Berry is a business executive in Nashville, Tennessee.

San Antonio Off-Campus Center Opens

The trustees approved the opening of a third off-campus study center in San Antonio, Texas. Other centers were located in Houston, Texas, and Shawnee, Oklahoma. Each of these centers represented Southwestern Seminary's commitment to provide seminary training to the many church staff persons who serve local congregations without the benefit of formal seminary education.

The San Antonio center was the outgrowth of a joint request submitted by nine San Antonio area Baptist associations. This new center allowed students to pursue either the Master of Divinity degree or the Master of Religious Education degree. Classes were held on Mondays, with professors from the Fort Worth campus teaching the various courses. The Mexican Baptist Bible Institute hosted the classes. The San Antonio center was expected to have as many as 70 students in its first class.

Enrollment Reaches New Peak

The cumulative enrollment figures for 1976-1977 academic years reached a new peak. 3,851 persons enrolled during the past academic year. This was an 11 percent increase over last year's cumulative count of 3,470. The individual school count was astounding: the School of Theology had 2,246; the School of Religious Education had 1,221; and the School of Church Music had 384. A record 1,320 new students enrolled during the year. Not only were these figures staggering, but 3,101 returning students had signed up for the spring term compared to 2,813 last spring.

L.L. Collins said, "The significance of the enrollment is we have lost fewer students to attrition than ever before. Noting that even with a record 643 graduates and a record new student enrollment last year, we have more students than ever before staying to complete their degree programs."[63]

Course Description Manual Progressing

Preparing for a lifetime of ministry was the key behind the new curriculum manual for the seminary's School of Religious Education. According to Dean Jack Terry and LeRoy Ford, professor of foundations of education, the new course description manual for the Master of Religious Education degree plans was possibly the only one of its kind among seminaries in the United States. What made the manual so unique was the description of courses offered by the religious education school. Each course was described in competency terms or performance skills needed for the student to minister effectively. Each course description enabled a student to understand how that course contributes to the entire seminary educational experience.

Each student was expected to develop certain skills by taking each of the courses. In time, this should lead to a lifetime of meaningful creative ministry. The course indicators, such as tests and projects, demonstrate whether or not the student was acquiring the necessary skills to do educational ministry. This was the first time the religious education manual had had all of the courses stated in competency terms. The National Association of Professors of Christian Education and the National Association of Bible Colleges gave each of their members a copy of this book because it was the first model in seminary education ever developed.

As the School of Religious Education established additional master's degrees, each of the courses in those degrees would have residence in the Course Description Manual. By studying the manual, each student could determine the educational competencies, indicators, skills, and exit outcomes that would be learned during the course of a degree program in order to practice educational ministry in the church and denomination more effectively. The Course Description Manual is a living organism and would be improved or corrected as the students gave indication of their learning during the course of a degree program. New insight from the learning acumen of each student would greatly improve the competencies in the manual.

Specialized Educational Conferences

A major regional conference on Child Life Problems was co-sponsored by the School of Religious Education and the Southern Baptist Sunday School Board (LifeWay). Experts from a variety of fields were featured at the conference.

A panel including Judge Oswin Chrisman, of the Dallas Domestic Relations Court, and C. Edwin Cooley, head of the Fort Worth

Parenting Guidance Center, discussed "Children in Crisis," a careful look at the effects of death, child abuse, and divorce. Edward C. Frierson gave the keynote address at the opening banquet. Frierson was the executive director of the Nashville Leaning Center, an educational center offering a wide range of services to families in middle Tennessee. He coordinated doctoral training programs in the area of learning disabilities and gifted education at George Peabody College and served as a lecturer at the University of Tennessee. David Elkind led a discussion on religious concepts of children. He was the professor of psychology, psychiatry, and education at the University of Rochester. His research was in areas of cognitive and perceptual development in children. Jeroline Baker, professor of childhood education, organized the program.

A Church Architecture Conference was the second major seminar on October 24-26 with representatives from the church architecture department of the Southern Baptist Sunday School Board. The architecture leadership met classes, talked with staff members of area churches, and served as consultants to local churches in need of advice concerning church buildings. Three specialists from the department were Jerry A. Privette, building program and resource consultant; Debie Bower, design draftsman; and Robert E. Crowder, secretary of the church architecture department. Charles Tidwell, professor of church administration, identified two purposes for the conference: to help students become familiar with the services offered by the church architecture department, and to give area churches an opportunity to discuss specific building needs with the experts.

The Southwestern Baptist Religious Education Association (SWBREA) had met annually on the Southwestern campus since it was first organized in 1921 by J.M. Price and other religious education leaders of the Southern Baptist Convention. Over 260 religious educators gathered for the 57th annual meeting. The theme of the conference was "The Ministry of Religious Education." Sunday School Board personnel, religious educators, and seminary professors led multiple conference workshops dealing with the subject "Developing Trends in Religious Education" as well as vocational interests.

A major emphasis of this conference was the publication of a book in the field of religious education written by selected religious educational leaders and the participants at the conference. Those in attendance who chose to participate in writing the book were organized into three group emphases: foundations for religious education, religious educational programs for the church, and the vocational role of religious education. Other religious education experts contributed additional chapters to the book that were evaluated and edited by the conference registrants. The completed book was published by Broadman Press.

An added feature in this year's meeting was a renewed emphasis about the Jerry Lambdin Memorial Scholarship established in the School of Religious Education since 1964 as a special scholarship for worthy older religious education students. The J.E. Lambdin Memorial Scholarship paid tribute to a longtime innovator of the Training Union movement in the Southern Baptist Convention. Lambdin was called to head the Training Union Department of the Baptist Sunday School Board in 1925. In 1929, he was named secretary of the department, a position he held until 1961. Following his death in 1961, his wife established the memorial fund in the School of Religious Education. After the fund's principal had grown sufficiently, the first scholarship was awarded in 1964 and each year thereafter.

Russell H. Dilday Assumes Presidency

The conversation in the faculty lounges, the student center, and student chat corners all over the campus was about the coming of the new president. Russell H. Dilday assumed the presidency of Southwestern Seminary on August 1, 1978, following what was deemed the smoothest transition in Baptist history.[64] Wayne Evans, vice president for business affairs, said, "The transition has been tremendous. It is amazing how the right person always seems to be in the right place, at the right time, and I think this is exemplified by the way these three great men have been called to the helm of Southwestern Baptist Theological Seminary."[65] Dilday was the third president Evans had served under since coming to the seminary in 1954 during the administration of the late J. Howard Williams.

The Called—Will They Continue to Come?

Inaugural ceremonies for the seminary's sixth president were scheduled for Wednesday, October 25, in Truett Auditorium. A full week of special activities was planned in conjunction with the inauguration. Dilday had been working with President Naylor since January 1, 1978, in preparation for assuming the official duties as president.

The inaugural day was a brisk October morning when all the academics gathered in Truett Conference room, adjacent to Truett Auditorium, to robe in their 13th-century academic regalia for the ceremony. Over 2,000 people attended the ceremony, which included more than 80 delegates from colleges, universities, seminaries, and learned societies. Southern Baptist Convention leadership and agency representatives, members of the boards of trustees, members of the Southwestern Seminary Advisory Council, and state convention executives from Texas and adjourning states were also present. Additionally, several pastors and church leaders from Dallas/Fort Worth area churches attended the ceremony.

The inaugural address was delivered by Baker James Cauthen, executive secretary of the Southern Baptist Foreign Mission Board (now IMB) and an alumnus of Southwestern. In the address, Cauthen discussed the outlook for Southwestern Seminary and the outlook for Southern Baptists around the world. He said,

> We face an awesome challenge in the world today to make Christ known. We are trembling with anticipation and in awe and fear of failure. God has opened a door for His people that they dare not ignore. It is a world-wide ministry for which we are called today. Christianity is on trial everywhere in the world today. But we (Southern Baptists) are strategically placed across the world as never before. There are nearly 3,000 Southern Baptist missionaries on fields of service around the world with a potential goal of 5,000 in the very near future. Southwestern Seminary has had a vital role in providing the missionary personnel for the tasks that lie ahead. [66]

Dilday, with his Bible in hand and a firm commitment to its content, was inaugurated the sixth president of Southwestern Seminary. Jesse Northcutt, vice president for academic affairs, presided, and the Seminary Medallion, signifying the office of president, was presented by Ray L. Graham, chairman of the board of trustees. Dilday graciously accepted the medallion and made a stirring acceptance speech outlining his vision for the future under his leadership.

With the coming of a new presidential administrator, so came new appointments and readjustments of administrators from the last administration. At the October 24, 1978, meeting, the trustees were prepared for the new president to add to the administrative staff as well as adjust new nomenclature and assignments for several administrative officers.

Two new vice presidents were named. Lloyd Elder, assistant to the executive director of the Baptist General Convention of Texas, was named executive vice president. John Newport, former faculty member, was elected as vice president for academic affairs. A change in title nomenclature was made for John Seelig, who became vice president for public affairs. Felix Gresham received a new assignment as seminary chaplain and director of financial aid.

Other academic positions were reaffirmed. Supporting the vice president for academic affairs were the academic deans of the three schools—James McKinney, School of Church Music; Jack Terry, School of Religious Education; and Huber L. Drumwright, School of Theology. Not long after the new president began his tenure, Huber Drumwright resigned his faculty position (1980) to become executive director of the Arkansas Baptist Convention. After Drumwright's resignation, the trustees elected William B. Tolar as the dean of School of Theology.

Notable Trustee Actions

A notable action of the board was the proposal for a new learning center, which would allow the new administration to begin planning for the new library facility that would be the largest in the nation when completed. The seminary's library was previously located in what is now Fleming Hall in the Memorial Building, with additional facilities in

Cowden Hall and Price Hall. A tentative location for the new building was planned for the east side of the campus on Stanley Avenue.

Preliminary plans called for a four-story building with two floors underground. The building would have a maximum of 117,430 square feet.

Enrollment Continues an 11-Year Trend

The spring and fall enrollments during the academic year 1977-1978 continued the 11-year upward trend. The spring enrollment of 3,321 reflected a 7 percent increase over last spring's enrollment and continued to break records.

Jesse Northcutt, vice president for academic affairs, projected that the 1977-1978 count would reach the cumulative projected enrollment for the year 1982, which would be 4,170. He indicated that the basic growth factor was a spiritual one of God calling out those whom He declares to do His ministry.

By schools, the spring count registered 1,981, School of Theology; 1,048, School of Religious Education; and 292, School of Church Music. The fall enrollment showed a slight decrease from the 1977 fall enrollment, but one probable reason was the large graduating class of 858 in 1977-1978. Preliminary figures for the fall semester indicated 746 new students as compared to the 859 graduated the previous year. The largest concentration of students was in the School of Theology (2,017), with the School of Religious Education at 1,125 and the School of Church Music at 305. The three off-campus centers reported a total of 187 signed up for courses with 121 in Houston, 26 in San Antonio, and 40 in Shawnee, Oklahoma.

Conferences and Workshops Invite Alumni for Continuing Education

Two major educational conferences met on the campus during the year 1978. A conference emphasizing the special needs of families convened April 3-5. "Counseling Today's Families" highlighted the research of O. Hobart Mower, research professor emeritus at the University of Illinois. His topic was "The Fragility of the Nuclear Family."

In his speech, he reminded the family leaders that "the church for its own self-preservation must save and revitalize the family. It was once said the family was the cornerstone. If this is true, the cornerstone is crumbling."

Mower explained the causes of this breakdown in the nuclear family: increased mobility, greater privacy, and a range of conveniences. Mower said, "These things come in the name of progress and a free enterprise system but let it be known, technology is no longer the servant, but the master."[67] He concluded his address with an injunction to the church to step up and reclaim the family presence by sponsoring marital retreats, family educational programs, and Christian Life weeks that are inclusive of the entire family.

The second conference was the Southwestern Baptist Religious Education Association in its 58th annual meeting. The theme of the conference was "Common Focus … Religious Education, Bold Mission Thrust." Keynote speaker Harry Piland, the Sunday School Department Director of the Baptist Sunday School Board (LifeWay), illustrated the theme of the conference by saying, "A vision without a task is a dream. A task without a vision is a drudgery. But a vision and a task together is the hope of the world."[68]

Religious Education Faculty Publish

Three religious education professors published during the 1978 academic year. Charles Ashby wrote a book entitled *31 Great Years of Texas BSU Happenings*, which honored his mentor W.F. Howard, retired director of Baptist Student Work in Texas. The book was a history of the student work in Texas under the leadership of Howard from 1943 to 1974. Texas Baptist Student Union work began in 1920, but the first chapter provided a brief history of student work in the United States from 1600. Succeeding chapters highlighted the development of Howard's life and ministry to Texas Baptist students during his tenure as director. At the writing, Howard was serving as an adjunct instructor in campus ministries in the School of Religious Education.

John W. Drakeford, professor of psychology and counseling, published his 22nd book, *Wisdom for Today's Family*. The book framed a study of family life based on the book of Proverbs. Using a thematic framework, Drakeford studied multiple subjects: youth life, wisdom, temper, sex, fatherhood and motherhood, and family communication. At the end of each chapter, Drakeford provided a list of different proverbs to emphasize the chapter headings.

Jack Terry, dean of the School of Religious Education, authored the book *The Administration of Learning Resources Centers*. The book contained a practical guide for establishing an administrative procedure for a learning resource center (a library). The book studied principles and management models as well as the kind of equipment needed for an adequate learning resource center. The book emphasized administration and leadership components more than the audio-visual hardware and software or even library services. It was aimed at helping educational institutions improve their resource centers or initiate a program.

Recreation Aerobics Center Dedicated

The culmination of a long-awaited 70-year dream was realized March 19, 1979, with the dedication of the Recreation/Aerobics Center (RAC). In the dedicatory speech, President Emeritus Robert Naylor reminded the audience of the dreams of the founding president B.H. Carroll and his successors, who desired that seminary students maintain strong bodies as well as strong theological minds. President Carroll made plans for the construction of a gymnasium on the campus, and copies of the architect's concept are in the seminary's archives.[69]

Agnes Pylant, the first secretary at the Baptist Sunday School Board's Church Recreation Department and former faculty member, told the audience that "we have come a long way from the first anemic attempts of recreation in churches."[70] Dr. Kenneth Cooper, founder of the Aerobics Center in Dallas and a member of the Southwestern Advisory Council, graciously allowed the seminary the privilege of using the term "aerobics" in the naming of the building. (Dr. Cooper holds the copyright on the word "aerobics.")

The $2,219,073 complex provided the 10,000 members of the seminary community a place for Christian recreation and personal physical fitness. It was used by students involved in recreational ministry as a laboratory as they worked in church recreational programs. A classroom provided the academic setting for various courses offered by the School of Religious Education, and the building is a model for churches who want to visit an ideal recreation/family-life-type building. Over 6,000 persons a week had used the facility since its operation began in January.

During the March 1979 trustee meeting, the trustees approved three new degree programs designed to correlate courses between and among the three schools. Those degrees included a Master of Divinity degree with a church music minor, a Master of Religious Education with a church music minor, and a Master of Church Music with a religious education minor. Each of these degrees would meet various needs of graduates who required additional skills in education administration or music leadership. The Master of Religious Education degree with a church music minor and the Master of Music degree with a religious education minor were developed to fill a need of combination ministries. The majority of churches who searched for a combination staff member generally wanted educational responsibility along with music responsibility, or youth ministry with music responsibility. A major response to the new combination degrees was anticipated.

The trustees elected two new faculty members for the School of Religious Education during the academic portion of the meeting. Bob Wayne Brackney was elected as assistant professor of social work. He was one of the best trained social workers in the Southern Baptist Convention and was professor of social work and human services at Wingate College in Wingate, N.C. Byron A. (Pat) Clendinning was elected associate professor of psychology and counseling. Clendinning was a former Southern Baptist missionary and professor at the Baptist Theological Seminary, Ruschlikon-Zurich, Switzerland, teaching religious education, psychology, and counseling (1958-1964). He was also the director for the program of family ministry in the Sunday School Board of the Southern Baptist Convention (1964-1971).

The growing enrollment in each of the three schools encouraged the trustees to look at 30 adjunct and guest professors for the fall of 1979. Several adjunct professors were appointed for each of the three schools. The School of Religious Education had 10 appointed as adjunct professors. Mrs. Monte Clendinning, the wife of Pat Clendinning, taught as professor of religious education and missions education. R. Othal Feather, retired professor of administration; Harvey Hatcher, retired professor in drama and public relations; and Joe Davis Heacock, retired dean in education administration, all continued teaching adjunctively. W.F. Howard, Baptist Student ministries; Grady Lowery, director of the RAC, in recreation; Lawrence Klempnauer, minister of education at Travis Avenue Baptist Church, Fort Worth, Texas, in education administration; William McKinney, professor at the University of North Texas, in foundations of education; Bob Oldenburg, minister of adult education at North Richland Hills Baptist Church, in musical drama; and Gary Waller, minister of education, Lamar Baptist Church, Arlington, Texas, in church administration were all enlisted as adjunct professors for the year.

The Baptist Sunday School Board made a request to the trustees to establish a Doctor of Education (Ed.D.) center at the board in Nashville, Tennessee. The center would offer Ed.D. seminars in conjunction with the staff development program at the board. All who participate in the program were approved Sunday School Board personnel and met all the requirements for the Ed.D. degree. School of Religious Education professors conducted the seminars at the board along with qualified adjunct professors (i.e., Harry Piland) from the board. The entire program was financed through the board with tuition and grants given to personnel who were qualified to participate. It was a total financial recovery program. The request was approved at this trustee meeting.

Enrollment Hits All-Time High

The cumulative enrollment for 1978-1979 academic year represents the largest enrollment in the 71-year history of the seminary. This was the 12th consecutive year the seminary had experienced an enrollment increase. Preliminary reports indicated there would be 1,061 first-time students. Again, the largest concentration of students was enrolled in the School of Theology (2,347). There were 1,402 students in the School of Religious Education and 378 in the School of Church Music. A total of 251 students matriculated at the centers this academic year, with 149 at Houston, 47 in San Antonio, and 55 in Shawnee.

Coupled with this cumulative enrollment report was the fall 1979 enrollment figures indicating the largest fall enrollment ever. The record for fall enrollment was 3,475 (set in 1977). The 1979 fall enrollment was 3,564, and this was about 3 percent higher than the fall enrollment of 3,447 in 1978. In the fall semester, there were 2,062 enrolled in the School of Theology, 1,163 in the School of Religious Education, and 339 in the School of Church Music. Southwestern was the largest of the six Southern Baptist seminaries and the largest of any denomination in the world.[71]

Changes in the Air

The faculty of the School of Religious Education had been extremely busy developing the final touches for the *Course Description Manual for the Master of Religious Education Degrees*, and with that publication in print, the faculty turned its attention to some needed internal matters. The old administrative structure of single, standalone disciplines (i.e., principles, administration, youth, preschool, etc.) in the School of Religious Education did not fit the growing number of new educational ministries that the school addressed. In the curriculum committee meeting, January 9, 1979, the committee requested that Dean Jack Terry develop a composite organizational chart for the religious education faculty to consider.[72] The dean, with assistance from the department heads, developed the new departmental design.

The structure clustered like disciplines into four major divisions. The four divisions were foundations (foundations of education and communication arts), administration (education administration and church administration), behavioral sciences (psychology and counseling and social work), and human growth and development (adult education, youth education, childhood education, and preschool education). Each division had a chairman who would convene the division for discussion and recommendation as well as represent the division in the division council with the dean. Ancillary to each of the divisions were 15 major committees such as field education, graduate committee, curriculum committee, house and grounds committee, etc., which could draw membership from each of the four divisions. The structure was approved at the February 1, 1979, meeting and passed unanimously. The division organization served the school well for two decades.

George R. Wilson, professor of education administration since 1973, was reappointed by the Foreign Mission Board (IMB) to Hong Kong. Wilson served in Hong Kong 13 years before coming to Southwestern. Upon his return, he taught in the Hong Kong Baptist Seminary and will help individual churches on a consulting basis. He also worked on a special project of developing a learning resources center for the seminary.

Youth Lab: RAC Riot

The summer Youth Lab used the new Recreation/Aerobics Center as its major location for the 12th annual meeting. The theme was "He Is The Wind I Soar On," taken from the musical by Buryl Red, "Celebrate Life." The theme was illustrated using hot air balloons to decorate the new Recreation/Aerobics Center. This year's meeting was highlighted with a "RAC riot," a recreational extravaganza in the new center. The emphasis centered on the numerous possibilities of using recreation buildings on church campuses for multiple ministries during the entire church year.

The use of a building like the RAC added a dimension to church life like never before. The program discussed the various ministry activities that could be planned for a family life center or a recreation center on a church campus. Discussion groups examined various ministries that could effectively use a recreation center such as Vacation Bible School, inter-church and inter-departmental leagues and tournaments (basketball, baseball, volleyball, flag football, tennis, racquetball, etc.), physical fitness classes, weight-loss classes, family game nights and activities, Mother's Day Out programs, health and wellness clinics, parenting classes, pre-natal classes, child-birth classes, and physical activities for pre-natal moms, to name a few. Plus, the building would be there for use by the members of the church any time it was available. There were over 400 full-time youth ministers and college and seminary students who attended the three-day workshop.

SWBREA: "The Challenge of Change"

Paul Geisel, of the University of Texas at Arlington Institute of Urban Studies, delivered the keynote addressed entitled "The Challenge of Change" and set in motion the 59th meeting of the Southwestern Baptist Religious Education Association, April 14-16, 1979. The theme of the meeting had a futuristic note—"Looking at Learning in the '80s." The conference was developed to provide attendees an opportunity to explore different activities as a minister in educational work. Conferences focused on single parenting, writing for publication, open-room teaching for youth, senior adult ministries within the range of their abilities, and a learning resource center in the church. Each of the conferences spoke about the growing problems in many local churches and gave practical help to those who were struggling while trying to develop and administer the much-needed new ministries.

Dorothy Pulley, administrative assistant to three deans—J.M. Price, Joe Davis Heacock, and Jack Terry—was recognized for 20 faithful years of service to the seminary as well as the SWBREA. A gift of $1,200 was gathered for her from contributions made by friends, former students, and faculty.

SBC Changes Leadership

The June 1979 meeting of the Southern Baptist Convention in Houston was the beginning of a game changer for the future of the convention then under the control of a more moderate bureaucratic leadership. Although prior elections of convention presidents included a few conservatives, they seemed to accomplish little in changing what was considered a "strong liberal drift" in the convention. A strong SBC bureaucracy rendered the more conservative members ineffective in most of their attempts to change the direction of the convention because they did not have the support of the SBC team behind them. They were forced to rely on the bureaucracy, and any attempt to do anything without working with the bureaucracy's guidance was difficult if not impossible.

The powerful committee on nominations was heavily influenced by the president of the convention and the executive secretary of the executive committee. The committee on nominations and other important committees that selected board members for all the major agencies (i.e., mission boards, seminaries, commissions, etc.) were controlled by the moderate group presently in leadership. The only way the convention could be changed was for a strong-willed conservative to be elected president of the convention and to begin placing more conservative leadership as trustees on the boards of the numerous agencies.

Adrian Rogers, a strong conservative, was nominated and elected without a run-off in 1979. It was a small beginning, but it would grow into a "fire-storm" during the next few conventions. The "Conservative Resurgence" was alive and determined to change the drift of the Southern Baptist Convention by eventually naming conservative trustees for the various boards and agencies. The conservative leaders were in a stronger position and could eventually change the direction of the convention toward a more conservative stance.

Notes
[1] Southwestern News, February, 1970, p.1.
[2] Trustee Minutes, 3 March, 1970. P. 41

3 Southwestern News, January, 1970, p.1.
4 Ibid.
5 Trustee Minuets, 3 March, 1970, p. 42.
6 Trustee Minutes, 5, May, 1970, p. 49.
7 Trustee Minutes, 3, March, 1970, p. 42,
8 Trustee Minutes, 24, November, 1970, p. 51.
9 Trustee Minutes, 5, May, 1970. p.49.
10 Trustee Minutes, 24, November, 1970, p. 52.
11 Trustee Minutes, 5, March, 1970, p. 42.
12 Southwestern News, November, 1970, p. 1-2.
13 Ibid., p. 6.
14 Ibid., p. 8
15 Ibid., p. 10.
16 Southwestern News, February, 1970, p. 11.
17 Southwestern News, February, 1971, p. 6.
18 Southwestern News, October, 1971, p. 4.
19 Ibid.
20 Southwestern News, December, 1971, p. 7
21 Trustee Minutes, 22, November , 1971, p. 76.
22 Ibid., p. 1.
23 Trustee Minutes, 2, March, 1971, p. 69.
24 Southwestern News, "Annual Report to the Trustees 1970-1971, December, 1971, p. 2.
25 Baker, Robert A., *Tell the Generations Following*, Broadman Press: Nashville, 1983, p. 390.
26 Southwestern News, March, 1972, p. 1.
27 Trustee Minutes, 14, July, 1972, p. 96.
28 Southwestern News, May, 1972, p. 3.
29 Ibid., p. 9.
30 Baker, Robert A., *Tell the Generations Following*, Broadman Press: Nashville, 1983, pp. 393-394.
31 Ibid., p. 396.
32 Southwestern News, "Children Assist in Breaking Ground for Children's Building" February, 1973, p. 1 & 4.
33 Ibid.

34 Trustee Minutes, 2, March, 1973, p. 121.
35 Baker, Robert A., *Tell the Generations Following*, Broadman Press: Nashville, 1983, p. 413.
36 Ibid., p. 414.
37 Southwestern News, April, 1974, p. 10.
38 Heacock, Joe Davis. *J.M. Price: Trailblazer in Religious Education*, Unpublished Founder's Day Address, March 14, 1974.
39 Southwestern News, April, 1974, p. 3.
40 Ibid.
41 Ibid., p. 5.
42 Southwestern News, November, 1974, p.1.
43 Southwestern News, March, 1975, p. 4.
44 Southwestern News, October, 1975, p. 1.
45 Ibid.
46 Ibid., p. 4.
47 Ibid.
48 Trustee Minutes, 30, September, 1975, p. 187.
49 Southwestern News, May, 1975, p 9.
50 Southwestern News, February, 1976, p. 1.
51 Ibid.
52 Ibid., p. 3.
53 Southwestern News, July, 1976, p. 1.
54 Trustee Minutes, 24, February, 1976, p. 194.
55 Ibid.
56 Trustee Minutes, 23, November , 1976, p. 9.
57 Curriculum Committee Minutes (School of Religious Education), 19, February, 1976, p. 1.
58 Trustee Minutes, 24, March 1977, called meeting 15, June, 1977, and November , 1977.
59 Southwestern News, December, 1977, p. 2.
60 Trustee Minutes, 24, March, 1977, p. 225.
61 Ibid., p. 228
62 Trustee minutes, 15, March, 1977, p. 232.
63 Southwestern News, February, 1977, p. 7.
64 Southwestern News, September, 1978, p 1.

65 Ibid.
66 Cauthen, Baker James, Unpublished Presidential Inaugural Address, October 25, 1978.
67 Ibid., p. 8.
68 Southwestern News, September, 1978, p.11.
69 Southwestern News, February, 1979, p. 4.
70 Southwestern News, March, 1979, p. 5.
71 Southwestern News, October, 1979, p. 1.
72 Curriculum Committee, School of Religious Education, January 9, 1979, p. 1.

Photos

Page 46 – Portrait of Joe Davis Heacock.

Page 48 – Religious Education faculty circa 1965.

Page 51 – From left, George Wilson, Harvey Hatcher, and Joe Davis Heacock, 1961.

Page 53 – Joe Davis Heacock and J.M. Price in front of Price Hall.

Page 81 – Joe Davis Heacock and Jack Terry in front of Price Hall.

Page 84 – Huber L. Drumwright, dean of the School of Theology; Jack Terry, dean of the School of Religious Education; and James McKinney, dean of the School of Church Music.

Page 89 – Religious Education faculty circa 1957. On the front row, J.M. Price is the third person from the left. On his left is Joe Davis Heacock.

Page 111 – Professors Paula Brooks and Phil Briggs, Youth Ministry Lab 1979.

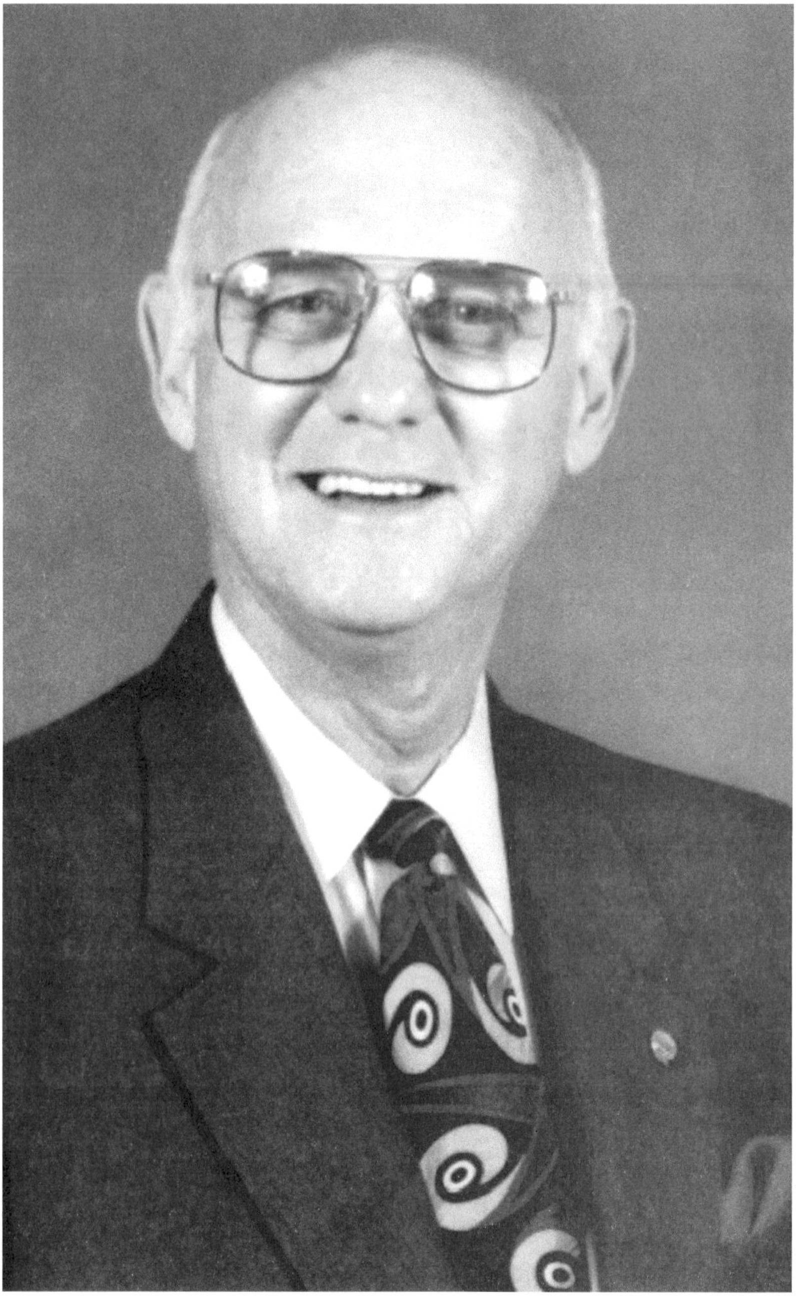

Chapter 3

Unprecedented Growth Continues 1980-1989

Decade of Unprecedented Growth

A report of the growth of Southwestern Baptist Theological Seminary during the 1970s was an impressive introduction to the March 1980 spring trustee meeting. This unprecedented growth was seen in budget requirements, total assets, endowment, and student enrollment that more than doubled during the preceding 10 years. Student enrollment increased from 2,096 during the 1969-1970 academic year to 4,154 during the 1979-1980 academic year. The budget rose from $2.7 million to $8.4 million during the same period. Total assets grew from $20 million to more than $40 million, and endowment increased from $6.7 million to more than $13 million.[1]

During the 1970s, the Goldia and Robert E. Naylor Children's Center and additional student housing were constructed. Renovations were completed on Truett Auditorium, Price Hall, and some of the married student housing. The fundraising effort met its goal of $8 million nearly one year ahead of schedule. The success was boosted by a single gift of $1 million in land given by Mr. and Mrs. J. Roy Slover of Liberty, Texas. Future plans included the funding and construction of a new library/resource center, the establishment of a World Missions/Church Growth Center, and a continuing education center.

The reorganization of the seminary's administrative structure was approved by the trustees in 1973, and three vice presidents and a chaplain were named: Wayne Evans, vice president for business; John Seelig, vice president for administration; Lloyd Elder, executive vice president; John Newport, academic vice president and provost; and Felix Gresham, seminary chaplain. Academically, the Doctor of Ministries degree program was approved in 1973 to provide additional advanced professional training in ministry. The Doctor of Philosophy degree replaced the Doctor of Theology degree in 1973. Field education was added as a permanent part of the theology and religious education curriculum. An important academic achievement was the accreditation by the Southern Association of Colleges and Schools (SACS), as was the reaffirmation by the Association of Theological Schools (ATS) of Southwestern Seminary's accreditation after the 10-year self-study.

EEOC Lawsuit Settled

Early in 1980, the seminary received word from the Equal Employment Opportunity Commission (EEOC) that it did not have jurisdiction over Southwestern Seminary. U.S. District Judge Eldon Mahon ended a two-and-a-half-year court battle by ruling that the EEOC did not have the right to seek employee records at the Southern Baptist institution. What the ruling meant was that the EEOC could not force the seminary to provide records on the race, sex, or salaries of employees, nor could the federal agency take any action against the seminary while enforcing federal laws on discrimination.[2]

The lawsuit was filed in May 1977 by the EEOC attorneys when the seminary refused to provide the records they requested based on the grounds that it would violate the first amendment, the right of separation of church and state. At the time of the ruling, the seminary administration did not know if the EEOC would appeal to the 5th Circuit Court in New Orleans.

Jenkins Garrett, Southwestern's attorney in 1979, argued the fact that the seminary is a wholly religious institution in its purpose and is not subject to federal jurisdiction by the agency. Mahon said the wording of the 1967 Civil Rights Act appeared to give the EEOC jurisdiction, but he emphasized that the operation of the seminary is a religious activity entitled to the highest degree of protection. In a lengthy opinion, Mahon said the seminary sought to create an integrated, homogenous community where all employees were expected to contribute to a unified religious endeavor and maintain a commitment to spiritual life.[3] The real issue at stake was that the seminary and all its employees were engaged in a totally religious function unlike other

Record Budget and the Election of New Faculty

The trustee adoption of a $9.6 million budget and the election of seven new faculty members highlighted the March 1980 meeting. Dilday noted that the budget was a 14 percent increase over the current $8.4 million budget and included salary raises of up to 13 percent for some faculty and staff. He reminded the trustees that the Southern Baptist Convention would provide 56 percent of this year's budget, down 2 percent from last year's 58 percent. The seminary's projections for the coming year allowed the seminary to operate in the black for the 26th year.

The trustees unanimously approved the election of seven new faculty members—five in theology, one in religious education, and one in church music. The religious education faculty member elected was Robert P. Raus as associate professor of church recreation. Raus' service background was in ministry as well as secular recreational employment. He served as director of Christian recreation at Tower Grove Baptist Church, St. Louis, Missouri (1951-55), and taught at schools in Indiana, Oregon, and West Virginia.

Recreation Concentration Added

The election of Raus in church recreation gave rise to a number of new courses added to the curriculum in the School of Religious Education. The courses added were Educational Programing for Family Life Ministry Recreation, Philosophical Foundations of Church Recreation, Administration and Church Recreation Facilities, Sports and Games, and Aerobics Fitness.[4] Three additional courses in administration, social work, and campus ministry internship were also approved.

In preparation for a surge of interest in the ministry of recreation, the School of Religious Education became the first among all the Southern Baptist seminaries to offer a concentration in recreation in its Master of Religious Education degree. The four recreation courses that were being taught had now expanded to nine with the addition of Raus.

Grady Lowery, director of the Recreation/Aerobics Center, said, "Church recreation is expanding across the convention and we see the need for leading in this new emerging ministry field."[5] The Baptist Sunday School Board reported that there were about 1,500 church recreation centers with at least a gym in 1979, and a 30 percent increase in the number of full-time recreation directors. There were 1,500 church staff members with "recreation" in their title.

The School of Religious Education felt that ministers of recreation should first be trained as ministers; secondly, as educators; and thirdly, as church recreation specialists. The five new courses approved by the trustees were added to the present recreation curriculum, which included camp leadership, recreation leadership, religious drama, and production of religious drama.

One last religious education program approved by the trustees during the 1980 academic year was a Baptist Student Union internship. The program provided for future BSU workers to receive academic credit for on-the-job-training with a practicing BSU director on a college or university campus. The intern received 12 hours credit for the experience. To be eligible for the student ministry internship program, a student had to have completed 30 hours of seminary course work on the Master of Divinity or the Master of Religious Education degree, including the courses The Baptist Student Director, Campus Ministry, or The Church's Ministry with College and University Students.

The response was strong, with initiated requests from many college/university BSU directors across the state of Texas. W.F. Howard, retired director of the student work division of the Baptist General Convention of Texas, noted that the opportunity for a BSU internship could come from several different directions. A student could explore with BSU directors on a college campus to see if such a program could become a part of that BSU ministry, or a BSU minister could contact the seminary to see if there was a student interested in exploring the possibility of working with him in a campus BSU ministry. When the contact was made, the final decision about the internship would be determined by the seminary (field education committee) and the interested college or university. Howard concluded that this program would become a continuing academic program that provided excellent clinical experience gained on the field of BSU ministry on a college or university campus.

The report of the cumulative enrollment for 1979-1980 was 4,336, the 13th consecutive record-setting enrollment and the largest in seminary history. There were 863 graduates during the year, which set a record. The individual school records for the year were the largest in the history of the seminary, as well. The School of Theology, with its new dean, William B. Tolar, had 2,436 enrolled with 460 degrees and diplomas conferred. The School of Theology had 48 permanent faculty members, 30 adjunct teachers, and one guest professor. The School of Religious Education had 1,501 enrolled with 325 degrees and diplomas conferred (also a record). The School of Religious Education had 19 permanent faculty members and 17 adjunct teachers and teaching fellows, and the upgraded and expanded curriculum in church recreation was added. The School of Church Music had 399 enrolled with 71 degrees conferred. The School of Church Music had 18 permanent faculty and 18 adjunct teachers and teaching fellows.

The off-campus centers set record enrollments as well, with 160 at Southeast Texas in Houston, 57 at Southwest Texas in San Antonio, and 67 at the Oklahoma Center in Shawnee. The new off-campus center established at the Baptist Sunday School Board in Nashville had 14 students enrolled for the initial year of its operation.

Conferences, Institutes, and Workshops in Abundance

The year 1980 was filled with conferences and special events on the campus. The advent of the new recreation center provided the impetus for a "Christian and Physical Fitness Seminar" sponsored by the Southern Baptist Sunday School Board in March. The intensive laboratory sessions held in the RAC were aimed at qualifying church staff members or volunteers to test church members and to design individual fitness programs. Richard B. Couey and Bonnie Luft, specialists in physical fitness from Baylor University physical education faculty, led the sessions qualifying attendees for testing church members for the various fitness programs.

The 31st Annual Student Missions Conference was scheduled for March with the theme "Why Missions … Why Me." The conference was designed for college, university, and seminary students who were considering the mission field as their future ministry. The major speakers were R. Keith Parks, executive secretary of the Southern Baptist Foreign Mission Board, and William R. O'Brien, administrative assistant at the mission board.

The "6th Annual Radio, Television and Cable Consultation" was sponsored jointly by the seminary and the Southern Baptist Radio and Television Commission. The consultation emphasis concentrated on program design to enhance church broadcasting both in radio and television. Southwestern President Russell Dilday and President of the Radio and Television Commission Jimmy R. Allen were the keynote speakers. Wayne Dehoney, pastor of Walnut Street Baptist Church, Louisville, Kentucky, and Clyde Fant, pastor of the First Baptist Church, Richardson, Texas, led workshops on radio and television broadcasting in local churches. Radio and television personalities headlined the individual conferences. Chip Moody, newsman at KXAS-TV; Frank Olsen, freelance writer and former ABC news writer; and Jeffrey K. Hadden, professor of sociology at the University of Virginia, rounded out the special professionals invited to speak at the consultation.

The youth division of the School of Religious Education sponsored the annual Youth Lab in April titled "On Your Mark, Get Set, Grow." The School of Religious Education's annual spring emphasis was "Church Administration." A major focus of the meeting was the celebration of the 200th anniversary of the modern Sunday School movement that was led by Robert Raikes in England in the 1780s.

The Southwestern Baptist Religious Education Association's August meeting promoted the theme "The Caring Fellowship." William Hull, pastor of First Baptist Church, Shreveport, Louisiana, was the lead speaker with the topic "Called to Care." The major topics discussed during the conference were "The Caring Growing Person," "Diagnosing the Growth Health of Your Church," "Taking Care of Your Time," "Taking Care of Your Finances," "Taking Care of Your Family," "Taking

Care of the Temple," "Growing as a Professional," "Training for Church Growth," and "Dilemma: Principles vs. People."

The Week of the Young Child was observed with special activities, displays, and an open house in the Naylor Children's Center. The observance was an extension of the national observance begun in 1971. David White, children's center supervisor, identified plans for picnics for children and parents on campus, parent/child play time, a children's cook book, and a parent/child paint time. Jeroline Baker, professor of childhood education, said, "The purpose of the week was to help people on campus and in the community be aware of and to understand the needs of the young child."[6]

Another First...

The social work department at Southwestern Seminary was awarded an Association of Theological Schools grant to design a curriculum for training specialists for church-related social work. For the first time in the history of Southwestern Seminary or the School of Religious Education, two faculty members were awarded a grant together. Working on this project were Derrel Watkins, associate professor of social work, and Bob Brackney, assistant professor of social work. The ATS grant provided the funds necessary to design a specific program for Southwestern and accredited by ATS and the Council on Social Work Education. At present, no Southern Baptist seminary provided this option.

Watkins hoped to have a skeleton program by the fall of 1980 and a firm proposal by the spring of 1981 for the meeting of the trustees. From this design, a full-fledged program for training specialists for church-related social work began in the fall of 1981.

Contract Awarded for Construction of New Library

The trustees awarded a contract for the construction of the nation's largest theological library to the John W. Ryan Co. in 1980. Construction began immediately. The $8.5 million project included the furnishings, equipment, landscaping architects' fees, and engineering fees.[7] Groundbreaking ceremonies were planned for March 24, 1981, at 10:00 a.m., with the completion of the structure expected sometime during the summer of 1982. The three-story library center was designed by Geren and Associates of Fort Worth, Texas.

The 100,000-square-foot facility was constructed on the east side of the main campus. The center has a capacity of 700,000 volumes and seating for 1,045 persons. Special features included an archives and rare books collection area, archaeological and heritage museums, computer systems to enhance circulation and inter-library loan systems with other colleges and university libraries, an extensive security system, and expanded audio-visual facilities.[8] The new building replaced Fleming Library, which was constructed in 1949 and had a capacity of 400,000 volumes and seating for 600 persons.

March 24, 1981, the official day for groundbreaking of the new library, dawned with a chilly breeze for those who attended the ceremonies. Davis Cooper, trustee from Colorado and the principal speaker for the ceremonies, called the building "evidence of that which is transcendent expressed in temporal ways. With hands of men and bricks that man made, we will build a place to house the eternal Word of God. We should thank God that He will allow us to touch for a brief moment in time that which will house the eternal."[9]

During the ceremony, Dilday called the new building "the conclusion of the dreams of many people. We are here to set aside this place for the holy and significant purpose of furthering God's work."[10] Representatives from several seminary constituencies participated in the groundbreaking ceremonies, including students, trustees, alumni, faculty, and civic and advisory council representatives. Dignitaries assisting in the groundbreaking were President Emeritus Robert Naylor; Mrs. Frank Sanford, daughter of the late J. Howard Williams; Mrs. Browning Ware, great niece of the late E.D. Head; and Mrs. Lee Brewer, great-granddaughter of the late L.R. Scarborough. The principal participants in the actual shovel ceremony were Keith C. Wills, director of libraries; President Russell Dilday; Kenneth Chafin, board of trustees chairman; and Preston M. Geren, architect.

The endorsement of the program plan for the Center of Christian Communications Studies, which was established in October 1980, was approved by the trustees. The center provided graduate professional training for men and women preparing for Christian ministries in the field of Christian communications. The program was sponsored jointly by the seminary and the Southern Baptist Radio and Television Commission. In addition to a communications concentration within the seminary degree programs, the center provided continuing education internship opportunities with the Radio and Television Commission. Future plans included a Master of Arts degree in communications. A seven-member steering committee appointed by the presidents of the seminary and the commission developed the policies, guidelines, programs, budgets, and many other facets of the center. An important action in relationship to the establishment of the Communications Center was the acquisition of Darrel Baergen, who was named professor of communication arts and acting director for the Center of Christian Communications Studies.[11]

Baergen had served as professor of communication and theater at Southwest Texas State University, San Marcos, Texas. He had also held positions at Oklahoma Baptist University, Baylor University, and the University of Denver. Baergen acted in over 25 different stage productions; directed 18 stage productions; wrote stage plays; wrote, directed, and acted in radio and television productions; produced programs for ACTS and BTN of the Radio and Television Commission; and wrote two books, *Communication Strategies for Churches in Their Marketplaces* and *Training the Speaking Voice*.

William R. Yount was elected as instructor in the foundations of education. Yount served as minister to the deaf for First Baptist Church, Irving, Texas (1973-1976) and as minister of education for Columbia Baptist Church, Falls Church, Virginia (1976-1981). He authored *Called to Teach: An Introduction to the Ministry of Teaching* (1999), *Created to Learn: A Christian Teacher's Introduction to Educational Psychology* (1996), and *Be Open! Introduction to Ministry with the Deaf* (1976).

The trustees changed the leadership of the Baptist Marriage and Family Counseling Center from its founder, John. W. Drakeford, to Theodore (Ted) H. Dowell, professor of psychology and counseling. Drakeford relinquished the directorship on August 1, 1981.

The center began in 1960 as an opportunity for psychology and counseling students to put into practice what they had been learning in the classroom. Students came to the psychology and counseling professors for counseling, and their need for counseling made the development of the counseling center inevitable. During the center's 21 years, the clientele had become more diverse. At first, only seminary students came for counseling, but now, counseling was available to anyone in the community. In fact, the counseling center was listed in the Yellow Pages along with other Christian counseling centers in the area.

Drakeford continued teaching as distinguished professor of psychology and counseling. He also continued his writing ministry that included 27 books, plus leadership in conferences, institutes, and workshops across the U.S. and around the world.

Record Cumulative Enrollment

Both the spring and fall enrollment soared to another record. A record 3,514 students enrolled for the spring semester. The figure was a record for any spring semester and represented a 2 percent increase over the spring 1980 enrollment of 3,437. The total included 2,015 in the School of Theology, 1,172 in the School of Religious Education, and 327 in the School of Church Music. The off-campus centers in Houston, San Antonio, and Shawnee enrolled 207 students as part of the growth enjoyed by the seminary as a whole.

Coming right on the heels of a record spring enrollment was also a record fall enrollment. The record fall enrollment was 3,837, which included a record of 900 first-time students. This figure represented the fourth consecutive fall enrollment increase. It was a 4.2 percent increase over the 1980 enrollment of 3,684. The cumulative total enrollment for the 1980-1981 year was 4,412. Enrollment by schools included 2,467 in theology, 1,535 in religious education, and 410 in church music. The report of the seminary enrollment did not necessarily indicate just immediate college graduates, nor did it reflect college populations or other sociological demographics. Many students were in their 30s and 40s. This is particularly true of the off-campus centers, where men and women were coming to seminary later in life for various reasons. In response to the high cumulative enrollment, Dilday stated,

> The total number of different persons enrolled in *all* semesters of one year is reported as the annual cumulative head count. The cumulative enrollment at Southwestern in the current year (1980-1981) is 4,421, the highest in the school's history. Ten years ago (1970-1971) the cumulative enrollment was 2,171, an increase of more than 100 percent. Southwestern is carrying the load for our convention in the basic degree task—41 percent of all students enrolled in the master's degree programs of our six seminaries are enrolled at Southwestern.[12]

Three Programs Developed by the School of Religious Education

The RAC implemented stress testing under the direction of Dr. David J. Pillow, the seminary physician, and the recreation department of the School of Religious Education. Cardiac stress testing was the most recent implementation of the RAC for determining the physical fitness of the minister and his family. The stress tests were designed to determine an accurate level of physical fitness and to prescribe ways a student's fitness could be improved. Grady Lowery, director of the RAC, said, "While spiritual fitness is the most important part of our lives, our ability to perform our ministry is often directly related to our physical level. When the minister is fatigued his body can limit him physically."[13]

Mike Lofland, aerobics coordinator for the RAC, coordinated the stress testing. Lofland, a M.R.E. student from Longview, Texas, worked on staff at the Cooper Clinic in Dallas for more than two years before coming to Southwestern. Cooper was the originator of the aerobics program and trained Lofland during his tenure on the Cooper staff.

In the short time the program had been engaged at the RAC, several immediate problems were discovered and referred by the technicians to cardiologists and doctors for immediate care. Without the stress tests, these problems may not have been discovered for a long period of time, and serious cardiac results could have occurred in the lives of the students. It was imperative for a physician to compile the information of the stress tests. David J. Pillow administered the tests while serving on the seminary medical staff. After looking at the results, the technician and nutritionist compiled the data in a notebook for the student to use as a guide to better health. A coronary risk profile was developed so the participant could see the level of fitness in proportion to the norms.

Baylor University and Southwestern Seminary established a new joint gerontology program—the first of its kind between a seminary and a major university. Gerontology, the study of aging, had become a growing concern among Americans. Ben Dickerson was the director of the graduate program in gerontology at Baylor University. He believed that most congregations were generally characterized by an age higher than 30. Churches had youth directors, but few had an adult director, much less a senior adult director. A certificate in gerontology became available with any degree program at the seminary. A Master of Science in gerontology was available but required 42 hours of study beyond the Master of Religious Education degree.

James Williams, professor of adult education and associate dean for advanced studies in religious education, identified a growing interest in older adults among seminary students in the ministry. Proposed classes between the two schools would include courses on death and dying, religion and the aging, physical fitness for older adults, etc. Southwestern faculty who participated in the program were given status as Baylor professors, and Baylor professors were given Southwestern faculty status. There was no need for course transfer of credit between the two schools because the courses were listed in each of the school's catalogs. Objectives for the program included emphasis on the wholeness of the aging adult; sharing resources of faculty and staff; and offering credit courses, internships, and field placement at the graduate level. The collection of information on aging and case studies as well as conferences, institutes, and workshops to enhance the continuing study of gerontology were being developed as part of the consortium. Research gathered from the study would be used by Southern Baptists and other religious groups in preparing to reach, teach, and assist in ministry with the aging adult.

James Williams studied the hospice movement in England while on sabbatical leave in the late 1970s. The School of Religious Education offered a conference on hospice during its annual spring emphasis in 1981. The title of the conference was "The Hospice Concept: A Better Way of Caring for the Dying." The conference was open to students, health care professionals, chaplains, church and denominational staff members, social services personnel, and adult educators. The senior adult section of the Baptist Sunday School Board's family ministries department, Buckner Baptist Benevolences, and the Baylor Medical Center sponsored the workshop in conjunction with Southwestern Seminary.

The purpose of the workshop was fourfold: to enhance awareness of the hospice concept; to describe how a hospice is developed within health support systems; to interpret the helping roles of the interdisciplinary hospice team; and to address critical problems of the hospice services, including ethical, legal, economic, social, and spiritual. The major purpose of hospice was to develop a specialized family-centered healthcare program that emphasized the management of pain and other symptoms experienced by patients with limited life expectancy. The goal of hospice was to carry on an alert and pain-free existence through the administration of drugs and other modalities of therapy.[14] The family as a unit in hospice was a vital part of meeting the needs of both patient and family members. The service to patients and family was provided by a medically directed nurse and coordinated team of professionals and volunteers.

Shoemakes Establish Chair of Personal Growth and Ministry

A chair established anonymously in 1974 was made public by Southwestern Seminary on February 3, 1981. The Earl L. and Vivian Gray Shoemake Chair of Personal Growth and Ministry was established in the School of Religious Education and provided for study in the role assessment of family relationships in the ministry. The desire to assist ministers and their families to understand themselves, their calling, and their relationships before they entered their field of service was deemed imperative to effective ministry. Shoemake said,

> In our ministry we have seen so many instances where people had a poor understanding of the role of ministers. Problems were created because of this lack of understanding of self and family relationships. There are so many pressures in ministry of which people are not aware. The commitment to establish a study was planted in our hearts when we were poor. While in seminary and during the early days of their ministry money and other resources were scarce. An inheritance has provided funds to establish such a trust.[15]

Earl and Vivian Shoemake are graduates of Southwestern Seminary who served churches in Georgia, Florida, and South Carolina. They had also been in associational missions work in Kentucky for the last several years.

All Records Shattered in 1981-1982

A record cumulative enrollment of 4,604 students for 1981-1982 shattered all other cumulative records. The total was a 4.2 percent increase over the 1980-1981 cumulative enrollments. The new figure represented the 15th consecutive cumulative record increase.

The record fall enrollment of 3,837 and spring enrollment of 3,691 represented 1,400 first-time students—a 5.4 percent increase over the 1980-1981 total of 1,324. One contributing factor to the increase in enrollment was the record enrollment at the four off-campus centers in Houston, San Antonio, Shawnee, and Nashville, which provided students an opportunity to receive seminary training while continuing to live on their church field. The centers enrolled a record 330 students.

The increase in adult education had a major effect on the seminary's enrollment, as well. Many older adults decided to pursue college education, and the seminary attracted these non-traditional college students. More than one-fourth of the seminary's students were 30 years of age or older. Additionally, many new specialized programs in missions, church growth, communications, church recreation, gerontology, instrumental music, and other areas contributed to the seminary's growth.

A numerical milestone was passed in January 1982. Southwestern had enrolled 40,202 students since its founding in 1908. Robby Wes Barrett, a Master of Church Music student from Midland, Texas, became the 40,000th student to enroll during the spring registration in January 1982. Also, 20,033 degrees had been awarded in the seminary's 74-year history.[16]

In the fall of 1982, a record 3,854 students enrolled for classes. This was a slight increase over the preceding fall of 1981, when 3,837 students enrolled in all programs. This was the 16th record fall enrollment of the last 17 years. However, new student enrollment decreased to 822 from the fall 1981 total of 900. Multiple economic factors probably affected new student enrollment, including relocation to a seminary campus, limited housing, limited new jobs at the seminary, an established ministry career where they were serving, and the choice to attend an off-campus center near their place of ministry. Another factor was the new satellite program sponsored by the six seminaries through the Seminar External Education Department, which may have had some effect on new student enrollment at some campuses, including Southwestern.

Trustees Name Recreation/Aerobics Center and Memorial Building Complex

The naming of two major campus buildings and the adoption of a record budget were the focus of the spring board of trustees meeting, March 12-14, 1982. The Recreation/Aerobics Center was named for Myra K. and J. Roy Slover of Liberty, Texas. The Slovers gave property valued at $1 million to Southwestern in February 1979, the largest single gift in seminary history. The recreation complex was part of the capital projects of the seminary's "Eight by Eighty" campaign. It officially opened in January 1979. The Slovers gift was the largest contribution to the campaign.[17]

The board voted to name the Memorial Building complex for B.H. Carroll, founder and first president of Southwestern Seminary. The complex included three major wings of the building: Scarborough Hall (which housed the School of Theology), Truett Auditorium, and Fleming Library. The three wings retained their original names, with the entire complex to be known as the B.H. Carroll Memorial Building.

In 1980, a new Master of Arts in Communication degree was developed with the Radio and Television Commission of the SBC. At a June 16, 1982, meeting in New Orleans (during the Southern Baptist Convention), the trustees approved the implementation of the degree beginning in the fall of 1983. The new degree was part of the seminary's Center for Christian Communications Studies for students planning ministry careers in communications-related ministries. The degree included the basic courses in each of the seminary's three schools, in addition to required and elective communications courses. A thesis or creative project was required of all students in the new degree program. A specialization in radio/television/film, public relations, editing/writing, drama, or speech was available for all enrolled.

At the same meeting, the trustees announced the establishment of the Bessie M. Fleming Chair of Childhood Education and named Jeroline Baker, professor of childhood education, to be appointed to this chair for the academic year of 1982-1983. They also approved two new degrees: Master of Arts in Marriage and Family Counseling and Master of Arts in Missiology.[18] Theodore H. Dowell was named the director of the Marriage and Family Counseling Center to replace the founding director, John W. Drakeford, who retired after 20 years as director.

August 31, 1982, was identified as the official starting day for Southwestern Seminary's 75th anniversary celebration year. The celebration began with the first day of classes during the 75th annual academic session. As spokesperson for the traditional president's convocation, Dilday introduced a series of special events for the entire academic year and involved constituencies from every facet of seminary and convention life.

The theme for the celebration year was "Heritage/Reality/Vision," with major focus on Southwestern's past, present, and future. The thematic Scriptural text for the anniversary celebration was Psalm 48:12-14, focusing on the phrase "tell the generations following."[19] Robert Baker, professor of church history, delivered the traditional Founder's Day address on March 22, using this passage as the general theme. Baker was completing a history of the seminary to be published under the same title, *Tell the Generations Following*, in March 1983.

Bill Moyers, correspondent for CBS News and Public Broadcasting System and an alumnus of the seminary, spoke in chapel on March 23. A luncheon honoring the community and municipal leadership of the Dallas/Fort Worth Metroplex was held in Naylor Student Center.

An original historical drama was presented in chapel and in an evening performance on March 24. The drama, written by Karen Oakerson, a Master of Religious Education student from Mt. Pleasant, Texas, focused on the six presidents and their wives, highlighting the contributions of each in the formation of Southwestern's unique history.

A major event for the celebration year was the dedication ceremonies for the A. Webb Roberts Library. This event took place on October 19, 1983, during the gathering of the state alumni presidents for the "Fall Homecoming Events."

Throughout "Founder's Week," "Seminary Day" observances were held in area churches. Southwestern Seminary students were invited to participate in worship services on the two Sundays and the Wednesday of that week, emphasizing the relationship between the seminary and local area churches.

All other seminary events were focused on the anniversary year celebration. The celebration year climaxed at the 1983 national Southwestern Alumni Luncheon during the June meeting of the Southern Baptist Convention in Pittsburg.

In a final presentation to the trustees, Dilday reported the completion of the accreditation self-study. The Association of Theological Schools (ATS) and the Southern Association of Colleges and Schools (SACS) reaffirmed the seminary's institutional accreditation for another 10-year period. The next accreditation self-study would not take place until 1991-1992, when the 18-month process began again to determine the seminary's progress and accomplishments in light of the self-study criteria. The trustees prepared a resolution to be read to the administration and faculty expressing sincere appreciation for the hard work done in securing the accreditation reaffirmed for another 10-year period.

Gerontology Classes Boom in First Year

Whoever said "the only certainties in life were death and taxes" oversimplified the statement. The process that gets us through life also ensures another certainty: aging. Declining birth rates and longer life spans go hand in hand. The cooperative agreement between Baylor University and Southwestern Seminary met this need. The joint venture, the first of its kind at Southwestern, allowed both institutions "to benefit for the other's resources."[20]

At least 300 students had taken senior adult courses in each of the first two semesters. Not only were religious education students interested in the courses for their degree plans, but many theology students were taking the courses such as Death and Dying, taught on the Southwestern campus by Tilman Rodabough of the Baylor faculty.

In addition to visiting professors and course cross-listing in the catalogs, the two institutions co-sponsored workshops dealing with the hospice movement and a senior adult leadership conference for church leaders. Ben Dickerson of the Baylor faculty wrote, "Where past senior adult ministry has been limited, emphasis moving toward survival and instrumental needs of older adults, we hope to provide assistance and ministry in programs such as nutrition, economics, legal problems, retirement housing and health care affecting senior citizens."[21] Many seminary students who were active in the Southern Baptist Association of Ministries with the Aging (SBAMA) were presently in ministry positions in the local church and with denominational agencies. There were over 100 full-time ministers with "senior adult" in their ministry titles in the SBC. Many churches had substantial senior adult populations available to practicing senior adult ministers. An awareness of the resources available from both schools and the denomination ensured continued growth in this exciting new arena of full-time ministry. The program moved to the cutting edge of ministry with older persons.

CBS Produces Documentary for SWBTS

On April 13-16, 1982, Southwestern Seminary was the subject of a documentary film on the CBS television network. Film crews were on campus during this four-day period filming the series "For Our Times," which was aired by CBS on 40 stations across the United States. Robyn Mendelsohn, the series' producer, said,

> Southwestern was chosen because it is the largest theological seminary in the world and because of the 75th planned anniversary celebration during the 1982-1983 academic year. It seemed very appropriate that an ecumenical series feature such a significant subject at such a significant time. I personally was amazed to learn that training for ministry was not just theological at Southwestern. Here you train the mind and the body and provide specialized training in so many things like music, communication, recreation and other areas.[22]

Mendelsohn also noted that she was impressed with the spirit of the faculty and the students. She said, "Many people do not know what seminary is. It will be a wonderful revelation for viewers to see that seminary is not pious people praying all day but rather wide and encompassing studies and activities."[23]

75th Anniversary Conferences Kick-Off Celebration Year

The Day-Higginbotham Lecture Series at Southwestern Seminary that spring emphasized the main purpose for personal recreation, or "play." Theologian Robert K. Johnson of Western Kentucky University was the main speaker for the series, noting that "Americans are having difficulty learning, as a society, how to play."[24]

Johnson discussed the theology of play as part of American society. Although work hours are shorter than they were a century ago, he said, Americans still have failed to understand the value of play. He continued,

> Hard work with sufficient time off for vacations and recreation seems to be the formula for a meaningful life. But increased leisure time seems to pose a threat. We have a continuing inability to escape our compulsion to work. Christians have discovered the need for play. In a world full of ulcers and high blood pressure, play has become important. Americans still seem unsuited to authentic play because either we work at work or we work at play.
>
> … God played meaningfully with His own possibilities. And He rested—or played—as part of the creation process. Israel used the Sabbath as a day of "play" to qualify their working world and to realize that life is a gift, as well as a task. The Sabbath was viewed as having ethical implications: all creation was in travail and needed recreation. We are called to our work, but we are also called to refrain from work, to play. Play, too, is a gift from God. We should enjoy and work and give ourselves wholly to all we do. We are told to work playfully and to play playfully. We are not to work at play. Work-dominant models have destroyed our personhood. Man must seek to rediscover the sacred in the common things of life. We must live now as if playing.[25]

Unprecedented Growth Continues

"Strengthening the Family" was the theme for the School of Religious Education spring emphasis, April 1982. The emphasis was sponsored by the Social Work Department and coincided with the current Southern Baptist Convention emphasis on the family. The Southern Baptist Home Mission Board (now NAMB) requested the seminary's emphasis to be a regional conference to highlight the beginning of the convention-wide emphasis. The conference focus was the prevention of family problems, family enrichment, and dealing with problems of family life. Workshops dealt with marriage, parenting, parents no longer in direct parenting roles, single parents, foster homes and children's homes, day care centers for children and senior adults, family financial planning, and family recreation. A Sarah Walton Miller Drama Festival was also featured during the conference. Mrs. Miller produced several plays dealing with the family, and she was present for the presentation of the series of her four dramas presented by the seminary's Center for Christian Communications Studies.

The 1982 National Conference of Broadcast Ministries was held on the campus April 26-28. Sponsored by Southwestern Seminary and the Southern Baptist Radio and Television Commission, the conference was directed primarily at pastors, church staff personnel, and members of churches that had broadcast facilities or hoped to have facilities in the near future. The keynote speaker was Charles L. Allen, pastor of the first United Methodist Church of Houston. Allen's Sunday morning services were televised over Houston's KTRK-TV and KENR radio. Another feature was a speech by Mollie Pauker of the Federal Communication Commission's Broadcast Bureau. Other major topics to be addressed dealt with the practical aspects of broadcasting the worship service, the worship as a local television ministry, the potential of cable in the spreading of the Gospel, and 30- and 60-minute production formats.

The 15th Annual Youth Lab theme "Youth Ministry: Promises ... Possibilities" began on April 30 and continued through May 2, 1982. Program personalities included Richard Ross, minister to youth at Royal Haven Baptist Church, Dallas, Texas; Ewing Cooley, psychologist at the Metro Counseling Center, Dallas, Texas; Wesley Black of the church training department of the Sunday School Board, Nashville, Tennessee;

Steve Seelig, minister to singles at the North Phoenix Baptist Church, Phoenix, Arizona; and Barbara Kent, youth teacher, curriculum writer, and conference leader, Fort Worth, Texas. Worship was led by Darrel Baergen, professor of communication arts at the seminary, with music provided by Doug Wood, youth minister at Champion Forest Baptist Church, Houston, Texas. The lab was opened to full-time, part-time, and summer youth work leaders. An attendance of over 400 participants energized the entire three days of worship, workshops, and personal meetings with outstanding youth leadership from around the Southern Baptist Convention.

An original drama written, directed, and produced by students was the "icing on the cake" in preparation for Southwestern's 75th Anniversary Celebration during the 1982-1983 academic year. The production was a major student contribution to the celebration. Darrel Baergen chaired the play selection committee, with the winning play receiving a $250 prize. The winning selection was announced May 6, with production beginning in the fall of 1982. The play was scheduled for its premiere performance on March 24, 1983, during a special Founder's Week celebration.

Pastors, ministers of education, and other people responsible for the teacher training programs in their churches were invited to a workshop specifically aimed at training Sunday School teachers and class leaders. LeRoy Ford, professor of foundations of education, and Jack Terry, dean of the School of Religious Education, led the workshop. The presentations focused on the philosophical aspect of teaching and the practical aspects of teaching, such as lesson plans, learning activities, teaching aids, goal analysis, and goal-setting. Participants developed a better understanding of the multiplicity of learning activities that are available for teachers as they develop week-to-week Sunday School lesson plans.

75th Diamond Anniversary in Full Swing in 1983

Southwestern Seminary began the celebration of the 75th Diamond Anniversary Year with a multiplicity of special events on and off the campus. The Diamond Founder's Week, March 20-27, featured local and denominational leadership from around the nation highlighting the special Founder's Observance Week commemorating Southwestern Seminary's 75th anniversary. Special events throughout the previous year had pointed to this Founder's Week, traditionally a one-day observance, but this year a full week. During this year, all three schools, alumni, trustees, and students enjoyed a full week to remember March 14, 1908, the day the state of Texas granted Southwestern Seminary's charter.[26] Students and faculty were invited to churches in the area and around the state to tell the story on "Seminary Day in the Churches," Sunday, March 20 and 27. Wednesday, March 23, was designated as "Seminary Night in the Churches" and featured students and faculty in local churches in the Fort Worth/Dallas Metroplex telling the 75-year story of Southwestern Seminary.

"The Imperishable Vision," an original drama written by a student on the history of Southwestern Seminary, was presented in Truett Auditorium at 10:00 a.m. on March 24. The play was written by Karen Oakerson and depicted scenes from each of the six president's terms in office, incorporating drama, music, and audio-visuals. The play was presented a second time that evening for the Fort Worth community. At a special "Student Chapel" during Founder's Week, Carl Barrington, Master of Divinity student from Marlow, Oklahoma, gave a historical synopsis of the seminary from a student's perspective.

Special luncheons on Monday, Tuesday, and Wednesday of Founder's Week drew attention to the heritage, reality, and vision of Southwestern. All of the luncheon themes were tied to the Scriptural theme of "tell the generations following" from Psalm 48. The celebration week recounted the historical and spiritual foundation of what had become the largest theological seminary in the world.

Outstanding denominational and secular personalities were featured speakers during the week's celebration. Robert E. Naylor, the fifth president, spoke to over 300 Southern Baptist pastors and denominational leaders from the Tarrant and Dallas Baptist Associations on Monday, March 20. Harold C. Bennett, executive secretary of the Southern Baptist Convention executive committee; Herbert H. Reynolds, president of Baylor University; and William M. Pinson, executive director of the Baptist General Convention of Texas, addressed a luncheon on March 22. Robert A. Baker, professor of church history, authored a history of Southwestern Baptist Theological Seminary from 1908-1983 titled *Tell the Generations Followi*ng. The history was published by Broadman Press, and a copy was presented to President Dilday with additional copies available for all who attended. Chapel was followed by a luncheon featuring present and past members of the seminary's board of trustees. There was a special dinner that evening specifically for faculty, trustees, and administration. Following the dinner was the climax of the day, a concert at 8:00 p.m. in Truett Auditorium with a joint performance by choirs from Baylor University and Southwestern Seminary presenting a new musical, "King David," one of the four musical pieces commissioned specifically for Founder's Week.

On Wednesday, March 23, John Sullivan, first vice president of the Southern Baptist Convention, spoke in chapel, which was followed by a luncheon honoring the B.H. Carroll Award recipients. The B.H. Carroll Award is the highest award given to laypersons by Southwestern Seminary. The award was given annually during the Founder's Day Celebration and recognized outstanding ministry partners who had been especially beneficial to Southwestern Seminary. Receiving the B.H. Carroll Awards during the 75th Anniversary Celebration luncheon were George Ann Carter and Amon G. Carter, Jr. (posthumous), philanthropists from Fort Worth, Texas; John and Jane Justin, Jr. (Justin Boot Corp., Fort Worth, Texas); and Evelyn and Tom Lineberry, philanthropists from Midland, Texas.

The final chapel of the Diamond Anniversary Celebration Week, Friday, March 25, featured Dilday, who addressed the chapel audience on the theme "Tell the Generations Following" by setting out his vision for the future of Southwestern Baptist Theological Seminary, pointing toward the 100th Centennial Year Celebration in 2008. It was a fitting culmination of a magnificent week of historical remembrances; fellowship with former alumni, professors, and denominational representatives; and honoring the world's largest seminary, Southwestern Baptist Theological Seminary of Fort Worth, Texas.

The School of Religious Education sponsored a Religious Education Emphasis Week during the 75th Diamond Anniversary Celebration

Unprecedented Growth Continues

Year, April 4-6, inviting religious educators to the campus for a combination homecoming and workshop emphasis. The week was sponsored by the individual departments of the School of Religious Education and included topics such as administration, counseling, social work, childhood education, youth ministry, church recreation, and adult religious education. Each of the conferences was led by national denominational leaders including Jimmy Allen, president of the Radio and Television Commission; J. Oscar Jeske, professor of psychology at Oklahoma Baptist University; and many area consultants from the Baptist Sunday School Board.

An April 4 banquet featured Philip Harris, former professor of youth education and the current secretary of the Church Training Union department of the Baptist Sunday School Board, speaking on the advancement and achievement of church training in SBC churches. At a second banquet on April 5, Elaine Dickson, author and consultant at the Baptist Sunday School Board, addressed the banquet attendees about the "Future of Religious Education." Four noteworthy denominational spokespersons responded to her address: Bernard Spooner, state Sunday School director for the Baptist General Convention of Texas; June Cooper, missionary to Japan; Bill Rogers, New Orleans Seminary professor of history and philosophy of religious education; and Bob Edd Shotwell, minister of education and administration at Hyde Park Baptist Church, Austin, Texas.

Harry Piland, minister of education and administration at First Baptist Church, Houston, Texas, concluded the week as the chapel speaker on April 5 in Truett Auditorium. Piland shared historical documentation of the cooperative relationship between Southwestern Seminary and the Southern Baptist Sunday School Board. Piland was the former director of the Sunday School department of the Baptist Sunday School Board in Nashville, Tennessee.

Trustees Meet during Anniversary Week

The 75th diamond anniversary week was crowded with special events on the campus, but the week-long observance also included the 1983 spring meeting of the board of trustees. The School of

Religious Education had several major activities that needed the attention of the board during this meeting, including the election of two faculty members.

A major change in the nomenclature for the Master of Religious Education degree (M.R.E.) was brought to the attention of the trustees. The recommendation was to change the nomenclature of the Master of Religious Education (M.R.E.) to the Master of Arts in Religious Education (M.A.R.E.). It was also recommended that persons who currently held the M.R.E. be permitted to exchange the degree for the M.A.R.E. by a procedure to be worked out in consultation with the registrar. This exchange referred to the M.R.E. only and not to the Master of Arts in Marriage and Family Counseling or the Master of Arts in Communication.

A second recommendation was to add eight new courses to the communication curriculum. The addition of Darrel Baergen to the communication department required many additional courses that needed to be added to complete a total communication curriculum. A new directed study course that could be taken in any department in the School of Religious Education with the approval of the professor and by a student with a 3.0 GPA, was likewise added. Two new courses in the counseling department on staff relationships and personality theory and one in the childhood department on the director of children's work were made a part of the curriculum.[27]

The trustees elected two new professors to the faculty of the School of Religious Education. Lucien E. Coleman was elected as a tenured professor in adult education. Coleman previously pastored churches in Kentucky, Arkansas, and Indiana and joined the faculty at Southern Seminary in 1965. He authored several books: *Understanding Adults*, *How To Teach the Bible*, *Understanding Today's Adults*, *How to Generate Excitement for Bible Study*, and *Why the Church Must Teach*—his most notable book. Wesley O. Black was elected as associate professor of youth education. Black was a first lieutenant, U.S. Army, Ordnance Corps.; band director, Sam Houston High School, San Antonio, Texas; minister of youth in several churches in Texas and Oklahoma; and consultant in youth education, Baptist Sunday School Board, Nashville,

Tennessee. Black published several articles for the youth leadership materials of the Baptist Sunday School Board and was a contributing editor of *Disciple Youth Notebook* and the *Baptist Parent Enrichment Program* learning module.

The trustees approved two new degree plans in the School of Religious Education, the Master of Arts in Social Services and the Master of Arts/Master of Science in Social Work (MA/MSSW). Both degrees prepared students to provide social services in conjunction with community/mission centers, children's homes, retirement homes, homes for the aging, hospitals, local congregations, state conventions, and denominational agencies.[28]

The MA/MSSW was an integrated degree with the University of Texas at Arlington. A student enrolled in both schools graduated from both schools upon completion of 82 required course hours.[29]

Dilday noted in his article, "From the President,"

> While the seminary is not in the business of equipping public school teachers, we have discovered that a very effective bi-vocational minister is available to people who can teach in the public school and at the same time serve as a pastor or staff minister in local churches. Many school districts and foreign governments (such as Brazil) have not recognized the master's degrees of our seminary graduates and additional preparation for teaching until the terminology of some of our degrees was changed to be more consistent with standard terminology. Hence, the change from M.R.E. to M.A. in religious education and the change from [Master of Church Music] to [Master of Music], is the standard terminology for music teachers. This change has already proven to be a great blessing to foreign missionaries and many bi-vocational ministers across the convention. The curricula for these degrees remains essentially the same even though the terminology is different. These and other changes in no way suggest that the seminary is becoming a secular university or is moving away

from its traditional purposes. It does illustrate the sensitivity on the part of Southwestern to the emerging needs of the churches and denominational mission agencies and the desire of the seminary to be responsible and creative in attempting to meet these needs.[30]

During the year of the 75th anniversary, all the new degree plans were approved by the trustees to provide training for church-related vocations that had emerged in recent years. The M.A. in Christian Communications is a prime example. Churches were calling for ministers of media, and this new degree gave the student not only basic theological courses but also specialized courses in the use of media in ministry. The M.A. in church social services was also approved, and the M.A. in marriage and family counseling certified a person called to the ministry of counseling to be prepared for a specific ministry position on the staff of a local church.

A record enrollment was reached during the 75th anniversary year. There were 4,337 students enrolled for the fall semester across all campuses of Southwestern Seminary. The total was up 12.5 percent from 1982. The enrollment number also included 1,029 new students, which was a record. This was the fifth consecutive record fall enrollment and the 17th in the last 18 years.[31]

The Fort Worth campus had the largest numerical gain from 3,574 to 3,890, an 8.8 percent gain. The extension centers had a total of 447, with 157 at Houston, 107 at Shawnee, and 183 at San Antonio. The School of Theology had 2,459 with 255 doctoral students, the School of Religious Education had 1,508 with 72 doctoral students, and the School of Church Music had 370 with 31 doctoral students. For the first time in the School of Church Music, all new master's-level students were enrolled in the Master of Music degree.[32]

Church Business Administration Certification

Several major emphases were held during the 75th anniversary celebration. With a mind to assist churches, the administration faculty in the School of Religious Education developed a program specifically designed for church business administrators. As budgets, church buildings, various insurance necessities, and custodial instruction outgrew the attention of some part-time staff member, the role of a full-time church business administrator became a more popular ministry field.

In June 1983, William G. Caldwell, associate professor of education administration and church business administration, with the assistance of F. Marvin Myers, executive director of the National Association of Church Business Administrators, developed a two-week certification seminar on the Southwestern campus for the National Association of Church Business Administrators. Southwestern was one of two institutions offering this academic certification. Presently, professional church business administrators were only certified at the Candler School of Theology in Atlanta, Georgia. The Southwestern program took place during two summers to complete a similar four-week program being offered at the Atlanta seminary.

Caldwell reported that many churches had million-dollar budgets and membership of well over 1,000 members, and church business administrators were in demand. Students with an undergraduate degree in business administration and Southwestern Seminary's four-week program provided a tremendous opportunity for finding a vocational ministry opportunity. Interest in church administration had been on the increase since Caldwell had been teaching at Southwestern for the last seven years. He admitted that current chances for a church position without experience were negligible and slim at best. Churches needed Church Business Administration (CBA)-certified ministers and seldom hired a novice.

During a sabbatical leave, Caldwell visited nearly 150 churches of all sizes and denominations to see how they would utilize a church business administrator. He found they were frequently the second staff member hired in many denominations. Southern Baptist churches hired youth, children's, and music staff members before hiring a business administrator. The church business administrator did not just keep books but much of the time was in charge of financial records, office personnel, facilities, food services, insurance, security, vehicles, and tax issues. The need of church business administrators to free other staff members and lay members for the task more related to their ministry was sorely needed. Graduates of the four-week program were certified as Fellows in Church Business Administration.

Bob Keeshan (aka Captain Kangaroo) Headlines Television Emphasis

During the anniversary celebration, the childhood education department, under the direction of Jeroline Baker, invited an international television personality to the campus. Bob Keeshan, better known to a generation of young adults as Captain Kangaroo, addressed 225 childhood educators from Fort Worth churches and schools. During his address to the educators, Keeshan told them they were not just making a difference in the lives of the young children, but they were training others to make that difference as well.

Keeshan noted that his show had its best effect in homes where children knew they were loved. He said, "Youngsters who are ignored or abused need more help than my show can give them."[33]

Sitting next to the president of the Radio and Television Commission, Jimmy Allen, at a press conference, Keeshan told reporters that Baptists do not stand much more chance than he did of getting people to watch "family entertainment" over the new ACTS Network. However, he did say that Baptists had a distinct advantage over him in a built-in communication network in the churches. The churches were the key locations where major family communication responsibilities could be developed. He said,

> Pastors can let parents know such programming exists and recommend it. As soon as a parent says, "why don't we watch this program?" you're 99 percent home because concern has been shown by the parent. Parents should not throw the television out the door because television is a fact of life and is no more intrinsically evil than a vacuum cleaner. It is an appliance to be turned on to do a job and be turned off when that job is completed.[34]

Baptist Childcare Research Documents Acquired

Major social work documents were delivered to the social work department in the School of Religious Education by the Association of Childcare Executives. The seven-volume set included research papers delivered at its meetings since they began in 1948.

Bob Brackney, associate professor of social work, received the papers on campus from Wade East, superintendent of childcare for the Louisiana Baptist Convention. The papers included the history of some important years in Southern Baptist childcare work, which was not available elsewhere. The volumes showed that Baptist childcare was second to none among denominational agencies in the U.S. The papers are now on reserve in Roberts Library.

Campus Landscape Drastically Changed

By the spring of 1984, the landscape on Seminary Hill had changed drastically. The new A. Webb Roberts Library stood majestically on the east side of the campus between Barnard Hall and Cowden Hall, just adjacent to the B.H. Carroll Memorial Building's Fleming Hall. The southwest side of the campus boasted the new Slover RAC, complemented by the Naylor Children's Center and the Walsh Medical Center to the north. The previous five years had been a flurry of groundbreakings, building construction, and building renovations.

The $3 million renovated Fleming Library building project began in 1982 and was completed in early 1984. It involved the restructuring of space that once housed the books and other resource materials now in the Roberts Library. The newly renovated space included the new location of the public affairs and student affairs divisions on the main level. Student Affairs was housed in a suite named for the Sid Richardson Foundation of Fort Worth, Texas, with another suite on the lower level housing the audio-visual services, also named for the Richardson Foundation.

Gracing the far end of the main level of Fleming was the Lucille Freeman Glasscock World Mission and Evangelism Center and the Jane and John Justin Conference Center. Mrs. Glasscock, a Corpus Christi philanthropist and former seminary student, was a major donor for the renovation project. John Justin, boot-maker, industrialist, and former mayor of Fort Worth, along with his wife Jane displayed a portion of their Western American art collection in the conference center named in their honor.

The renovation of the lower level included the Charles D. Tandy Center for Archaeological Research, named for the founder of the Fort Worth-based Tandy Corporation. The upper third floor area included faculty offices and student study carrels.[35]

Five-Year Strategic Plan, "Upward 90 – 1985-1990"

The spring trustee meeting was totally consumed with the presentation of a new five-year strategic plan, "Upward 90 – 1985-1990." The strategic plan virtually included every area of seminary life. Amid other activities of the meeting, President Dilday gave concluding remarks on Vision/85. The new strategic plan, Upward 90, proposed to raise $50 million for capital needs and endowment, funding 10 endowed teaching chairs, enlarging the faculty, and developing a more involved alumni relations division that would be responsible for church leadership development.[36]

The capital needs plan called for major renovations to existing buildings, additional faculty, student housing, and a major emphasis on the planning and construction of a continuing education conference center. A final piece of the strategic plan was the expansion of computer services, library acquisitions, and a major thrust at energy conservation for the entire campus. The five-year strategic plan consumed the energy and direction of the board of trustees for the next several years.

A $16.3 million budget was approved that included $6.8 million from the Cooperative Program of the Southern Baptist Convention. Included in the meeting was the election of four professors, naming the seminary's new physical plant for its director, James R. Leitch, who also served as the seminary's director of bi-vocational training. Leitch had directed the seminary's ongoing maintenance and physical plant program since 1953.[37] An array of new courses, numerous chair designations, faculty promotions, and tenure designations were included in the meeting.

Three faculty additions were made to the School of Religious Education. Wynona Tipton Elder, assistant professor of psychology and counseling, was a licensed psychologist who had been in private practice in Carrollton, Texas, since 1977. Gary W. Waller, assistant professor of administration, had previously served as minister of education and evangelism at the First Baptist Church of Waco, Texas. Daryl R. Eldridge, instructor in foundations of education, had served in multiple churches and written several youth discipleship training procedures such as *Group Covenants, Creative Ways to Study Doctrine,* and *Why Youth Should Study Doctrine.*

Jeroline Baker, professor of childhood education, was named to the Bessie M. Fleming Chair of Childhood Education; William G. Caldwell was named professor of administration; Pat Clendinning was named professor of psychology and counseling; and Alva G. Parks was named associate professor of administration. Rounding out the promotions was Rick Yount, assistant professor of foundations of education.

James D. Williams resigned his position as professor of adult education at Southwestern Seminary to become the associate to the president for planning and research at the Baptist Sunday School Board. The board's new president, Lloyd Elder, had served as executive vice-president at Southwestern from 1978-1983. Williams was a member of the faculty since 1962 and had served as associate dean for advanced studies. Under his direction as professor of adult education, the seminary developed a hospice program with St. Joseph Hospital and a cooperative program in gerontology with Ben Dickerson and Baylor University to provide training, research opportunities, and placement for students interested in ministries with senior adults.

While recognizing new faculty members in the School of Religious Education at the spring 1984 meeting, the trustees also said farewell to two long-term professors—Harold Dill and LeRoy Ford. Dill had served as youth education and field education professor since 1959. He was the founding impetus that began the Youth Lab emphasis in 1968, which had grown to be the largest attended conference for youth ministers and lay-youth leaders in Texas and throughout the Southern Baptist Convention. From the small beginning of 125 in 1968, upward of 1,000 had been in attendance each year at the spring meeting during the past 17 years.

LeRoy Ford was professor of foundations of education. He introduced programmed instruction into the curriculum of the seminary and was the guiding educational architect for the development of the *Course Description Manual for the Master's Degree Program* for the School of Religious Education. A prolific author and programmed instruction design architect, Ford was engaged in the design and promotion of Theological Education by Extension (TEE) on multiple foreign mission fields.

A retirement dinner was held on April 26 for four professors and two administrators. Aside from Dill and Ford, those honored were Jack Gray, professor of missions since 1956; Jesse Northcutt, professor of preaching, dean of the School of Theology, and vice-president for academic affairs since 1939; Wayne Evans, vice-president for business affairs since 1954; and Keith Wills, director of libraries since 1966.[38]

A final recommendation presented to the trustees by the faculty of the School of Religious Education was to phase out the Graduate Specialist in Religious Education degree (G.S.R.E.). The G.S.R.E. degree was designed especially to meet a specific requirement of the Foreign Mission Board. The Foreign Mission Board, prior to 1974, required each candidate to have 98 hours of theological studies. Since the M.R.E. degree was a 66-hour degree, the candidate in religious education was 32 hours short of meeting that requirement. An additional 32 hours had to be earned in either the theological school curriculum or the religious education school curriculum.

To provide a religious education base for the additional hours, the faculty designed the G.S.R.E. This was a 32-hour degree with an 8-hour project. Not only did it meet the 98-hour mission board requirement, it also gave the mission volunteer additional hours of specialized training in theological education.

But in 1974, the Foreign Mission Board changed this policy. The new requirement was 20 hours of theological studies, already part of the M.R.E. degree. With the number of new M.A.R.E. degrees, the continuation of the G.S.R.E. put a drain on the human resources of the school because of the project requirement at the end of the degree.[39]

The trustees approved the recommendation, and the G.S.R.E. was phased out over a period of two years. Those enrolled in the program were allowed to continue to graduation, but no new applications for that program were received.

A Record for Southwestern and Theological Education

Another milestone was reached in enrollment during the 1983-1984 academic years with an accumulated enrollment of 5,120. This was a record enrollment not only for Southwestern Seminary but for all of theological education. The enrollment record took into consideration students who had enrolled since summer 1983 and had taken courses on the main campus in Fort Worth as well as at branches in Houston, Shawnee, and San Antonio. President Dilday said, "We are overwhelmed that God continues to draw students to Southwestern for ministry preparation. It is encouraging and exciting to be a part of the largest gathering in history of men and women preparing for Christian ministry."[40]

Added to this accumulated enrollment record was a report of 1,506 new students, also a new record. The spring 1984 semester registered 383 new students to add to the 1,123 who had previously matriculated. Additionally, 56 percent of Southwestern's students were enrolled in the School of Theology, 36 percent in the School of Religious Education, and 8 percent in the School of Church Music.

One fascinating factor was that 25.8 percent of the student body were mission volunteers in 1981-1982, but in 1983-1984, 30.5 percent were mission volunteers—a significant growth in two years. Courses of study with the highest enrollments for the academic year were the Master of Divinity degree, 2,226 students; Master of Arts in Religious Education, 1,421; and in various facets of church music, 414 students were enrolled.

In the last 76 years, a total of 44,406 students enrolled for classes at Southwestern Seminary. Of that number, 22,259, or 50.34 percent, had received degrees. In addition to the 5,120 students who enrolled in credit courses, 3,519 audited classes or participated in a non-credit institute for Christian studies, elevating the number of people served by Southwestern this academic year to 8,639.[41]

Mission Education Emphasis in Religious Education

Lucien Coleman, professor of adult education, spent two weeks in Japan speaking to Japanese church leadership about the importance of adult Sunday School. Coleman, the author of *How To Teach the Bible* and *Why the Church Must Teach*, was part of a seven-member team that shared insights into church-wide Sunday School methodology with Japanese Baptists.

Adult Bible study was not a major emphasis in Baptist churches in Japan. Sunday School was considered an activity for children and not for adults. Coleman helped the Japanese pastoral leadership understand that adult work is key to the development and growth of Japanese Baptist churches in the future. He observed that we have so much adult work in America that we have become inoculated against seeing it as crucial to the growth of the church. Coleman was persuaded that the future growth of the church in any culture depends greatly on the strength and vibrancy of the adult population of that church. Coleman told the Japanese pastors that he had never seen a church in the U.S. or any other country that is growing and developing without a strong program for adults. Other members of the team who accompanied Coleman were Harry Piland, director of the Sunday School Board's Sunday School division; and Marcie Creech, director of childhood education at Fielder Road Baptist Church, Arlington, Texas.

Monte Clendinning, adjunct professor of missions education in the School of Religious Education and conference coordinator of Southwestern Seminary's Glasscock World Mission and Evangelism Center, led a consultation on mission education within churches. The consultation was specifically developed for pastors and mission education strategists from five states and denominational agencies, all of whom were actively involved with missions education. During the consultation, notable representatives from churches and denominational agencies outlined their missions education efforts and highlighted various innovations in promoting missions education programs.

Reginal McDonough, Southern Baptist Convention associate executive director, reviewed the historical significance of Bold Mission Thrust, calling it God's gift to our denomination. But only 13 percent of the people in the Southern Baptist Convention were members of a missions education program. He pointed out the gap between God's vision and the denomination's response to missions. He concluded by saying, "We must grow up a generation that understands that missions is every Christian's vocation."[42]

Justice Anderson, director of the Glasscock World Missions and Evangelism Center, reminded the attendees that they cannot sit back on their laurels and enjoy life while the world is in abject darkness. A second consultation was planned to begin developing a comprehensive missions education strategy that would be made available for use in the local churches when completed.

Conservative Resurgence Moving Forward

The Conservative Resurgence movement that began in 1979 with the election of Adrian Rogers and continued with the election of conservative presidents—namely, Baily Smith (1980-1982) and Jimmy Draper (1982-1984)—continued to have a major impact on the boards of seminaries, agencies, and commissions with the addition of more conservative trustees. Dilday was asked to deliver the convention sermon at the Southern Baptist Convention in Kansas City, Kansas, in 1984. In his sermon entitled "Higher Ground," the message appeared to be more actively engaged on the side of the moderates. This gave the conservative leadership considerable consternation and apprehension about the future direction of Southwestern Seminary. Southwestern was popularly known as the most conservative Southern Baptist seminary at that time, and this more moderate indication by its president was of grave concern to the Southern Baptist Convention conservative leadership. The convention-wide debate had come to Southwestern, and Dilday was the point man.

A Tale of Two Semesters (1985)

The ebb and flow of enrollment from semester to semester was enough to keep even the bravest academic heart in a tailspin of awe and wonder. The 4,027 students who enrolled in the spring of 1985 was the second highest enrollment in the school's 77-year history. Enrollments had been booming for the last several years, and it appeared the figures were just going to continue to escalate into the 1990s.

However, the 1985 spring's enrollment was a 2.44 percent decline from last year's spring semester, when the enrollment was 4,128 on all campuses. Dilday responded to the decline and noted, "We are always grateful when the Lord continues to send us so many men and women whom He calls into ministry from such broad backgrounds."[43]

Dan McLallen, director of admissions and registrar, in an attempt to lessen the blow of a small downturn, noted that there were presently 15 file drawers of applications, and the pool was still as large as ever. McLallen identified that denying admission to a person who wishes to train for the ministry is a tough decision, but a more demanding policy was a necessity. If Southwestern was going to be the leading theological institution in the nation, standards would have to be set. Increased enrollment required an institution to keep the student/teacher ratio at a level that promotes the best possible environment for learning. Present facilities were 99 percent filled in Fort Worth.

A final count for the spring at each of the campuses was 3,615 in Fort Worth, 56 in San Antonio, 117 in Shawnee, and 102 in Houston. This enrollment included 2,314 in theology, 1,396 in religious education, and 317 in church music.[44]

The overflowing facilities caused the administration to be concerned through the spring and summer semesters because a larger than expected enrollment was looming on the horizon for the fall of 1985. In fact, the fall enrollment of 4,375 was the largest number ever enrolled in a theological school.[45] This record broke Southwestern's previous record of 4,337, which occurred in 1983. Enrollment for the Fort Worth campus was 3,796. Two of the three off-campus extension centers posted enrollment increases in the fall semester, with Houston leading the way with 172 students, Shawnee with 114, and San Antonio with 59. In addition, there were 147 taking courses for no credit, which enlarged the theology school to an enrollment of 2,543, or 58 percent of the total enrollment.[46]

The important fact was that the enrollment occurred with tougher admissions standards in place. Upward 90, Southwestern's five-year plan, placed a major emphasis on student quality that required all applicants to have a personal interview before being admitted along with a mid-degree program evaluation to check the student's progress. The student-teacher ratio improved and placed a greater emphasis on the goal for student quality. McLallen said, "We worried that enrollment might go down because we have a more stringent enrollment standard."[47] However, there appeared to be a surge in the fall enrollment, with the theology school having the highest enrollment with 2,543, the religious education school with 1,485, and the music school with 347.

Calm Following a Busy Celebration Year

The 1983-1984 academic year was extremely busy with the 75th Anniversary Celebration, and the trustees seemed to slow down a bit in the spring meeting of 1985 in order to take a deep breath and get to the business at hand. Business as usual seemed to be the theme of the spring trustee meeting. A report from the budget affairs committee for the sale of shares from Allied Bancshares, given by Charles Brinkley, for student scholarships was approved. The business affairs committee report concerning the Member's Employment Contributions Account with the Annuity Board was accepted, along with a report from the investments subcommittee about investments with the Baptist Foundation of Texas.[48] Several courses in the School of Religious Education were deleted because of the retirement of professors or were incorporated in the newer courses in the communications division of the school.

The spring meeting was very docile even though a few new conservative trustees had been appointed by the committee on committees under the leadership of SBC presidents Smith and Draper and were finding their place on the seminary's board of trustees. Prior to the trustee meeting in October 1985, Dilday spoke to the faculty at a general faculty meeting, September 30, 1985, and presented his perspective concerning the SBC that the Conservative Resurgence ferment appeared to have calmed down a bit. He said,

> There is little mail, discussion or interviewing in the media. There is a hopefulness concerning the work of the Peace Committee. The Executive Committee in its September meeting appeared to use the Peace Committee as a reason to postpone some action of matters arising in the past year, especially from the Dallas meeting of the SBC.[49]

The fall 1985 trustee meeting picked up a little more steam than the earlier spring meeting because of some of the motions that were fostered by a few newly elected conservative members on the board. One motion was a special recommendation by Hugo Lindquist, a new conservative member on the board of trustees from Oklahoma, to have the names of prospective faculty submitted to all the trustees at least 60 days prior to their election by the board of trustees. The motion included a request for all available information regarding prospective faculty members to be submitted with their names. Milton Cunningham offered a substitute motion strongly encouraging the administration to share with the trustees all of the state information and plans that were being made about this serious information-gathering. A second substitute motion was made by Rheubin South to have the motion referred back to the academic affairs committee to discuss and study all the items mentioned in the foregoing motions and to bring a report to the board at the March 1986 meeting. The second substitute motion passed.[50]

The appointment of new, more conservative trustees was beginning to reveal a felt suspicion about the theological positions of future faculty members recommended for election at Southwestern. The new trustees were asking for more information about where prospective faculty members stood theologically to determine whether they were acceptable to the more conservative members of the board.

In the October 1985 meeting, two faculty members in the School of Religious Education were promoted in rank. Leon Marsh, professor of foundations, was promoted to distinguished professor of foundations;

and Rick Yount, instructor in foundations, was promoted to assistant professor of foundations predicated on the completion of his Ph.D. and graduation from North Texas State University.

Two new faculty acquisitions were recommended for election in the School of Religious Education. Dan Earl Clements was to be elected as instructor in psychology and counseling. He was the current correspondence counselor for the Radio and Television Commission, Fort Worth, Texas. Jim Woodrow Walter, Jr., was elected as assistant professor of adult education. He came with experience in service to the local church, consulting work for the Baptist Sunday School Board, and having authored *The Church's Ministry to Adults, Reaching and Teaching Through Vacation Bible School,* and *Reaching Adults Through Sunday School*.[51]

The trustees approved an academic chair in the School of Religious Education: the Paul Stevens Chair of Christian Communication. Paul Stevens had served as the executive director of the Baptist Radio and Television Commission. The chair named in his honor was especially important to the continued growth of the communication division in the School of Religious Education.

In an October 23, 1985, meeting of the general faculty, Dilday shared information about the trustee meeting and a final motion by the trustees. The motion was that the officers of the board, including those newly elected to office, and the chairman of each of the board's standing committees would form a "presidential review committee," which, after the conclusion of a regular board meeting, would appraise the work of the president during the previous year.[52] The reaction on the part of the faculty was an ominous feeling of distrust that seemed to pervade the intent of the motion passed by the trustees. It appeared that a cloak of dark suppression and restraint was being spread over the freedom and spiritual latitude of the seminary administration and faculty. The announcement was not received well by the faculty. Some faculty felt the academic freedom and tenure they had enjoyed for so many years was slowly being eradicated by the more conservative trustees appointed to the board.

Drakeford Retires After 30 Years

John W. Drakeford retired after 30 years of service to Southwestern Seminary. Drakeford was not retiring because he wanted to, but because the mandatory retirement age had caught up with him. He was not planning to spend the rest of his life fishing or just relaxing; he did not see any way that he would be slowing down because, he said, "movement is the essence of life, and complete absence of movement is death."[53]

Drakeford retired from Southwestern as distinguished professor of psychology and counseling. Although he owned 70 acres of beautiful East Texas country land, he had other plans for filling the hours of his new adventure as writer-in-residence at Southwestern. As writer-in-residence, Drakeford would concentrate on his writing assignments and advise professors and students needing help with writing projects. He taught two courses in counseling on occasion and, with his wife Robina, continued to do family enrichment conferences in Southern Baptist churches and denominational settings in the U.S. and around the world.

Joseph S. Johnson, an editor at Broadman Press who worked on several of Drakeford's books, called Drakeford "one of the most knowledgeable scholar/writers in the entire nation."[54] Johnson edited six of Drakeford's books, including *The Awesome Power of the Healing Thought, Wisdom for Today's Families,* and *Growing Old, Feeling Young.*

In addition to Drakeford's writing, he also founded the Marriage and Family Counseling Center and developed many of the seminary's counseling courses. But perhaps his greatest contribution to Christian life is in the area of the family. In an interview, Drakeford said he would like to be remembered as "Mr. Family Life," and Southwestern News reported that he did whatever he could to help the great institution of the family.[55]

Continuing Education Conferences Vital to Educational Ministry

The 1985 calendar was filled with outstanding conferences, institutes, and workshops directed by faculty members of the School of Religious Education. In January, there was a workshop led by Rick Yount, assistant professor of foundations of education, and Terry Bratton, director of computer services. The workshop was designed for church staff members and others interested in securing a computer system for a local church. Involved in the body of the workshop were topics on what computers can do for the church, preview of available software, and the necessary steps for developing a computer system in the church. The workshop was listed as a continuing education unit workshop (CEU) for all who attended.

In June, Bill Caldwell, professor of church administration, led a seminar for church business administrators who were interested in church business administration certification by the National Association of Church Business Administrators. The seminar was required for certification as a fellow in church business administration. Important areas of church business administration were included during the two-week session. CEU credit or graduate credit (by meeting seminary entrance requirements) was available in addition to certification through CBA.

Also in June, Lucien Coleman, professor of adult education, led a workshop for mature adult writers. The workshop was for persons 50 years of age and older who wished to sharpen personal writing skills. The workshop honed in on writing to improve communication, writing to be published, writing for religious publications, and strategies for writing one's life story. Other leaders for the workshop were John Gulledge, editor of Mature Living, and John Drakeford, writer-in-residence at Southwestern Seminary.

The RAC offered two recreation workshops, one in March and another in October. The October institute was led by Georgia Kostas, staff nutritionist at the Cooper Clinic in Dallas, under the title "Nutrition for the Christian." The course was designed to give knowledge of a biblical basis for nutritional stewardship, information for local church nutritional class instructors, an understanding of basic nutritional needs, and the organizing principles for beginning a nutritional class. CEUs were available for this class as well.

The second institute was "Physical Fitness and the Christian," directed by Dick Couey of Baylor University. The course included an understanding of physical fitness as spiritual stewardship, as well as a better knowledge of exercise physiology; testing, evaluating, and prescribing exercise programs; and principles and methods of programming a fitness emphasis for a local church.

The youth department's annual Youth Ministry Lab was conducted by Phil Briggs and Wes Black of the seminary; Esther Burroughs of the Southern Baptist Convention's Home Mission Board; Richard Ross of the Sunday School Youth Division of the Baptist Sunday School Board; Lamar Slay of Castle Hills Baptist Church, San Antonio, Texas; and Wynona Elder of the psychology and counseling department of the School of Religious Education. The theme was "Youth Ministry Breaking Thru…." More than 15 youth ministries were introduced during the three-day conference such as "Ministry on the High School Campus," "Ministry with Parents," "Ministry as it Relates to Teen Friends," and other youth ministry opportunities. This was the 17th annual meeting of the Youth Ministry Lab on the Southwestern Seminary campus.

Studies in Aging a Major Ministerial Need

Lucien Coleman, professor of adult education, had been studying the senior adult population in the Southern Baptist Convention and concluded, "As more Americans grow older, Southern Baptists will see a 'new generation of ministers with senior adults.' There are about 28 million adults in the United States, and by the year 2030, that number will double and predictions are that there will be more than 65 million senior adults."[56]

The baby boomer generation of the 1950s is one of the main factors involved in this number, but added to that is the fact that people are living longer and will need a ministry from the church for a longer period of time. The church needs to understand the aging population better in order to minister to them more effectively, Coleman said. Just as there are so many different needs with the 20- and 30-year-olds, there will be as many different needs with aging America.

One major factor Coleman pointed out was that the church needs to teach people how to grow old. "It's apparent that in the next 10 years, 1986 to 1996, the church will be calling one of its major staff members a Senior Adult Minister, and these senior adult ministers trained at Southwestern Seminary. It's kind of the frontier for Southern Baptists."[57]

Gulledges' Gift Ensures Future for Adult Ministry

While Coleman was writing about the needs for senior adult ministers in the church, in April 1986, a farming couple, Pat and Ruth Gulledge from Grenada, Mississippi, was praying about giving their cotton farm and other properties to fund the Kirk-Gulledge Gerontology Endowment. One day in August 1985, Pat Gulledge felt convicted to use whatever resources he could find to educate senior adult ministers for the church for ministry with the aging. He called Southwestern Seminary and was introduced to James Holcomb, the director of development. The astonished Holcomb led the couple to make their gift through the Baptist Foundation of Texas. He helped them understand how they could make their gift in such a way that they, their son Kirk, and the seminary would benefit from the trusts developed. A portion of the funds would benefit the Gulledges and their son and his wife (Mr. and Mrs. Kirk Gulledge) for the rest of their lives. Another portion would establish a future endowment for the seminary. Holcomb said, "These funds will care for the Gulledge family's needs and will ultimately provide major funding for studies in gerontology. Deferred giving through trusts benefits everyone."[58]

The Gulledges came to Southwestern in 1946 with not a penny in their pockets. During Pat's studies, their son was born. Pat graduated in 1949 (M.R.E.) and served churches in educational ministry in Virginia, Florida, and Georgia. When his father became ill, they went back to Grenada, Mississippi, to help with the farm. He continued serving churches as a volunteer or as a part-time educational worker while farming. During that time, Ruth taught school to help make ends meet. It was not until the 1970s that produce prices began to climb, and they began to reap significant profit.

Their only son Kirk grew up as the son of a minister of education and was called into educational ministry while in college. In a summer class with Derrel Watkins, professor of social work, Kirk discovered his ministerial desire for gerontology. He began a degree in gerontology at North Texas State University and started a business in Phoenix, Arizona, The Retirement Centers of America, a consulting firm for life-care centers. The need for this ministry in local churches spurred the interest in funding an endowed program of gerontology at Southwestern, his Alma Mata. Kirk said, "We hope Southwestern will become the headquarters for information and training in gerontology so that awareness can filter down to the smallest churches."[59]

Enrollment Drops (1986)

The 1986 enrollment fell a bit short of the record-breaking numbers of last fall from 4,375 to 4,146 on all campuses. However, Southwestern still held the title of the largest seminary in the world. Last year's record of 4,375 was the largest fall enrollment in the seminary's history. Several major events may have caused the slight decrease in enrollment. One such problem was that some students enrolled in special classes last fall that were only counted in spring and summer enrollment figures.

Even though there was a slight decrease, enrollments in off-campus centers were at an all-time high. Southwestern Seminary's three off-campus centers offered Monday-only classes for students unable to commute to Fort Worth. The Houston Center enrolled 180, up eight over last year. The Shawnee center enrolled 122, up from 114 last year. At the San Antonio campus, 74 students enrolled, an increase of 15 over last year.

Enrollment at Southwestern Seminary had been steadily increasing for the last 40 years, with a rapid expansion beginning in the mid-1970s. Stricter admission standards were instituted the previous year. The fall enrollment included 3,679 students on the main campus in Fort Worth. There were 2,371 in the School of Theology, 1,460 in the School of Religious Education, and 315 in the School of Church Music. During the fall graduation exercise, the 25,000th student graduated.[60]

Trustees Honor Heacock and Add Two Professors

As a major part of the fall meeting, the trustees honored Joe Davis Heacock, dean emeritus of the School of Religious Education, by naming the curriculum lab the "Joe Davis Heacock Curriculum Lab in the School of Religious Education."

The trustees made two additions to the faculty of the School of Religious Education. Terrell Mack Peace was elected as instructor in foundations of education. He had previously served with Campus Crusade for Christ and as minister of outreach at Central Baptist Church, Bryan, Texas, and North Fort Worth Baptist Church, Fort Worth, Texas. Royce Alan Rose was elected as assistant professor of administration. Rose also came with experience in local churches, and he wrote *Bi-vocational Ministry*, a church vocations pamphlet; *Profile of the Small Church*, a videotape series on small church administration; and seminar extension courses *Southern Baptist Heritage* and *Developing Leaders for Ministry*.[61]

The trustees approved the common core of learnings presented by the School of Religious Education for approval with the intent that it would be integrated into the four Master of Arts degrees in the school beginning with the fall semester of 1987. A number of professors in the School of Religious Education were promoted: Derrel Watkins, to professor of social work; Charles Ashby, to associate professor of foundations; Hazel Morris, to associate professor of childhood education; Jerry Privette, to associate professor of field education; and Wesley Black, to assistant professor of youth education. Jeroline Baker was named to the Bessie Fleming Chair of Childhood Education for the academic year of 1986-1987 for a third time.[62]

Dilday made a report to the trustees at the end of the October 1986 meeting about a meeting of the six seminary presidents with the SBC Peace Committee. He announced that another meeting was to be held in Glorieta, New Mexico, on October 20-22, 1987, with the members of the Peace Committee and all the heads of the SBC institutions and agencies. A motion was made by Bartis Harper and seconded by Stanley I. Hand "that the trustees communicate through their chairman with the SBC Peace Committee to affirm the work of the Peace Committee in their work toward the resolution of the conflict in our convention and to assure them, the Peace Committee, of prayer and support for the prayer retreat in Glorieta, N.M., on October 20-22, 1987."[63] The motion unanimously carried.

Several negative items from individual committees were reported to the faculty by Dilday at the general faculty meeting on October 17. The items included the perception that an unjustified "fortress mentality" on the part of the president existed; a desire to separate seminaries from each other; the claim by seminary administration that the controversy was political and not theological; pressure by the trustees to be more involved in the day-by-day operations of the seminary; concern that the seminary might be adopting the rules of its opponents' game; and concern about the theological stance of speakers invited to the seminary and for conferences and workshops attended by seminary faculty. Dilday requested the faculty to pray for the Peace Committee prayer retreat to be held in Glorieta in the following year.[64]

Youth Lab Makes Major Changes

The 18th year of the popular youth spring training conference offered a major change in the Youth Lab format. The lab separated the veterans from the rookies and offered specialized training conferences for experienced youth ministers. A veteran was a person who finished seminary in 1982 or earlier and was involved in full-time youth ministry. However, there was still a place for all people interested in youth ministry and wanted to attend the youth lab. This year's theme was "Illuminating the Way," encouraging all youth leadership to illuminate the way for the youth in their charge. This year's attendance had participants from 15 states, including Alaska.

"Obviously the folks who have been on the job for a number of years have mastered many of the topics we cover during a regular Youth Lab. We want other things that can help them with the challenges they are facing now; to that end the first Experienced Youth Minister's Workshop will be held April 17-19 in conjunction with the Youth Lab which is April 18-20," said Phil Briggs, professor of youth education.[65] Subjects for the veterans included "Understanding Today's Teens," "Dealing with Parents of Problem Teens," and "Ministering to Youth in Crisis." Outstanding leadership for the youth lab included Richard Ross, Baptist Sunday School Board; Charlie Dodd, First Baptist Church, Midland, Texas; Chris Liebrum, Baptist General Convention of Texas; Steve Ray, Union Baptist Association, Houston, Texas; Ann Sullivan, vice principal of Klein High School, Houston, Texas; and Chuck Gartman, minister of youth education, First Baptist Church, Conroe, Texas.

RAC's New Director

Grady Lowery, who had served as the RAC director since it opened, stepped down to become a private recreational consultant. David Lewis accepted the director's position on May 1, 1968. He moved from a similar position at First Baptist Church, Nashville, Tennessee, where he had served since 1980.

Before he moved to Nashville, Lewis was the assistant director of Christian recreation at Second Ponce De Leon Baptist Church in Atlanta, Georgia, and then associate minister of recreation at Travis Avenue Baptist Church, Fort Worth. In the past, he served as president of the Tennessee Baptist Recreation Association and taught at Belmont College in Nashville. As the director of the RAC on the Southwestern campus, Lewis directed a wellness and fitness program as well as a recreation program for the entire campus—students and faculty.

Three Major Continuing Education Courses Offered

Serving as a minister in a Baptist church calls for additional study and specific learnings in several areas of church ministry that were missed as a student. Besides the Youth Lab in April, three other continuing education courses were offered by several departments in the School of Religious Education. First, the Photojournalism Workshop was offered for photographers, editors, and others responsible for or interested in photojournalism for religious or secular publications. Small-group sessions included darkroom photo development, audio-visual techniques, shooting the single photo, visual grammar, available light photography, and preparing for an assignment. Opportunities for submitting work for critique by professionals during the workshop was encouraged.

Second, the Summer Institute for Aging, designed for pastors and staff members responsible for senior adult ministry who desire to receive certification, met for two weeks, July 6-10 and 13-17. The seminar was two weeks of a four-week program that led to certification. The first two weeks concentrated on senior adults in the church, nursing homes, and other such ministries examining the theological, biblical, and ethical foundations of these ministries. The institute was in cooperation with the Baylor University Institute of Gerontological Studies, with two of the weeks held on the Baylor campus.

Third, the National Association of Church Business Administrators offered a workshop on "How to Computerize our Church Office." Any staff member or other persons interested in establishing a computer network for a church office needed to attend. Information about what computers will do for the local church, the availability of software for churches, and learning the necessary steps in developing a computer system were a few topics considered. As an addition to this seminar, the Seminar in Church Business Administration Certification, in conjunction with the National Association of Church Business Administrators, offered those who attended continuing education credit toward certification CEU credit or graduate-level credit. The CEU or seminary credit was obtained by meeting the requirements for matriculation in Southwestern Seminary or the requirements of CBA for certification.

Enrollments Exceed Previous Highs (1987)

The world's largest theological seminary grew just a little larger during the 1986-1987 academic year. There were 5,247 enrolled students on all campuses during the year. This number surpassed the previous high of 5,120 in 1983-1984. The 1987 spring semester enrollment was 4,187, the highest spring enrollment ever in the history of the seminary. The individual schools enrolled 2,492 in the School of Theology, 1,191 in the School of Religious Education, and 304 in the School of Church Music. The off-campus centers set new records for enrollment during the academic year as well. The Houston center enrolled 221 for the year, an increase of 16 over the previous high. Enrollment at Shawnee reached 152, which was up nine students from its record high. And the San Antonio campus broke its old record of 82 by three students, with 85 enrolled. The Fort Worth campus enrolled 4,371 students during the academic year, with 1,099 new students coming to the mother campus for the first time.[66]

Southwestern Seminary graduated three times the number of students enrolled in the average American theological seminary at the spring commencement ceremonies, May 15, 1987. The average U.S.

seminary had an enrollment of 160. Dilday conferred 503 degrees, making the spring class the largest in the history of Southwestern Seminary. Previously, the largest graduating class was in May 1985, when 489 received degrees. The graduating class was divided among the three schools, with 259 in the School of Theology, 206 in the School of Religious Education, and 38 in the School of Church Music. There were 22 doctoral degrees awarded during the May ceremony.

Trustees Elect Four and Commend Dilday for the Glorieta Statement

In the spring 1987 trustee meeting, four new faculty members were elected, and approval was given to the new Master of Divinity (M.Div.) degree program that offered an optional non-language track for students who did not want to take biblical languages in their M.Div. degree plan. A two-hour course, Biblical Language Tools, was approved for the non-language M.Div. to assist the students in the use of biblical language tools for study in the non-language degree.

Jimmy Draper introduced a resolution expressing "appreciation to Dilday for his leadership in the composition of the Glorieta Statement."[67] This statement was issued by the six seminary presidents, October 20, 1986. In the Glorieta Statement, the six seminary presidents pledged to help bring an end to current controversy in the Southern Baptist Convention. Draper also noted that Dilday had been instrumental in presenting the statement and had not equivocated from it.

Following the completion of the Glorieta Statement was the Inerrancy Conference at Ridgecrest, North Carolina, on May 4-5, 1987. The seminaries brought together an expert faculty and 1,000 students of the Bible in an enormous classroom. The conference faculty included Southern Baptist leaders from both sides of the debate as well as non-Southern Baptist scholars who called themselves "inerrantists." The students were interested ministers and laypeople from across the convention. Dilday was asked by the other five presidents to take the lead in planning the conference, and all who attended were pleased at the positive evaluations at the conclusion of the conference. Paige Patterson, president of Criswell College in Dallas, who promoted the inerrancy doctrine, said, "I honor the seminary presidents for the idea of bringing together scholars from outside the convention. The inerrancy position did receive a very clear hearing both in terms of the major papers and the responders."[68]

The fall trustee meeting was filled with faculty elections and the approval of many new degree programs in all three schools. The School of Religious Education added several new courses that were necessary to complete the curriculum plan for several new degrees and concentrations. Thirteen courses no longer needed as a part of the curriculum structure were deleted, and 11 courses were renamed to give them a more up-to-date nomenclature for the educational ministry in the church (i.e., Survey of Adult Education to Adult Education in the Church, Preparation of Lesson Materials for Pupils to Curriculum Writing, etc.).

Several new courses were approved to enhance the new Master of Arts in Social Work degree for a better alignment with the cooperative relationship with the University of Texas at Arlington's M.S.S.W. Two new concentrations in adult education and in gerontology were approved. The new courses were added to the course structure of the new theology, religious education, and music core. The addition allowed a student to gain expertise in a broader range of theological and educational studies while completing the Master of Arts degree in religious education.

A major step forward was the approval of the new core curriculum for the master's degrees in the School of Religious Education. The core was firmly in place for the beginning of the fall 1987 semester.

> The implementation of the Core Curriculum this coming fall will conclude a curriculum revision and planning process that has been in process for the last several years. The new Core will provide common learnings which are the essential elements in an affective ministry of religious education in the church. With the inclusion of the Core as the center of the learning process in the Religious Education curriculum, the School of Religious Education will be in a position to assure churches that all graduates have the

basic learnings that are essential to effective educational ministry.[69]

The new Master of Arts/Master of Science in Social Work degree was approved. The number of hours required to complete both degrees was 94. In keeping with the new core curriculum design, a new curriculum plan was developed for the Associate in Religious Education (A.R.E.) degree requiring each of the three core curriculum designs (theology, music, and religious education) for a total of 68 hours for the completion of the degree.[70]

Attempting to meet the need of the growing body of communication studies courses, the trustees elected Dennis K. Parrish as instructor in communication arts. Parrish had previously served as a freelance television producer, Southern Baptist Radio and Television Commission (1983-1985); adjunct teacher, Southwestern Seminary (1985-1987); producer/director of on-air promotion for the ACTS Network (1985-1987); director of "The Company," Southwestern Seminary (1984-2004); and producer/director and choreographer of Youth Evangelism Conference, BGCT (1984-2003).

Promotions and tenure were also a part of the meeting. Daryl Eldridge, instructor in foundations of education, was promoted to assistant professor of foundations of education. Bob Brackney, associate professor of social work, and Pat Clendinning, professor of psychology and marriage and family counseling, were granted tenure.[71]

Lectureship in Gerontology Named

The trustees' recognized the rapid growth in gerontology and approved a new lectureship in gerontology. The lectureship was named the Kellogg Lectureship in Gerontology, established with the money given by the Kellogg Foundation and the Gulledge Endowment on Aging established in 1986. The lecturer named for the first Kellogg Lectureship was David Moberg, professor of sociology at Marquette University. Moberg was invited by the trustees to deliver the first series of lectures, July 7, 1987.[72]

"Southwestern Seminary has the potential to become a worldwide leader in education on aging," said the nationally known scholar in the inaugural address.[73] Moberg identified major challenges faced by Southwestern Seminary in the frontier that lay before them in gerontological education, continuing education, research, and publication. The sheer number of people in their senior adult years in congregations had contributed to the awareness of the importance and need for ministries with the aging. Outside of the theological educational world, very little attention had been given to religion and spirituality in the field of gerontology and geriatrics. Quoting from a Gallup poll, Moberg said,

> Three-fourths of Americans past 65 consider religion to be very important and more than four-fifths claim their religious faith is the most important influence in their lives. Ministers must cooperate with other professionals in meeting the needs of these again. It is the total person who is aging, so in the wholeness of existence there must be an interfacing and integrating of all the disciplines and professions that relate to him or her. Among these areas, the one that stands out as providing the most opportunity for continued growth in the later years is the *spiritual*. A first step toward wholeness is a salvation experience. A person cannot have spiritual life without a commitment to Jesus Christ as Savior. In the life of the aging adult, absence from religious meetings does not mean severed relationships. There is a great deal for older persons to offer the church, ministry in prayer, counsel and encouragement.[74]

Youth Ministry Named Tops at Southwestern

Southwestern Seminary had been named one of four schools in the United States "where youth ministry counts" by a national interdenominational publication read by over 55,000 youth ministers. The summer issue of Group magazine listed Southwestern Seminary as a "handful of colleges and seminaries that offer respectable youth ministry education."[75] The nomination came in an article titled "Are Christian Colleges Doing Enough to Educate Youth Ministers?"[76] The article, written by Greg Piburn, surveyed 567 Christian colleges, universities, and seminaries to learn how they deal with youth ministry, with responses from 110. Forty-three said they offered a bachelor's degree in youth ministry, 19 offered a master's degree, and six offered doctorates. A closer look, however, indicated that much of what was considered youth education was sometimes a token appearance of youth ministry in a required course.

Southwestern Seminary offered a Master of Arts in Religious Education degree (M.A.R.E.) with a youth concentration and a Doctor of Education degree (Ed.D.) with a youth education major. Southwestern Seminary's School of Religious Education had 18 different courses listed in youth education.

Some professors in religious institutions considered youth education as a stepping stone to a pastoral position, with the youth position as just an evolving part of their ministerial career. Phil Briggs and Wesley Black, professors in youth education at Southwestern, disagreed. They were convinced that many youth ministers considered the youth ministry task as a lifetime ministerial profession and not a stepping stone to some other ministerial position. These were not "pastors-in-waiting" but dedicated youth ministers for life. The other three top schools listed in the article were Eastern College, St. David's, Pennsylvania; Liberty University, Lynchburg, Virginia; and Gordon College, Gordon-Cromwell Theological Seminary, Wenham, Massachusetts.

Largest Class Ever Graduated (1988)

History was made at spring graduation when Southwestern Seminary graduated the largest class of any graduate theological institution in the world. Dilday conferred 520 degrees at the commencement exercises held at Travis Avenue Baptist Church, making the 1988 spring class Southwestern's largest graduating class.

This spring's class included 278 in the School of Theology, 212 in the School of Religious Education, and 30 in the School of Church Music. There were 19 who earned doctoral degrees.

Jesse Fletcher, president of Hardin-Simmons University and former Southern Baptist missionary, delivered the commencement address. Fletcher encouraged the graduates to care "what people think and say about them because it will affect their witness and ministry. Jesus has such concern because He asked His disciples, 'Who do men say that I am?' But Jesus wasn't anxious about how people perceived Him because He knew who He was. He knew He was the Son of God, and He understood His mission."[77]

During the fall semester, Southwestern Seminary enrolled its 50,000th student—Charles Frazier, a Master of Divinity student from Lithia Springs, Georgia. Dilday congratulated Frazier as the 50,000th enrollee. Frazier was the son of Southwestern graduate, Clay Frazier, who had close ties with Dilday. Frazier and Dilday were in seminary in 1955 and both pastored churches in Jack County, Texas, during their seminary years. The enrollment of the 50,000th student coincided with the celebration of the institution's 80th anniversary (1908-1988) and Dilday's 10th anniversary as president.

The fall enrollment at Southwestern Seminary, however, caused a bittersweet taste in the mouth of the largest spring graduating class in theological educational institutions with a slight drop in enrollment. Despite the fall of 1988 being the largest class of new students in the school's history, the large graduation class in the spring caused the fall enrollment to be 5 percent less than the 1987 enrollment. Of the 3,796 enrolled in the fall, 2,258 were in the School of Theology, 1,233 in the School of Religious Education, and 305 in the School of Church Music.

Dan McLallen, director of admissions, attributed the drop to economic difficulties, which forced older students to delay enrolling in the seminary: "The economy is so tight that older students just simply couldn't get enough money together to enroll."[78] Even though the number of new students accepted was the second largest number of new student applications in the history of the school, several who were accepted could not matriculate because of the tight economy.

Eighty and Ten

Two very significant events, the seminary's 80th year and Dilday's 10th anniversary, came together in the 1988 seminary calendar. Throughout 1988, the seminary family participated in an 80/10 Celebration to commemorate these two events. This celebration was observed at Founder's Day, March 10, 1988, and focused on the historical founding of the seminary by B.H. Carroll on March 14, 1908. These two celebrations were the central focus for the alumni meeting at the Southern Baptist Convention meeting in San Antonio, Texas, in June, as well as at state alumni meetings across the nation in the fall.

Dilday reflected on the founding of Southwestern Seminary and on the progress made since March 14, 1908:

> Southwestern has become the kind of institution Carroll envisioned, and he would probably be surprised that his dream has expanded to the entire world. We have built upon Carroll's founding vision. In every way of measuring the health of an institution like this, Southwestern is stronger than it ever has been in its history. The seminary is on the verge of the best years yet.
>
> The concentration of conservative, biblical scholarship in one place unlike anywhere else in the world creates an environment where faith grows, where positive attitudes about the Lord, His will and His Word are reinforced. Whatever a person brings to this campus in the way of a relationship to the Lord is inevitably strengthened and nurtured.[79]

The power of God's spirit working on Southwestern Seminary's campus enabled Dilday to accomplish these goals as the president. As he reviewed the goals of the last 10 years, he was amazed at how much had been accomplished and how much must be accomplished in the coming decades.

Trustees Meet During 80/10 Celebration Week

The budget and the reduction in Cooperative Program funding each year attracted the major attention of the spring trustee meeting. After adopting a $19.7 million budget for fiscal year 1988-1989, President Dilday reminded the trustees of the most recent percentage reductions in Cooperative Program funding. He told them, "The seminary is holding its own in a difficult financial context. Even the earning of the funds in the endowment has decreased due to poor economic conditions. Also, the percentage from the SBC Cooperative Program is decreasing each year."[80]

Because of the decreased funding from the convention, the trustees were forced to approve an increase in the matriculation fee from $350 a semester to $400. The trustees asked the administration to manage the budget funds carefully in order to keep student costs down in light of the increase in matriculation fees.

Turning from the budget to academic affairs, the trustees approved naming a new chair in student work in the School of Religious Education for Edgar "Preacher" Hallock, the longtime pastor of First Baptist Church, Norman, Oklahoma, who developed and organized the first Baptist Student Union program on the Oklahoma University campus. The chair was established after funding was secured. Tenure was given to Robert Raus, professor of recreation; and Dan Clements was promoted to assistant professor in psychology and marriage and family counseling, as was W.A. "Budd" Smith to associate professor of foundations of education.[81]

A report was made concerning the meeting of the Peace Committee. Jimmy Draper made an observation about the meeting of the Peace Committee on the campus of each seminary. "Only four or five questions have ever been raised about Southwestern. All of these concerns have been answered adequately. One concern was that not all the faculty believed in the 'historicity of Adam and Eve.' But John Newport convinced me this was not the case. I feel like we've been met with great cooperation and a good spirit."[82] The formal statement that was adopted by the trustees reflected that Southwestern had been dealing responsibly with the inerrancy question since as early as 1987. According to the adopted statement, a teacher's freedom is limited only by "the preeminence of Christ, the authoritative nature of the Scriptures, and the distinct purpose for which the seminary exists."[83]

School of Religious Education to Celebrate 75th Diamond Jubilee Anniversary

The Department of Religious Education was founded in March 1915 by J.M. Price. Religious education graduates like Lou Ella Austin, who graduated in 1917, and all who graduated since had scattered across the Southern Baptist Convention and in countries around the world. Many of these graduates and alumni were planning to return to the campus in the academic year of 1989-1990 to celebrate the 75th anniversary of the founding of the Department of Religious Education. A committee of School of Religious Education faculty members had worked tirelessly for a year planning and preparing for the celebration that began in the fall of 1989. Al Parks, professor of administration, chaired the committee.

Several major events were planned for the year-long celebration, including a history of the school compiled by Joe Davis Heacock, retired dean emeritus; a commemorative hymn composed by C.L. Bass, professor of music theory and composition; and several dramatic presentations. The celebration culminated in the spring of 1990 with a School of Religious Education homecoming, April 2-4. Other activities during the year included chapel services and the premiere of a documentary on the school's history. A major activity planned with the seminary's development department to fund the J.M. Price Chair of Religious Education was a vital part of the celebrative year. Members serving with Parks on the 75th anniversary committee were Charles Tidwell, professor of administration; Royce Rose, assistant professor of administration; Phil Briggs, professor of youth education; Jack Terry, dean of the School of Religious Education; and Joe Davis Heacock, dean emeritus.

1989—A Year Filled with Anticipation of the 75th Anniversary

Preparations for the celebration of the 75th Anniversary Diamond Jubilee were complete. Every means of special communication was employed in an effort to reach religious educators across the Southern Baptist Convention and around the world to invite them to the 75th anniversary activities in the spring of 1990. The theme for the celebration was "Proud Past – Promising Future."

Al Parks, chairman of the anniversary planning committee, put together an exciting slate of activities for the year culminating in April 1990. One event headlining the activities for the celebration was a history of the Southwestern Religious Education Association, which had been meeting on the seminary campus since its founding in 1921, compiled by Joe Davis Heacock. The history was illustrated by Doug Dillard, a graduate of the School of Religious Education and the cartoon illustrator for the Baptist Standard, the monthly news magazine of the Baptist General Convention of Texas. The commemorative hymn was composed by C.L. Bass, professor of music theory and composition, was performed at a celebrative chapel. This chapel service also featured the premiere of the documentary about the school's history.

A calendar for the 75th Diamond Jubilee Anniversary was composed of several specific activities in 1989-1990:

- A dramatic presentation of the history of the School of Religious Education during the October 3, 1989, chapel service.
- A special display case in Price Hall highlighting the history of religious education at Southwestern.
- A special insert about the Diamond Jubilee Anniversary in Southwestern News during the spring of 1990.
- A speech by Jack Terry, dean of the School of Religious Education, on Founder's Day, March 8, 1990.
- Homecoming week, April 2-4, 1990, which included:
  - A banquet featuring Dan McBride, Christian humorist, and Leon Marsh, professor of foundations of education.
  - The unveiling of an oil painting of Jack Terry.
  - The annual meeting of the Southwestern Religious Education Association.[84]

Since the founding of the Department of Religious Education in 1915 and the establishment of a School of Religious Education in 1921,

more than 9,000 men and women had graduated from Southwestern's School of Religious Education. Then-current statistics showed:
- 136 graduates served through Southern Baptist Convention agencies and auxiliaries, such as the executive committee, Woman's Missionary Union, and the Baptist Sunday School Board.
- 388 graduates served through the Foreign Mission Board.
- 137 graduates were employed by one of the six Southern Baptist seminaries, American Baptist Seminary, and the Seminary Extension Education Division.
- 610 graduates worked in Baptist colleges and universities, secular institutions of higher education, and non-Southern Baptist seminaries.
- 2,468 graduates were employed by Southern Baptist churches, while 125 served in non-Southern Baptist churches.[85]

Trustees Actively Engaged in Anniversary Year

A chill was in the air on that March 13, 1989, day when the trustees met, but the weather was not as discomforting as was discouraging news about budget freezes and salary cuts. The $18.5 million budget passed by the trustees was a 1.2 percent cut from the 1988 budget. The new budget froze all salaries and reduced some programs. The budget was passed but with grave concern on the part of the trustees. The concern resonated with the reduction of Cooperative Program funds allocated by the Southern Baptist Executive Committee of the Southern Baptist Convention.

As a result of the budget reductions, the board passed a resolution calling on the executive committee of the SBC to reconsider its procedures for the allocation of funds. The resolution offered by Wayne Allen, trustee from Carrollton, Texas, called to "express our concern about the way the Cooperative Program dollars are allocated and our concern about the support of the Cooperative Program by all of our churches. The purpose is to say to the 'grassroots churches' this is where it hurts."[86] This was the first time in over 30 years and maybe in the entire history of the seminary that the amount of denominational support was less this year than it was the year before.

Reflecting on the negative effects of the salary freeze, Jimmy Draper said, "I am fearful the salary freeze could cause a morale problem among faculty and staff at the seminary. Our concern and anticipation is that it's going to be better in the days ahead. We are not happy with the decrease."[87] Although the salaries were frozen this year, the budget planners pointed out to the trustees that much of the budget allocations represented a significant increase in benefit costs paid by the seminary for career employees and their families.

On the lighter side, the trustees looked with favor on the establishment of an endowed chair in the School of Religious Education named the J.M. Price Chair of Religious Education in honor of the founder of the school. The trustees encouraged the development officers to work diligently to find the funds that would endow such a chair. It was reported that the chair would not be established until all the funds had been secured.

Last but not least was the approval of a $2 million Phase 1 of the Cowden Hall building project. The approval of the project allowed the appropriate administrators to begin necessary design development and begin the bidding process for the renovation of major parts of the building that houses the School of Church Music.

Later in the year, an enrollment report was given to the trustees about the growth of Southwestern in the last 81 years. 51,000 students had passed through the school's doors to study and train for Christian ministry since the school opened in 1908. For the 1988-1989 academic year, Southwestern Seminary enrolled a total of 4,569 students, making it still the largest theological seminary in the world. Almost 40 percent of all students enrolled in the six Southern Baptist seminaries attended Southwestern Seminary. During the year, the School of Theology had a total enrollment of 1,782, the School of Religious Education had an enrollment of 1,458, and the School of Church Music had an enrollment of 329.

Exciting Conferences and Workshops Headline Pre-Anniversary Activities

"'Church Growth' has become a household item among all denominations,"[88] said Win Arn, a pioneer in church growth consultation. Arn, the president of Church Growth, Inc., was the major conference leader during the Religious Education Emphasis Week, April 4-5, 1989. Arn was joined by Bill May, director of church growth and development for the Arizona Baptist Convention, and Ron Lewis, a Southwestern Seminary trustee and the president of Church Growth Designs, Inc., of Nashville, Tennessee.

In the keynote address, Arn said,

> The early church grew by its members reaching out to friends, relatives and associates in household evangelism. Paul's strategy was to find receptive people, people whom God had prepared. Paul's pattern for establishing congregations was always the same. Paul followed the natural networks of people and started "pushing them out to the outermost possibilities." For a church to reach its growth

potential it must have the right mix of evangelism. What works for one church may not work for another.[89]

Ron Lewis asked questions about how well Southern Baptists were doing with church growth. Over the years, the Southern Baptist Convention had been a people-driven denomination. "In this period of Southern Baptist life, the church is struggling," Lewis said. "Emphasis needs to be put in the right place again and that focus is on the needs of the people. Most people claim they truly need church as a major player in their lives. It gives them a reason to get up on Monday morning and go to work."[90]

Youth ministers were entering a "new age," so announced the title of the 21st annual Youth Ministry Lab, April 7-9, 1989. The youth lab focus in this 21st year was on "The New Age: Outliving, Outloving, Outhinking" as youth ministers shared ideas gleaned while working with the New Age Movement and its effect on young people.

Recent declines in youth baptisms heralded the fact that it was time to discuss ways to combat the influence of the New Age syndrome as it drew young people into its philosophy and activities. The New Age Movement was widespread and getting a lot of attention. Emphasis was placed on looking at ways youth ministers assisted the members of their youth groups in understanding the Christian's response to New Age philosophies.

Neal Jeffery, youth minister at Prestonwood Baptist Church in Dallas and the lab's keynote speaker, spoke to this year's theme. All energy needed to be leveled at the youth and youth leadership as they attempted to minister in the sphere of youth new age.

Jeffery, an All-American Quarterback at Baylor University and a professional football player, told the 350 youth gathered that God's strength working through weakness is what makes an effective minister in this era of youth activities. Jeffery had a speech impediment all of his life and worked to overcome it in order to speak and preach to youth groups all over the nation. It follows the line of the old adage, "If God gives you a lemon, turn it into lemonade."

Notes

1 *Southwestern News*, March, 1980, p. 11.
2 *Southwestern News*, January, 1980, p.1.
3 Ibid.
4 Trustee Minutes, March, 1980, 18-19, p. 15.
5 *Southwestern News*, June, 1980, p. 1.
6 *Southwestern News*, April, 1980, p. 5.
7 *Southwestern News*, March, 1981, p. 1.
8 Ibid.
9 *Southwestern News*, April, 1981, p. 1.
10 Ibid.
11 Trustee Minutes, March, 1981, 24-25, p. 16.
12 *Southwestern News*, February, 1981, p. 2.
13 *Southwestern News*, April, 1981, p. 12.
14 *Southwestern News*, January, 1981, p. 2.
15 *Southwestern News*, March, 1981, p. 9.
16 *Southwestern News*, April, 1982, p. 2.
17 Ibid., p. 1.
18 Trustee Minutes, October ,1982, 19-20, p. 12 (with addendum).
19 *Southwestern News*, July, 1982, p. 4.
20 *Southwestern News*, November, 1982, p. 6.
21 Ibid.
22 *Southwestern News*, May, 1982, p. 11.
23 Ibid.
24 *Southwestern News*, April, 1982, p. 1.
25 Ibid.
26 *Southwestern News*, March, 1983, p. 3.
27 Trustee Minutes, March, 1983, pp. 11-14.
28 *Southwestern News*, November, 1983, p. 3.
29 Trustee Minutes, October, 1983, pp. 1-8.
30 *Southwestern News*, December, 1983, p. 2
31 *Southwestern News*, October, 1983 p. 3.
32 Ibid., pp. 2-3.
33 *Southwestern News*, April, 1983, p. 6.
34 Ibid.

35 *Southwestern News*, November, 1984, p. 4.
36 Unpublished News Release, March, 1984.
37 Trustee Minutes, March, 1984, pp. 4-5.
38 *Southwestern News*, May, 1984, p. 14
39 Trustee Minutes, October, 1984, Addendum I and p. 6.
40 *Southwestern News*, March, 1984, pp. 1 and 7.
41 Ibid.
42 *Southwestern News*, March, 1984, p. 12.
43 *Southwestern News*, February, 1985, p. 2.
44 Ibid.
45 *Southwestern News*, October, 1985, p. 3.
46 Ibid., p. 1and 4.
47 Ibid.
48 Trustee Minutes, March, 1985, p. 4.
49 General Faculty Meeting, September 30, 1985, p. 3.
50 Trustee Minutes, October, 1985, p, 9,
51 Ibid.
52 General Faculty Meeting, October 25, 1985, p. 2.
53 *Southwestern News*, June, 1985, p. 3.
54 Ibid.
55 Ibid.
56 *Southwestern News*, April, 1986, p. 2.
57 Ibid.
58 Ibid., p. 2-3.
59 Ibid.
60 *Southwestern News*, October 1986, p. 3.
61 Trustee Meeting, October, 1986, pp. 5-7.
62 Trustee Minutes, March, 1986, pp. 8-9.
63 Trustee Minutes, March, 1986, p. 6.
64 General Faculty Minutes, October, 1986, p. 3.
65 *Southwestern News*, March, 1986, p. 8.
66 *Southwestern News*, March, 1987,p. 1.
67 *Southwestern News*, April, 1987, p. 5.
68 *Southwestern News*, June, 1987, p. 1.
69 Trustee Minutes, March, 1987, pp. 10-12 and Addendum I.

Unprecedented Growth Continues

70 Ibid.
71 Trustee Minutes, October, 1987, pp. 8-9
72 Trustee Minutes, March, 1987, p. 9.
73 *Southwestern News*, July/August, 1987, p. 7.
74 Ibid.
75 *Southwestern News*, October, 1987, p. 1.
76 Ibid.
77 *Southwestern News*, June, 1988, p. 1.
78 *Southwestern News*, October, 1988, p. 5.
79 *Southwestern News*, January, 1988, p. 1.
80 *Southwestern News*, April, 1988, p. 4.
81 Trustee Minutes, March, 1988, pp. 8-9.
82 Ibid.
83 Ibid.
84 *Southwestern News*, May, 1989, p.3.
85 Ibid., p. 7.
86 *Southwestern News*, April, 1988, p. 1.
87 Ibid.
88 *Southwestern News*, June, 1989, p. 8.
89 Ibid.
90 Ibid.

Photos

Page 118 – Portrait of Jack Terry.
Page 133 – Religious Education faculty circa 1982.
Page 180 – The first three deans of the school of religious education: (from left) Joe Davis Heacock, J.M. Price, and Jack Terry.

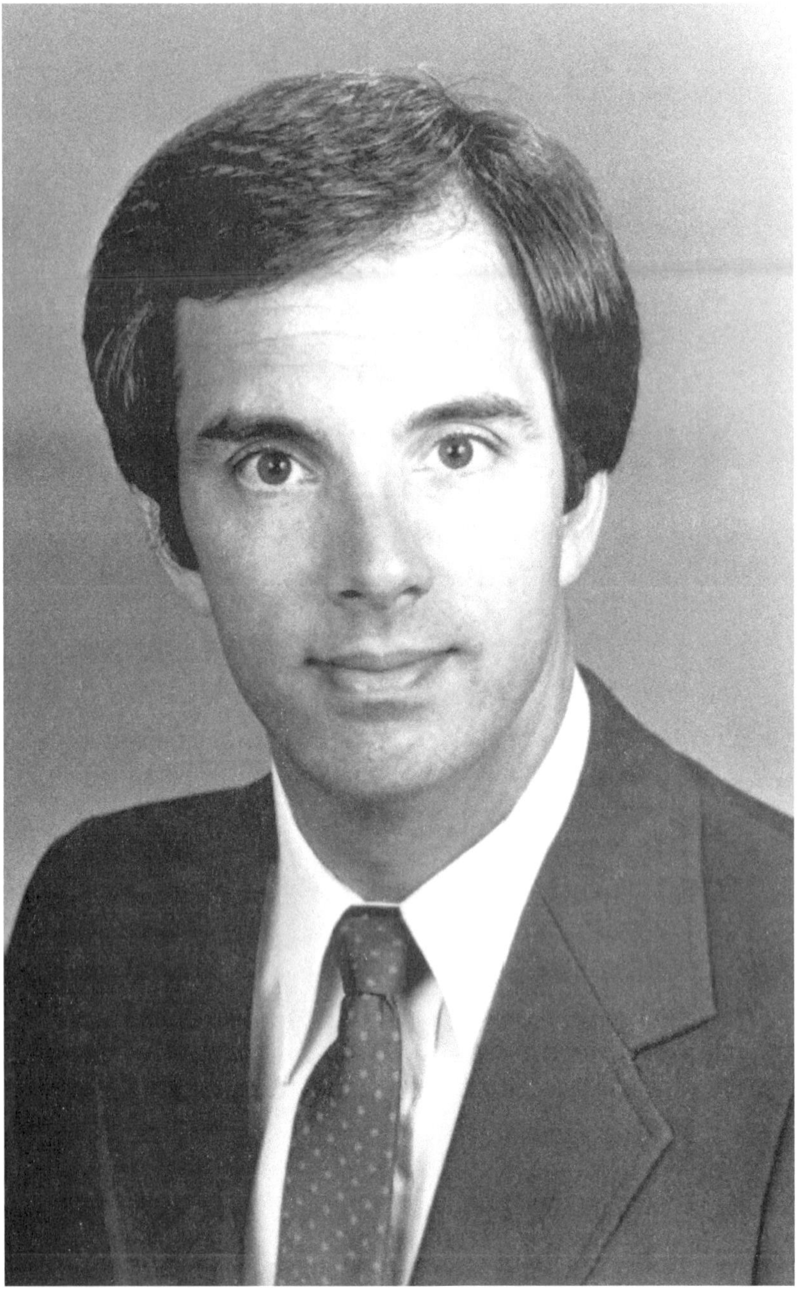

Chapter 4

Major Changes in Presidential Leadership 1990-1999

75th Diamond Anniversary Celebration – "Proud Past – Promising Future"

The diamond anniversary planning committee chaired by Al Parks, professor of administration, enjoyed seeing the fruit of the two-year planning cycle come to fruition during the year of the School of Religious Education's Diamond Anniversary Homecoming, held on the campus April 2-4, 1990. Parks said, "We felt it went very well, beyond all our expectations."[1] Several hundred School of Religious Education alumni returned to the campus for the celebration and homecoming events, visiting with old friends and making new friends of the students enrolled in the school. More than 500 people attended the anniversary reception, and 340 registered for the banquet of the Southwestern Religious Education Association (SWBREA); this organization and banquet are held normally in August, but because of the anniversary celebration, it met during the homecoming to honor Southwestern's impact on religious education.

Highlights of the week included the dedication of the Joe Davis Heacock Rotunda in Price Hall as well as the dedication of the Ann Bradford foyer in the Naylor Children's Center. Heacock was dean emeritus of the School of Religious Education, and Bradford was professor of childhood education emeritus. Both were at the celebration to meet with many of their former students as well as ministers of education and childhood education majors from across the Southern Baptist Convention.

A celebrative hymn, "Words of the Master," written by C.L. Bass, professor of music theory and composition in the School of Church Music, was composed in honor of the 75th anniversary celebration. An oil portrait of Dean Jack Terry was unveiled in the Price Hall rotunda to join the other portraits of deans J.M. Price (1914-1956) and Joe Davis Heacock (1956-1973). Terry had served as dean of the School of Religious Education since 1973. The Student Religious Education Association honored the week by placing a beautiful sundial in a small garden in front of Price Hall, across from the Naylor Student Center.

During his 75th anniversary chapel address on the life and ministry of J.M. Price, Joe Davis Heacock called Price "the most uncommon man I've even known. He was an innovator and with his insight, he could see the needs of religious educators of the future."[2]

Founder's Day Celebrates Religious Education School's 75 Years

As the world's first and largest School of Religious Education approached the 21st century, Dean Jack Terry delivered the 82nd annual Founder's Day address for the 75th Anniversary Celebration. Terry recalled the historical underpinnings of the School of Religious Education. Southwestern's founder, B.H. Carroll, first envisioned a school of religious pedagogy at the seminary to complete the scope of the training of young ministers. The school was established during the first term of L.R. Scarborough, only seven years after the founding of the seminary. The first man employed to lead the new school was J.M. Price, a pioneer in the field of religious education. When he arrived on the campus in 1915, there were no textbooks, no curriculum, and no degrees. Price offered five courses of study in religious education during his first year as part of the theological curriculum.

Price died in 1976, but despite the loss of the founding leader, the School of Religious Education continued to experience unprecedented growth and major changes. During the period from 1958 to 1978, the 20-year tenure of President Naylor, 143 new courses were approved, including an innovative counseling program, the Baptist Marriage and Family Counseling Center.

Terry concluded his remarks by saying, "The School of Religious Education is 'looking to the future' under the leadership of President Russell Dilday. The school boasts 27 full-time faculty members and 271 separate courses. What is in store for the School of Religious Education? Only God knows the answer. However, as its past has been—so may the future be."[3]

J.M. Price Chair of Religious Education

Price was called "the miracle man" by many of his religious education friends and students. So, in his honor and as a tribute to his gifts as a religious educator, the John Milburn Price Chair of Religious Education was established. Former students, family, and close friends joined together to raise enough money to endow the chair. The amount of money necessary to endow the chair into perpetuity was $500,000. The drive for the endowed sum was initiated by the 75th anniversary planning committee of the School of Religious Education. Stanton Nash, director of planned giving for the seminary, articulated the uniqueness of this quiet little man "who revolutionized religious education among Southern Baptists, and his influence extended far beyond that."[4]

The Price Chair honors the man who touched thousands of lives over a period of 41 years and who was the impetus that influenced religious education perhaps more than any other Southern Baptist. In the early stages of fundraising, the Price Chair had already received over $60,000, and the committee hoped to announce the underwriting of the chair during the 75th anniversary homecoming. Price did not live to see his chair funded but died at the age of 91 in 1967.

The Consummate Childhood Educator, Ann Bradford

Ann Bradford, professor of childhood education for 25 years, was known as a pioneer in children's work in the church. Bradford had a passion for the education of young children and spent a lifetime at Southwestern Seminary seeing that young children were properly cared for in the church. At 84, Bradford was honored during the 75th anniversary celebration by having the foyer of the Naylor Children's Center named in her honor.

After receiving a letter from J.M. Price, Bradford began teaching at the seminary in 1945 and taught until 1970. Bradford said, "Little children deserve the very best, and I would like to feel we were helping others to see that also. I felt that children were real personalities; that by teaching them I was laying a foundation for their future education."[5]

Bradford was instrumental in changes made in the kindergarten and childhood education departments and in the churches. Because of her many years of service at Southwestern, many students went on to become children's ministers, seminary professors, Sunday School Board Consultants, WMU workers, and missionaries. The construction of the Naylor Children's Center was the fulfillment of a dream for kindergarten education at Southwestern Seminary.

Trustees Meet Twice During 75th Anniversary Celebration Year

The trustees met for their semi-annual spring meeting March 12-13, during Founder's Week, and were present for the Founder's Day chapel, March 13, and the Founder's Day Address by Dean Terry, also on March 13. During the meeting, they recommended the election of a new academic vice president and provost to replace John Newport, who was retiring at the end of the year. They also recommended the election of a new public affairs vice president to replace John Seelig, who was retiring in January 1991. Several new faculty members for the School of Religious Education were nominated for faculty positions, and several promotions of present faculty were considered.[6]

Dilday made a request to the trustees about his proposed recommendation for the election of William B. Tolar as vice president for academic affairs and provost to replace Newport. A motion was made and seconded that the academic affairs committee join with President Dilday in this special recommendation to the board for Tolar's election.[7]

Several faculty members in the School of Religious Education were promoted during the spring trustee meeting: Tommy Bridges to professor of administration; Wynona Elder to associate professor of psychology and counseling; Gary Waller to associate professor of administration; and Daryl Eldridge to associate professor of foundations of education.

In the semi-annual fall meeting, October 15-17, 1990, the trustees followed through on the election of three new faculty members for the School of Religious Education to begin in the spring semester of 1991. The three new faculty members were James Scott Floyd, Norma Sanders Hedin, and Robert Horton Welch.[8]

James Scott Floyd, associate professor of psychology and counseling, previously served as program coordinator in the adolescent unit of the Charter Hospital, Fort Worth, Texas; associate professor of psychology, Howard Payne University; and minister of counseling, Travis Avenue Baptist Church, Fort Worth, Texas. He was a licensed professional counselor and a licensed family therapist.

Norma Sanders Hedin was the representative/seminar leader for Pioneer Clubs in Wheaton, Illinois; director of education, Liberty Baptist Church, Plano, Texas; an editorial assistant, Southwestern Journal of Theology, Southwestern Baptist Theological Seminary; and an adjunct instructor in Southwestern's School of Religious Education. Her publications include *The Teaching Ministry of the Church* and *Education in the Bible*.

Robert Horton Welch had served in the U.S. Navy for 22 years and had subsequently been an associate professor at the University of Oklahoma; church business administrator, Trinity Baptist Church, Norman, Oklahoma; adjunct professor, Southwestern Baptist Theological Seminary; and assistant professor, Liberty Baptist Theological Seminary. His publications included *Leadership Handbook of Practical Theology Vol. II*; *The Church Organizational Manual: Implementing and Coordinating Church Operations and Functions*; and *Maintenance Manual for Southern Baptist Churches*.

As the dawn of a new decade approached, the trustees approved 288 students to receive degrees at the fall commencement, December 15, 1989. Dilday conferred 288 degrees on the class, with six students receiving dual degrees. Degrees were awarded to 19 from the School of Church Music, 122 from the School of Religious Education, and 146 from the School of Theology.

Norman Wiggins, president of Campbell University, Buies Creek, North Carolina, told graduates that change was on the horizon for the future, and they should not be afraid of change. "We expect change from you because we believe that you can perform miracles. We know that God performs miracles through human beings."[9]

A second commencement was held on May 11, 1990, with 462 graduates receiving degrees. The awarding of 462 degrees made the spring class the second largest ever graduating class. Degrees were awarded to 22 students from the School of Church Music, 183 from the School of Religious Education, and 257 from the School of Theology.

Louis Drummond, president of Southeastern Baptist Theological Seminary, told the graduates, "It is an exciting time and an exciting experience to serve Christ. As with the early church, the present-day local church is the place today where leadership is vital to Kingdom progress."[10]

Children's Television Program Produced

A children's television show titled "The Construction Company" was created in the Center for Christian Communication in the School of Religious Education. The concept of the program was birthed in a studio operations class and blossomed into a full-blown production in the TV drama for children class. Four scripts that dealt with a variety of childhood issues were completed, and the students planned to have these tape-ready for release on the ACTS Network in Fort Worth that year. Some of the scripts included "Feeling O.K. in New Situations" and "How to Deal with Anger and Fears and Phobias." One script, "Definitely Different," was produced especially for hearing-impaired children and some other handicaps.

The shows were dramatized with puppets, who always stole the show. A communications student, Jeff Fitzwater, worked with a national puppet production company for four years, traveling the nation and teaching the use of puppetry in churches. He had the lead role in developing the puppets for these shows. He said, "Puppetry is part of my life blood right now, and we're trying to make the puppets more life-like, to let the camera be the state. It's been exciting to push my artistic limits and really work at making the characters believable."[11] Darrel Baergen, professor of communication arts, and his wife Judy served as executive producers of the show. The programs were aired on the ACTS Network in the spring of 1991.

The 22nd annual Youth Lab was held in conjunction with the 75th anniversary celebration calendar on April 6-8, 1990. The theme for the year was "Youth Ministry: A Cut Above." The theme was based on Daniel 12:3ff: "Those who have insight will shine brightly like the brightness of the expanse of heaven." The faculty consisted of 25 youth ministers, consultants, and other professionals from across the country who led seminars, worship activities, and fellowships. The threefold purpose of the Youth Lab was continuing education for those already serving in youth ministry; reaching laypeople and youth leaders of local churches; and providing fellowship, new insights, and an update on what was happening in youth ministry. There was no doubt that youth education must be made a major priority in all churches of all denominations everywhere.

Chairman of 75th Celebration Committee Resigns

Al Parks, professor of church administration at Southwestern for 16 years and the chairman of the steering committee for the 75th anniversary celebration, was named executive vice president at Dallas Baptist University by President Gary Cook. Parks assumed his new duties August 1, 1990. His duties included shared responsibilities of coordinating the day-to-day operations of the university, coordinating the school's long-range planning evaluation of personnel, and overseeing the update of job descriptions for all employees. Parks' long-time experience as a minister of education in several Southern Baptist churches and his church administration professorship at Southwestern prepared him for this new responsibility at Dallas Baptist University.

Following the hectic year of the anniversary celebration, time for a breather was certainly appreciated and in order. The year 1990 had been long and exhausting, and a brief reprise from all of the celebration activities was more than deserved. The School of Religious Education needed some time to sit back and appreciate the 75 years of heritage just celebrated, relish in the past year's exciting activities and accomplishments, and look forward to new, innovative programs developed in the future. The new year (1991) would provide tremendous opportunities to begin developing plans and improving many of the strong programs that were in place. It would be a year of reflection and continued growth. The prospect of additional endowed academic chairs was a major priority moving forward.

Future Academic Chairs and Professorships

In both semi-annual meetings, March 11-12 and October 21-22, the trustees dealt primarily with academic questions about endowed chairs, endowed professorships, new degree programs, and the promotion of present faculty members who had performed admirably. A special task force to study and bring a recommendation regarding a special training program and degree programs for pioneer and bi-vocational pastors was formed. Chairman Jimmy Draper appointed this special task force that included members from Southwestern Seminary's faculty and staff, plus a request for participation from the Home Mission Board and members from active pioneer ministry areas.

> The task force will study considerations such as: survey questionnaire, screening tool to identify suitable pioneer prospects, 6-12 months of directed field work, training in specific vocational skills, modified curriculum to meet the issues and practical needs of pioneer ministers, inclusion of the minister's wife in the process and periodic evaluations to provide appropriate adjustments.[12]

The task force was to report to the trustees at their next meeting.

In response to the trustees' interest in new endowed chairs and professorships, a recommendation was made by Jim Bolton and seconded by T. Bob Davis in the academic affairs committee that a new Professorship of Marriage and Family Counseling be approved in the School of Religious Education.[13] The naming of the professorship would be determined by the Institutional Advancement committee of the trustees. During the October 21-22, 1991, meeting, the Institutional Advancement committee made the following recommendation:

That the Professorship of Marriage and Family Counseling in the School of Religious Education be named for Robina Drakeford. Background information: Robina Drakeford is the wife of Distinguished Professor of Psychology and Counseling, Emeritus, John Drakeford. A gift of $100,000 is required for the endowment of a Professorship. The Drakefords have provided a gift of $100,000 in their estate plan for the funding of this professorship.[14]

Why Academic Chairs and Professorships?

Academic chairs are a vital part of any educational institution, and all educational institutions have as many different varieties of academic chairs as one can imagine. But the chair that one cannot see is the chair that is so vitally important to any educational institution; it is an *endowed academic chair* that was a major priority at the two semi-annual trustee meetings. In academic parlance, an endowed academic chair is an academic post named in honor or in memory of a special person or persons. Every academic chair is located in a specific area of study in an institution and is presided over by an academically qualified person who "holds the chair." The earnings gained from the endowed fund are used to assist the budget in paying faculty salary, benefits, and other pertinent amenities of the person who is installed in the chair.

At Southwestern, the salary and benefits of a faculty member are paid from the earnings of the endowed gift. At the time, an amount of $500,000 fully endowed an academic chair. The endowment principal is protected into perpetuity, with only the interest earnings used to pay the needs of the faculty member installed. Jay Chance, vice president for Institutional Advancement, said, "New chairs make possible programs which otherwise might not be included in Southwestern's budget."[15]

The seminary had nine fully funded academic chairs: six in the School of Theology, two in the School of Religious Education, and one general chair, the Fred and Edith M. Hale Chair of Prayer. There were 11 chairs in the process of being funded: three in the School of Theology, seven in the School of Religious Education, and one in the School of Church

Music. An academic chair can only be installed in an institution when it is fully funded.

Graduates Honored at Fall Commencement (1991)

William Crews, president of Golden Gate Baptist Theological Seminary (now Gateway Seminary), was the speaker for the fall commencement at Travis Avenue Baptist Church. Crews spoke to the graduating class on the subject "Will Success Mark Your Ministry?" Using Joshua as a model, Crews said, "Some would say success depends on who you are and others will say it depends on where you are. But, if God can find a person on whom He can put His hand, then you will be successful, and God desperately needs those kinds of people to bless."[16]

Dilday conferred degrees on 284 graduates, including 33 who received doctoral degrees. Degrees were awarded to 11 from the School of Church Music, 128 from the School of Religious Education, and 159 from the School of Theology. There were five students who received the Diploma in Christian Ministry, awarded by the seminary under the Ethic Leadership Development Program of the Baptist General Convention of Texas.

A special member of this graduating class was Carl Burns. Burns was the first African-American to receive a Doctor of Education degree in the School of Religious Education. During his tenure as a student at the seminary, Burns taught at the Sidney Lanier Vanguard Elementary School for Creative Arts and also pastored the Brighter Hope Mission Church, where he was a role model for hundreds of African-American children.

Burns commented about his life as a role model, "I don't preach Christianity in the classroom, I just live it. My own role model here at the seminary was the professor I wrote about in my doctoral dissertation, Leon Marsh, senior professor of foundations of education. My first day at seminary, Marsh greeted me in the foyer with a hug, and 11 years later, I ended my academic career with the same person and another hug."[17]

Major Changes in Presidential Leadership

Two Major Conferences Continue in 1991

The annual Kellogg Lectures in Gerontology, April 4-5, featured David Oliver, the renowned vice president for Physical Medicine and Rehabilitation Chronic Care Services at the Heartland Center in St. Joseph, Missouri. Kirk Gulledge, a private consultant specializing in retirement communities and whose parents funded and endowed the Gulledge Gerontology program activities, hosted Oliver during the lecture series and delivered three lectures as well. Oliver's lectures included "A Wholistic Approach to Ministry with Older Persons: A Pastoral Care Perspective" and "Can the Church be the Extended Family?" Gulledge's lectures included "Clergy Attitudes Toward the Aging: Implications for Curriculum Development" and "Housing and Health in Later Adulthood."

The 23rd annual Youth Lab, April 5-7, took its participants into the "Faith Lane." This year's theme was "Life in the Faith Lane." The planners were attempting to grab kids out of the fast lane and exercise caution regarding what methods they were using to accomplish that feat. It was an emphasis on using faith rather than the fads and fashions that catch youth up in their glitter and glitz and hype of the day's culture. This year, there was a brand new feature never attempted before: specialty conferences for Hispanic and African-American churches.

Outstanding leaders from across the Southern Baptist Convention leading the worship services and workshops included Richard Ross and Art Herron of the Baptist Sunday School Board, Marti Solomon from Woman's Missionary Union, and Chuck Flowers of the Baptist General Convention of Texas. As with other years, this year's Youth Lab endeavored to speak to current critical issues in youth ministry and to give encouragement and support to youth ministers, pastors, and volunteer youth workers.

Trustees Evaluate "Vision for Excellence" Fundraising Goals

In 1992, the 10-year fundraising plan, "Vision for Excellence," was in its second year of activity, and the trustees were interested in what the future of the program would look like. Dilday had challenged the trustees and the supporters of Southwestern to raise $36 million dollars over that 10-year period.

The goal would be separated into three phases, with $25 million going toward the endowment and $11 million funding major capital projects. The report to the trustees indicated that the first phase general endowment was imperative for continued growth of the seminary, no matter what economic indicators might show. These funds, wisely invested, would provide annual income for the seminary's budget and would not invade the principal but allow it to continue well beyond the present situation. A goal of $8 million was designated for general endowment.

A second phase of $4 million was designated for endowed chairs, professorships, and scholarships, and a third phase of $11 million was designated for capital projects that identified the need for expanded facilities and services to meet the growth of the seminary. The projects included new buildings and the renovation of some existing buildings. Major projects targeted were:

- Center for Continuing Education: a state-of-the-art center that would serve as a visitor's center and a conference center, with guest rooms for use by all who visited the seminary campus each year. $7 million were designated for this project.
- Student/faculty housing: would provide affordable housing for students and faculty to assist them in their continuing ministry as students and as faculty members. $2 million were designated for this important project.
- Computer equipment: would provide a new up-to-date computer system, which was vital to the efficient operation of an institution such as Southwestern Seminary. $1 million were designated for the computer replacement.
- Bowld Music Library completion: $500,000.
- Robert E. Naylor Student Center renovation: $500,000.

The "Vision for Excellence" fundraising goals were well-received by the trustees, and Dilday was encouraged to begin working diligently toward its 10-year completion.[18]

In response to the president's presentation of "Vision for Excellence," the trustees recommended two new academic chairs—the establishment of a Chair of New Testament in the School of Theology and a Chair of Music Ministry in the School of Church Music, to be named by the Institutional Advancement committee of the trustees. In other academic activity, four faculty members in the School of Religious Education were promoted: Wesley Black was promoted to associate professor of youth education, Bob Brackney to professor of social work, Wynona Elder to associate professor of psychology and counseling, and Gary Waller to associate professor of administration.[19]

As a part of the October 19-20 meeting, the trustees responded to the challenge of Dilday to seek funding for endowed academic chairs. The trustees made a recommendation that a Chair of Philosophy and History of Education be established in the School of Religious Education. A motion was made by T. Bob Davis and seconded by Olin Collins that the chair be named the Jack D. Terry, Jr. Chair of Philosophy and History of Education. The chair would be installed when all funding ($500,000) was received.

The trustees raised serious questions about the present convention-wide debate over the Bible. These questions were part of the conservative movement that began at the Southern Baptist Convention of 1979 with the election of Adrian Rogers and subsequent elections, including that of trustee board president Jimmy Draper. A bit of uneasiness was fermenting among the trustees concerning the administration's slow timetable for mailing the printed materials to the trustees prior to the meeting. The printed material contained all the information about the election of new faculty, promotion of present faculty, tenure offered to faculty, as well as reports about important Southern Baptist Convention correspondence and procedures that were to be considered and voted on at the meeting. The printed material was being mailed less than 20 days prior to the meeting and, on too many occasions, sometimes fewer than 10 days before the meeting. A motion was made by Lyle Seltmann and seconded by Olin Collins that the trustees receive the materials, in order to be better prepared for the meetings, no less than 20 days in advance of the meeting. The motion carried.[20]

Women's Leadership Consultation

Extensive planning by Southwestern Seminary and Woman's Missionary Union was developed carefully in anticipation of the Woman's Leadership Consultation, January 28-30, 1993. The consultation featured leading women from across the Southern Baptist Convention who led inspirational worship, conferences, and workshops over the three days. The featured speakers included Esther Burroughs, assistant director of lay evangelism for the Southern Baptist Home Mission Board, and Dellanna O'Brien, executive director of Woman's Missionary Union in Birmingham, Alabama.

Sheila West, president and CEO of AIM Concepts, Inc., led a seminar on helping women to discover their purpose in the church's ministry. Humorist Rosemary Rumbley provided creative Texas homespun entertainment for the meeting. Monte Clendinning, conference coordinator for the World Mission/Evangelism Center, said, "The consultation is designed to help women develop organizations and ministries in their own churches, help them find what makes a well-balanced ministry and what blends well together."[21] Various sessions during the three days focused on themes such as "Resources for Effective Ministry to Women"; "Joint Relationship of WMU and Women's Ministries"; "Beginning a Women's Work in Churches and Associations"; "Evangelism Through Women's Ministries"; and "Phases of Women's Ministries."

Youth Lab's 25th Birthday

The Youth Lab, now a young adult, celebrated its 25th birthday in 1993. The lab began in 1968 as a fledgling upstart in the Christian youth educational world at its home, Southwestern Baptist Theological Seminary. Planning was now in progress for next year's 1993 lab with the theme "Youth Ministry…So What?!" The lab would explore how youth work had its roots in local church youth work and attempt to examine and determine future youth trends. 1992's theme was "Youth Ministry: Gang Busters," with sessions on helping youth to become more interested in church youth groups rather than in the gang scene that was so prevalent. Experts who had had extensive experience in working with street gangs taught how to encourage youth to participate in church-related youth groups rather than street gangs.

Since 1993 was a birthday celebrative year, the youth planning committee was attempting to encourage every former seminary student who served on any of the steering committees over the past 25 years to come home for this celebration. Outstanding Southern Baptist leaders headlined the lab's stellar faculty: Richard Ross, youth work consultant for the Baptist Sunday School Board, and Joe Palmer, a church recreation specialist with the Baptist Sunday School Board. Also returning as faculty for the birthday celebration was Don Mattingly, minister of education and administration at Pioneer Drive Baptist Church, Abilene, Texas, one of the founders of the first youth lab in 1968 along with Harold Dill, retired professor of youth education at Southwestern Seminary. Originally established to provide training for summer youth workers, the Youth Lab had grown to include more than 400 participants ranging from full-time youth ministers to lay volunteers in youth work in local churches, as well as youth from those local churches.

Farewell to a Loving Professor of Childhood Education

Jeroline Baker spent three decades as professor of childhood education at Southwestern Seminary. During her tenure, several times she occupied the Bessie M. Fleming Chair of Childhood Education, and she served as consulting design architect, along with Ann Bradford, for the Goldia and Robert E. Naylor Children's Center in 1974. Baker watched children's ministry evolve from just a Sunday morning necessity to a viable weekday ministry for children and parents.

While a student at Georgetown College, Lexington, Kentucky, Baker heard R.O. Feather, professor of education administration at Southwestern Seminary, speak to students about the various kinds of seminary education available for students desiring to enter some kind of ministry. Baker said she felt she was called to some kind of ministry, "but since I couldn't preach, I supposed the mission field was my only choice."[22] Feather told the students about the various kinds of ministries in the School of Religious Education at Southwestern, and when childhood education was mentioned, Baker knew that was where she would go.

As she visited the campus in August 1954, she recalled that, having come from beautiful, lush, green Kentucky, she thought it was the most God-forsaken place in the entire world. She remembered everything was brown and dusty with not a blade of green grass.

After graduating from Georgetown College in 1956, she came to Southwestern, completing her Master of Religious Education in 1958. Returning to Kentucky for six years, she taught elementary school and served as a children's director on a church staff and completed her Master of Education degree in elementary education from the University of Kentucky. In 1964, she was elected to the faculty of the School of Religious Education to work alongside Ann Bradford, then professor of childhood education and kindergarten. She completed her Doctor of Education (Ed.D.) at North Texas State University.

Upon her retirement, Baker said she planned to stay involved in children's ministry through writing and leading children's workshops in Kentucky and surrounding states. "I also plan to enjoy my home, Kentucky, the lush green state I left for the God-forsaken plains of Texas 35 years ago."[23]

Former Dean of Women, Floy Barnard, Dies at 97

One of the pioneer educators who joined the School of Religious Education faculty in 1933, died at the age of 97. Floy Barnard was professor of missionary education and educational arts until her retirement in 1960. She was a graduate of Colorado College of Education with B.A. and M.A. degrees. Barnard later matriculated at Southwestern Baptist Seminary in the School of Religious Education, earning her M.R.E. degree in 1929 and D.R.E. degree in 1939. Barnard also served the seminary as dean of women and was in charge of the women's residence hall until her retirement.

As dean of women, Barnard had close association with all the women in the residence hall, serving as surrogate mother, confidant, counselor, and friend to all the young women who lived there. Trustees voted to name the women's dormitory Floy Barnard Hall at her retirement in 1960 because of her gracious spirit and total dedication to the seminary and the seminary women.

Major Changes in Presidential Leadership

Following her retirement, Barnard led conferences at several mission field meetings in Argentina, Brazil, Chile, Mexico, and Guatemala. She wrote two books, *Drama in the Churches* and *Christian Witnessing*. This pioneer woman on the plains of Texas was sorely missed by all who knew her at Southwestern Seminary and all the other ministry engagements she filled so admirably.

A Flurry of Activity

The trustees had cause for a "hallelujah and praise the Lord!" moment during the March 7-10, 1993, trustee meeting. A report to the board affirmed Southwestern Seminary had all notations removed from its accreditation. Notations that were levied on the seminary by the National Association of Schools of Music and the Alliance for Higher Education have subsequently been removed. The seminary was accredited by the American Association of Theological Schools (ATS), Southern Association of Colleges and Schools (SACS), the National Association of Schools of Music, and the Alliance for Higher Education with no notations. The new accreditation statement would be in place for the next 10 years.

A report was given from the Children's Work Task Force that had been reviewing the entire children's program at Southwestern. The task force was commissioned to look specifically at the possibility of the seminary sponsoring a private Christian school to meet the needs of seminary students, faculty, and the local community children. The school would serve as a laboratory for the training and education of private Christian school teachers.[24]

Another report was given on the successful women's leadership consultation, which was held on the campus in January 1993, bringing women to the campus from across the U.S. and across a wide theological spectrum. Monte Clendinning and Betty Dilday coordinated the event, which could become a model for women's consultations at other seminaries and convention enterprises.

The campus master plan was progressing well. The new official entrance to the seminary was constructed on Seminary Drive, across from J. Howard Williams Student Village, at the entrance to the B.H.

Carroll Memorial Building complex. The designated entrance had been at the corner of James Avenue and Seminary Drive. A green belt around the campus and the median on Seminary Drive had been adopted by the seminary under the new city parks program. New signs in front of each of the buildings on campus identified the facility's name and purpose. The Rosemont Apartments located three blocks east of James Avenue were renamed the E.D. Head Apartments. Southwestern won the Fort Worth "Beautiful Award," given by the city to locations in the community that enhanced the appearance of the location and the city.[25]

School of Religious Education Elections and Promotions

In the fall trustee meeting, October 11-13, a new professor in childhood education was elected to the School of Religious Education faculty. Marcia Granger McQuitty, who had taught adjunctively, was elected as assistant professor of childhood education. McQuitty's experience in childhood education spanned a period of 20 years. She was the Acteens director, Hawaii Baptist Convention; minister of preschool education, Travis Avenue Baptist Church; minister of childhood education, First Baptist Church, Colleyville, Texas; director of preschool education, Southcliff Baptist Church, Fort Worth, Texas; and director of international students, Southwestern Baptist Theological Seminary. Her publications include *Baptist Youth Curriculum*, *Religious Herald*, and *Preschoolers at Church*.

Dean Jack Terry was named consultant in planned giving by Dilday with approval by the trustees during the spring meeting. Terry assisted the seminary in developing, promoting, and maintaining a program of deferred gifts, or planned giving. Tom Chism, executive director of development, said,

> Terry is a natural for the position because he comes out of many years of service with the seminary and involvement in the denomination. He is well-known and respected. As dean of the School of Religious Education, Terry has helped Southwestern raise numerous major gifts for the

School of Religious Education. He has also been active in major fundraising campaigns.[26]

Terry continued his duties as dean as he took on this new adventure in fundraising.

A Price Chair challenge gift of $50,000 was received from an anonymous donor with the promise of an additional $50,000 if the school was able to match the donor's challenge of raising an additional $100,000 in the next 18 months. With this $200,000 challenge added to the funds already raised, the total amount of money given toward the project was more than $400,000. The total needed for the chair to be endowed was $500,000. The recent challenge gift provided an opportunity to complete the funding for the chair.

Woman's Leadership Consultation Huge Success

Baptist women from the Southern Baptist Convention and around the world were called on to "penetrate the culture with the Gospel."[27] The call was given during the third Women's Leadership Consultation on Southwestern's campus, January 28-30, 1993. With an attendance of over 200 women from the U.S. and four foreign countries, consultant Ester Burroughs from the Southern Baptist Home Mission Board encouraged women to take the Gospel of the grace of Christ to the world. She said, "We are going to have to get out of our organizations, outside the walls of our churches and cross barriers to penetrate the culture with the Gospel."[28]

Betty Dilday, President Dilday's wife and consultant spokesperson, said,

> We are blazing new paths. This consultation has allowed women to come together to understand each other and to try to work together. Baptist women have always been strong leaders in the church. It's just that they never really cared about it being acknowledged. There are still hundreds of women who have places of leadership in the churches who are unsung heroes.[29]

Summer School Offers Unusual Study Opportunities

Deans Bruce Corley, James McKinney, and Jack Terry announced that the 1993 summer school offered the broadest selection of courses in the history of Southwestern Seminary. The expanded summer school schedule in all three schools offered core classes and a full schedule of Doctor of Ministry seminars. The highlight of the summer schedule was the opportunity to take classes taught by renowned visiting professors. Visiting professors from various professions and ministries were enlisted to teach alongside faculty members in offering a plethora of courses in ministry.

Visiting professor courses were Doctrine of the Trinity by Millard Erickson, Strategies for Growing Churches by Paul Beasley-Murray, Music and Evangelism by Dick Baker, Sound Reinforcement Systems in the Church by Rick Robinson, Health and Fitness by Kenneth Cooper of the Cooper Clinic in Dallas, Fundraising for Church Endowment by Earl Murphy, and Substance Abuse by Ed Lilly. This kind summer school schedule was intended to encourage students to finish their degrees sooner.

Melton Social Ministry Institute Focusing on the Family

The School of Religious Education hosted the third annual Melton Social Ministry Institute Workshop, October 14-16, 1993. The theme of this year's institute was "Family Ministries: Process and Program" in keeping with the Southern Baptist Convention's "Year of the Family" emphasis. Social work professors and institute coordinators Derrell Watkins and Bob Brackney wanted the attendees to help church-community ministers and volunteers develop effective programs for two-parent families, single-parent families, or families with divorced parents. Sessions included studies involving the extended family, particularly senior adults.

Brackney said, "From a family development point of view, the family is definitely under fire today. People often enter marriage without having positive role models and are unable to deal with stress in their families. This year's workshop encouraged ministers and volunteers to reach out not only to the family of God, but also to families outside the church."[30]

The Melton Social Ministry Institute Workshop is named in memory of former missionary, community center worker, and professor Alpha Melton, Southwestern's first social work professor. She served on the School of Religious Education faculty from 1945 to 1971 and was responsible for the first degree-granting social work program at any Southern Baptist seminary. Specialists from the Home Mission Board and New Orleans Baptist Theological Seminary along with Harold Hime, Home Mission Board family ministries director, headlined the various workshop sessions.

Kellogg Lectures Explore "Images of Aging and Ministry"

The 1993 Kellogg Lectures, April 1-2, 1993, chose the theme "Images of Aging and Ministry" and featured keynote speaker Dennis Myers, assistant director of the Institute of Gerontological Studies at Baylor University. Meyers and Ben Dickerson, director of the Baylor Institute, served as speakers and resource persons during the lectureship series.

A special feature at the lectureship this year was the presentation of an honor given to Lucien Coleman, professor of adult education and gerontology in the School of Religious Education. Coleman was honored for outstanding service rendered to the program of gerontology established at Southwestern Seminary in conjunction with the Institute of Gerontological Studies at Baylor University.

Youth Ministry Lab Celebrates 25th Year

More than 425 youth workers from across the nation descended on Southwestern Seminary to celebrate the 25th year of the Youth Lab emphasis. The reunion theme chosen for this year was "Youth Ministry...So What?!" Participating in the celebration were two individuals who had a part in planning the first Youth Lab in 1968: Don Mattingly, a student who chaired the steering committee for the first lab, and Harold Dill, former professor of youth education in the School of Religious Education. Emphasis this year was placed on the dynamics of present-day youth ministry in relation to youth ministry of the past 25 years.

Wes Black, associate professor of youth education and co-sponsor of the Youth Lab, said, "Youth ministry has gotten to be more than a Coke and a joke. We still need to provide the fun elements, but it's much more than that. Needs have changed over the years, and these conferences need to recognize the dangers of at-risk teenagers, street gangs, peer stress, and adolescence (a critical stage of life)."[31]

The on-campus reunion of the youth leaders from the past 25 years was a brilliant idea. It provided an opportunity to renew old friendships, reestablish locations of ministry where friends were serving, and, in general, helped to catch up on the years that had passed. This was one of the greatest blessings of the 25th birthday celebration of the Youth Lab.

Trustees Dismiss President Dilday

The Conservative Resurgence that began with the election of Adrian Rodgers, the first conservative president of the Southern Baptist Convention, in Houston, Texas, in 1979 had been moving across the landscape of the Southern Baptist Convention over the past 15 years, with conservative SBC presidents being elected one after another. The election of the president of the convention placed that person in the strategic position of naming committees for the selection of boards of trustees for various agencies, commissions, and institutions. For the past 15 years, the boards of trustees were being filled with more conservative members who in turn began to change the nature of the agency, commission, or institution toward a more conservative mindset. A similar process favoring a change of presidency at Southwestern was in motion. This had already happened at Southern Baptist Theological Seminary with the election of Al Mohler; at Southeastern Baptist Theological Seminary with the election of Paige Patterson; and at Golden Gate Baptist Theological Seminary with the election of William Crews.

Unrest began to surface at Southwestern Seminary after Dilday appeared to side with the moderates in his 1984 convention sermon "Higher Ground." The convention debate about the Bible had finally reached Southwestern Seminary.[32] During the meeting of the board of trustees, March 7-9, 1994, the trustees in executive session voted to dismiss Dilday because of a number of unresolvable actions on his part toward the board. The actions seemed to predicate the need for immediate removal from the office of president. In an open letter to alumni and friends of Southwestern, the trustees listed more than eight serious charges that made it necessary to dismiss Dilday immediately.[33]

In a letter to the faculty and staff, Ralph Pulley, chairman of the board, said, "The trustees' decision allowed Southwestern to seek a new and fresh direction in administration for Southwestern Baptist Theological Seminary. We believe this is vitally important as we seek ways to effectively meet the challenges pastors and other Christian leaders face as we prepare for the next century."[34]

As part of their decision to dismiss Dilday, the trustees named Miles Seaborn chairman of the presidential search committee to begin the process for nominating a new president immediately. The other members of the search committee included Paul Balducci, Mobile, Alabama; Robert Burch, Knoxville, Tennessee; Pat Campbell, St. Charles, Missouri; Olin Collins, Watauga, Texas; Lynn Cooper, Madisonville, Kentucky; T. Bob Davis, Dallas, Texas; Edward Litton, Tucson, Arizona; and Damon Shook, Houston, Texas.

At a later meeting, the executive committee of the trustees appointed William B. Tolar, vice president for academic affairs and provost, as Southwestern's acting president. The announcement of Tolar's appointment came on March 29, 1994, at a press conference called by the executive committee of the trustees. Ralph Pulley noted, "Tolar is a man of impeccable character and unusual qualifications to fill this interim position. He is respected by faculty, students, and the Baptist constituency all over the world. We are indeed most fortunate to be able to secure his services. He gives a sense of security, and his stability will move the seminary in the right direction."[35]

Additional academic alignments were made during the meeting, with a motion that several new combined positions be established. One of the new administrative positions was vice president for development and campaigns. This position placed more direct and intentional administrative focus on fundraising. Jack Terry was asked to accept this new position and to continue as the dean of the School of Religious

Education. The workload had already been adjusted, and Terry enthusiastically endorsed the plan.

Two recommendations for faculty promotions in the School of Religious Education were made: Jerry Privette was promoted from associate professor of administration to professor of administration, and William A. (Budd) Smith from associate professor of foundations of education to professor of foundations of education.

Academic Chairs Funded

Significant advance was made in the endowment funding for the School of Religious Education academic chairs and was announced during the spring trustee meeting. Funding for the E.F. "Preacher" Hallock Chair of Baptist Student Work achieved total funding. The First Baptist Church, Norman, Oklahoma, where Hallock had been pastor for 46 years, led the funding operation and completely funded the chair at $500,000. The Hallock Chair would support Southwestern's first full-time professor in the area of Baptist student work.

Hallock served as pastor of the First Baptist Church, Norman, Oklahoma, and ministered to thousands of students who were members of his church as well as students at the University of Oklahoma. He was instrumental in beginning student work on the campus of the university. Terry said,

> Hallock was very interested in the spiritual lives of University of Oklahoma students. Many of the people giving to the endowment of the chair were people who were in his church and in the university BSU. Many of them served as BSU directors on college and university campuses. I am very excited about the new faculty position and actively seeking a professor. When the chair is inaugurated, it will be the only chair of Baptist Student Work in the United States.[36]

Trustees named the new landscaping building the Carl E. Norton Landscape Facility in memory of the seminary's first landscape supervisor. The new building allowed for the former landscaping building to be demolished and in its place provided 54 additional parking spaces for students on the main campus across from Fort Worth Hall.

Hubert Martin, vice president for business affairs, said, "Because of the 2,000 square feet of storage space, landscape equipment can be purchased in bulk and have a place to store them rather than buying them separately, which costs more in the long run."[37] The new building was much more energy efficient in heating and cooling.

Major Workshops Highlight Spring of 1994 as Seminary Life Goes On

A combined gerontology conference—the Kellogg Lectures and the Religious Education Spring Emphasis—encouraged ministers to take another look at their ministry roles and search out additional creative ministry activities. Three events were planned for April 4-6 to focus on senior adult discipleship. This year's Kellogg Lectures were delivered by David Maitland, emeritus chaplain and professor of religion at Carleton College in Northfield, Minnesota. In addition to the Kellogg Lectures, the Religious Education Spring Emphasis featured Ben Dickerson of Baylor University and other outstanding speakers from the Baptist Sunday School Board, who addressed senior adult evangelism and the troubling issue of assisted suicide.

Coinciding with the Kellogg Lectures and the Religious Education Spring Emphasis was a state meeting of the Texas Baptist Association of Ministries with the Aging on the seminary campus. The tri-emphasis was another step toward emphasizing the needs of seniors and of senior adult ministry in the church. Southwestern had long been recognized as the first accredited seminary to offer a senior adult ministry course.

The Baptist Religious Education Association of the Southwest (BREAS), formerly the Southwestern Baptist Religious Education Association, was organized by the late J.M. Price for the benefit and growth of ministers of education in all church and denominational positions. This year, it focused on intentionally involving the students enrolled in the School of Religious Education in the professional organization. The meeting dates were changed from August to November to include students on the campus who would be gone during the former August summer date.

Daryl Eldridge, associate professor of foundations of education and president of BREAS from 1994-1995, said,

> BREAS membership is open to all students from all Southern Baptist seminaries without regard to their majors. BREAS membership offers students an opportunity to hear about the work that is being done in the real world of religious education by those people modeling effective leadership. The theme for the meeting in 1995 is "Home Improvement: Strengthening the Family Through Religious Education."[38]

The 26th annual Youth Ministry Lab, April 8-10, followed the theme "Home Delivery," which proffered the idea of youth ministers reaching into homes and ministering to parents and teenagers alike. It was as important for youth ministers to minister in the homes of the teenagers as it was for them to minister to the young people at the church. For a youth minister to plan activities for the youth at the church was an easy task, but it was much more difficult for the youth minister to take the time to minister in the homes of the youth, getting better acquainted with their parents, observing the living conditions of the home, and assisting the parents in understanding how to give leadership to their teenagers in better Bible study, church attendance, and public and private school ministry activities.

Though such a ministry presents challenges, the benefits of a single-home ministry activity far exceeded the large group meetings at the church when it came to assisting the parents in learning how to minister to their own teens. The more the parents were involved in the spiritual life of the teenager, the more effective they became in ministering to their own children. The Youth Ministry Lab still trained nearly all the Texas Baptist summer youth workers and provided an excellent opportunity for full-time youth minsters to revitalize their own ministries.

The fourth annual Melton Social Ministry Institute Workshop was planned for October 13-15, 1994. This year's institute wrapped itself around the theme "The Synergistic Church: Ministry and Growth." Bob Brackney, Melton Institute coordinator and professor of social work, explained, "A synergistic church is inclusive, accepting, and reaching to all people of all walks of life. It lives the Gospel in all of its aspects, reaching people for Christ while meeting their physical, emotional, and relational needs."[39]

Brackney expected a larger attendance than the 1993 institute. The emphasis was to assist as much as 30 percent of those who attended this year's institute to become volunteers in local churches throughout the United States. The goal was to give attendees the essential tools for developing synergistic churches.

We've Found God's Man for the 21st Century

The presidential search committee was appointed during the March 1994 trustee meeting and went to work immediately in search of God's man for the 21st century. They found such a candidate, and at the July 28, 1994, trustee meeting, Board Chairman Ralph Pulley announced the election of Kenneth S. Hemphill as Southwestern Seminary's seventh president. Hemphill was elected by a unanimous vote, and his presidency was effective immediately. The announcement added that Hemphill was prepared academically with impeccable credentials. He was spiritually qualified with over 25 years of experience in the local church. He had been a successful pastor and was well-accepted throughout the Southern Baptist Convention and the Texas convention.

In a July 28, 1994, press conference with trustee chairman Ralph Pulley and presidential search committee chairman Miles Seaborn, Hemphill laid out his initial emphasis as Southwestern's president, which was to create a greater sense of family on campus. He said,

> A part of what I want to see happen is for this campus not only to be aflame with the Spirit of God for evangelism but to have a passion for the young men and women who come here so that there is a sense of family and community. I am

here by God's call to accomplish God's purpose through His supernatural empowering under His sovereign care for as long as He desires.[40]

Kenneth S. Hemphill Inaugurated

The two-day inaugural celebration began on May 1, 1995, and would continue into the evening of May 2. The crisp, cool May morning invigorated the students, friends, faculty and special guests as they joined the Hemphill family for an early prayer service, asking for God's blessings on the inaugural ceremonies and accompanying activities for the historic occasion. God's touch was felt throughout the prayer service and later in the day when several hundred participated in the inaugural ceremony. Special guests began to gather for the pre-inaugural brunch, which would be followed by the inaugural ceremony at Travis Avenue Baptist Church at 2:00 p.m. During the ceremony, Hemphill was presented the presidential medallion, and during his words of appreciation, he emphasized that Southwestern would remain a frontline bunker where students would participate in contemporary spiritual battles. "If the seminary is to build Christian character into its students, they must be taught how to walk in dynamic relationship to their God. Preparation for ministry is incomplete without a heart fully prepared."[41]

Nilson do Amaral Fanini, president-elect of the Baptist World Alliance and a 1958 graduate of Southwestern, delivered the inaugural address. He said, "God is the only person in the world who can accomplish all things alone, without the help of anyone. He doesn't need your money, your car, your strength. He is the Almighty and thus can do whatever He alone chooses, but permits us to work with Him."[42] Other inaugural program personalities were Jimmy Draper, president of the Southern Baptist Sunday School Board; Mark Corts, pastor of Calvary Baptist Church, Winston-Salem, North Carolina; Ralph Pulley, chairman of Southwestern's board of trustees; and Hemphill's spiritual mentor and personal friend, Charles Fuller, pastor of First Baptist Church, Roanoke, Virginia.

Following the inauguration, President Hemphill, his wife Paula, and their three daughters were honored at a reception at the South Educational Building at Travis Avenue Baptist Church. The evening activities included a special musical concert with the Southwestern Men's Chorus, the Southwestern Wind Ensemble, and the Southwestern Singers.

May 2 events began at 10:30 a.m. with a concert on the grounds featuring country/western singer Ricky Skaggs from eastern Kentucky. Skaggs said, "In a way, I am trying to convey not only my feelings, but the heart of God. I'm beginning to see much more clearly that the heart of God beats for the family. I can express those things through my music because I hear a cry from the world to have that."[43] The concert was followed by a western BBQ picnic from 11:00 a.m. to 1:30 p.m. catered by Cousin's Barbecue of Fort Worth. From its prayer beginning to its blue-grass country music concert finale, the inauguration of Ken Hemphill as the seminary's seventh president was one that united the seminary family and challenged them all to continue in ministry, fulfilling Hemphill's own motto, "Touch the World and Impact Eternity."

Trustees Meet Twice During Inaugural Year

The board of trustees had its semi-annual meetings during the inaugural year dealing with the new president, the change of administrators in some areas, and the election of one new faculty member in the School of Religious Education. During the spring meeting, May 1-3, the trustees elected John E. Babler as associate professor of social work and ministry-based evangelism. Babler had years' worth of experience in local church service, social work, and hospice care. He is a licensed childcare administrator, licensed master social worker, advanced clinical practitioner, and a certified biblical counselor with the Association of Certified Biblical Counselors (ACBC).

Two major administration changes were made during the October 16-18, 1995, trustee meeting following a re-alignment of administrators. Jack Terry, dean of the School of Religious Education for 23 years, was unanimously elected as vice president for Institutional Advancement. Terry, who had been serving as interim director of Institutional Advancement since May, assumed the new vice president's position

November 1, 1995. Terry filled the post previously held by Jay Chance, who resigned May 13, 1995, to assume the vice presidency of the Lockman Foundation. The other administrative move was the election of Daryl Eldridge, associate professor of foundations of education since 1984, as dean of the School of Religious Education on December 13, 1995.

Eldridge earned the Master of Religious Education and Doctor of Philosophy degrees from Southwestern. He served in numerous education, youth, and music positions in several churches in Missouri and Texas. Eldridge was a frequent contributor to youth and administration publications and was the editor of the textbook *The Teaching Ministry of the Church*, published in 1995.

In one other action, the trustees approved the addition of Dan Earl Clements as associate professor of psychology and counseling. Clements had served on the religious education faculty as associate professor in psychology and counseling from 1985-1990 but accepted a position at Criswell College and served as a psychotherapist at the Neuropsychological Association in Arlington, Texas. He earned the Master of Arts in Religious Education and the Doctor of Philosophy degrees from Southwestern Seminary.

Major Changes in Presidential Leadership

Tidwell Retires after 40 Years of Service

Charles Tidwell decided to "hang up his spurs" after 40 years of ministry in the School of Religious Education as a student, professor of administration, distinguished professor of administration, and, for the last 18 years, chair of denominational relations. Tidwell noted that he had been a student for 10 years before becoming a professor and then spent 30 years in his role as professor of administration. For the past 33 years, he had been in Price Hall, teaching, counseling, and mentoring students preparing to become ministers of education in Southern Baptist churches. He said, "As chair of denominational relations, I was the designated person on the campus to expedite relationships between the Sunday School Board and the faculty and students regarding services, materials, and programs the board provided."[44]

During his 30 years of teaching, Tidwell taught most of the courses offered in the School of Religious Education's department of administration, including Church and Denominational Administration, Church Staff, Church Business Administration, and Survey of Educational Administration. In addition to teaching these courses during his tenure, he developed three new administration courses: Leadership in Church Planning and Church and Financial Planning at the doctoral level, and Church Office Management at the master's level. Tidwell wrote two books, *The Educational Ministry of the Church* and *Church Administration: Leadership for Effectiveness in Ministry*.

Royce Rose, associate professor of administration and a colleague of Tidwell, wrote, "He is a man of integrity, a denominationalist and a caring person. He has always been true to his word and true to his character. He has genuine care for his fellow human beings."[45]

Ph.D. to Replace Ed.D. as Terminal Degree

The School of Religious Education replaced the Doctor of Education (Ed.D.) with the Doctor of Philosophy (Ph.D.) degree. The change of nomenclature enhanced employment opportunities for graduates. Many alumni with Doctor of Philosophy degrees reported they were more competitive in the marketplace, especially in the teaching and counseling fields. After five years of research and study on the merit and future importance of the degree to alumni, the change took place at the beginning of the 1994-1995 academic year. Robert Rause, associate dean for advanced studies in the School of Religious Education, said,

> Several graduates with the Doctor of Education degree had been passed over for certain positions simply because they did not have the Doctor of Philosophy degree. In addition, several foreign missionaries have had difficulty in getting the recognition they needed in other countries because the Doctor of Education degree was not a well-understood degree as was the Doctor of Philosophy.[46]

The change in nomenclature was a blessing for alumni with terminal degrees in psychology and counseling because of the resistance of insurance companies working with graduates with Doctor of Education degrees. Scott Floyd, associate professor of psychology and counseling, remarked, "Some insurance companies and health maintenance organizations require the therapist to have the Doctor of Philosophy degree before they will pay third-party insurance claims. Some medical professionals don't understand the Doctor of Education degree and think it is subordinate in some ways to the Doctor of Philosophy degree."[47]

Many people who came for counseling and therapy did not understand the nomenclature of the Doctor of Education degree but clearly understood the Doctor of Philosophy degree nomenclature because the Ph.D. degree has a wider and more reputable position in the academic world. Because of these and other distorted perceptions, the School of Religious Education was convinced the change was needed, and after five years of research and study, they received the approval of the board of trustees to change the degree nomenclature to Doctor of Philosophy (Ph.D.).

The trustees approved several degree name changes in the School of Religious Education. The Social Work Department changed its name to Department of Social Work and Ministry-Based Evangelism; the Master of Arts in Church Social Services degree was changed to the Master of Arts in Church and Community Ministry; and the

Master of Arts in Religious Education with Social Work Concentration degree was changed to the Master of Religious Education with Ministry-Based Evangelism Concentration. President Hemphill told the trustees, "Changing the names of these degree programs bonds our commitment to ministry and evangelism in these areas."[48] He later said of the change, "Ministry-based evangelism will be key to church growth in the next century and is an essential component in the church's outreach program. A program of social work that is biblically based and evangelistically focused will be a drawing card. Students will find these courses helpful."[49]

Changing the terminology from social work to ministry-based evangelism and church and community ministries reflected the emphasis that Southwestern Seminary had always had in its social work department. Brackney said, "What we have been doing for several years is now reflected in the new title. The bottom line is that if I'm a Christian social worker, I'm helping people deal with every aspect of life, especially at the point of their basic need for salvation. President Hemphill was one of the first to use the term 'ministry-based evangelism.'"[50]

In theological education, most students were taught propositional evangelism, where they meet someone and then question them about accepting Christ as Savior. In social-ministry-based evangelism, people are accepted where they are and their needs are being met. In the process of meeting needs, an opportunity for the claims of Christ to be presented to a person is a part of the natural process of doing church social ministry. Associate Professor of Social Work John Babler said,

> Changing the names of the degrees emphasizes that Southwestern offers an excellent ministry-based program to train people for social work positions, stressing that graduates will be prepared to work in children's homes, retirement centers, hospitals, nursing homes, and hospice units. We see our program as a modified secular approach to social work. The difference in our program is that others may see social work as a secular field that has been adapted

to the church, but we see it as a Scripturally based method of meeting spiritual needs."[51]

The new nomenclature was well-received by students interested in social work. The number of students applying this year was twice the number of a year ago. It appears the program, under its new name, was going down the right track toward success.

BREAS Conference Concludes the Inaugural Year

BREAS, the new name for the oldest professional religious educational organization of its kind, celebrated its 75th anniversary November 6-8, 1995, during the inaugural year. The organization met annually on the Southwestern campus for the purpose of updating educational skills and encouraging new colleagues in the field of Christian education to become a part of the organization. The theme this year was "Home Improvement: Strengthening the Family Through Christian Education."

Conference leaders from across the nation spoke about strengthening the family through Christian education. President Hemphill, who had written widely in the subject of the home and Christian education in the church, was a major spokesperson. Other speakers on program included Howard Hendricks, distinguished professor and chairman of the Center for Christian Leadership at Dallas Theological Seminary; Michael Anthony, associate professor of Christian education at Biola University/Talbot School of Theology; Dave and Claudia Arp, Family Life Education and co-founders of Marriage Alive International, Inc.; John Hendrix, professor of Christian education at Southern Baptist Theological Seminary; and Lela Hendrix, trainer, conference leader, and writer with emphasis in family education and marriage enrichment.

Teaching Text Written by Religious Education Faculty

Choosing the right text for the specific class to teach the exact materials desired for any given course is a daunting task at best, and a challenging one at worst. The time had come to choose a text for the new religious education teaching course required for every student entering any degree program in the School of Religious Education.

Major Changes in Presidential Leadership

"What text?" was the major question facing the dean and members of the foundations of education department, which was responsible for the teaching ministry of the church. The name of the course was The Teaching Ministry of the Church, and as the foundations faculty looked for an appropriate text, the process just became more frustrating.

Unable to find one, Dean Eldridge did the next best thing: He led the foundations faculty to write their own text. And write it they did.

The text, *The Teaching Ministry of the Church*, was published and released by Broadman & Holman Publishers and had its maiden run in 1995 and was solidly in place for the 1996 and following academic years. The subtitle for the book was *Integrating Biblical Truth with Contemporary Application*. Southwestern's School of Religious Education had always been concerned with the integration of the Bible with practical concerns. Dean Eldridge said, "If the church fails to teach, it fails to be the church. That's the focus of the book—that the teaching ministry of the church is done through every part, not just through Sunday School. It's all about discipleship because everything we do in church is part of teaching. For us to develop strong Christians, *we must teach*."[52]

Contributors to the book included Jack Terry; Norma Hedin and Terrell Peace, assistant professors of foundations of education; and William A. (Budd) Smith and William R. Yount, associate professors of foundations of education. Dean Eldridge said, "The basic premise in the book is that God is teacher, and He wants to reveal Himself to us. It is there we have the biblical rationale for teaching."[53]

Sam Cotter, an alumnus of the seminary and the director of religious education for the Colorado Baptist General Convention, purchased 20 copies of the book to give to the pastors around his state. He said of the book's usefulness, "Not only is the book biblically based and full of wonderful teaching principles, but it is also very practical for teachers of all age groups. This is the teaching book for the 21st century, and I wish every minister could read it."[54]

Trustees Grateful for a Slower Pace

After the full year of enormous energy-draining activities for the inauguration of Hemphill, the trustees were more docile in the two semi-annual meetings in 1996. The agendas were less power-packed, and the items to be discussed and decided seemed to fade into the sunset in relationship to the campus activities and meetings the year before. A major announcement was made to the trustees in their March meeting by William B. Tolar about his decision to step down from his administrative duties as vice president for academic affairs and provost in order to return to the classroom, his first love.[55] Tolar thanked Olin Collins for his leadership in chairing the committee for academic affairs and to the past chairmen of the committee, with whom it was his privilege to serve, he said. Tolar returned to the classroom effective August 1, 1996, and continued to serve as a special advisor to the president.

Several faculty members in the School of Religious Education were promoted during the spring 1996 meeting: Wynona Elder to professor of psychology and counseling; Terrell M. Peace to associate professor of foundations of education; Robert H. Welch to associate professor of administration; William R. Yount to professor of foundations of education; and Theodore H. Dowell to senior professor of psychology and counseling.

During the trustee meeting, October 21-23, 1995, the trustees elected two new faculty members to the faculty of the School of Religious Education.[56] The first was James A. Headrick, associate professor of psychology and counseling. Headrick had served in multiple churches in the preceding decades, most recently Cottage Hill Baptist Church in Mobile Alabama, where he served as associate pastor in family life and biblical counseling.

Also elected was Ian Frederick Jones, professor of psychology and counseling. Jones had most recently served as dean of the School of Social Sciences, professor of sociology, and chair of the department of sociology and social work at Howard Payne University.

The trustees expressed concern about the enrollment. For the last three years (1993-1996), the enrollment seemed to be slipping. In 1993, the total enrollment was 3,458. In 1996, the total enrollment in the fall was 3,027, a 400-plus enrollment loss from 1993. In 1996, the School of Theology enrolled 1,686; the School of Religious Education, 1,078; and the School of Church Music, 192.

Major Changes in Presidential Leadership

Hemphill assured the trustees that he was going to make every effort to make the campus student-friendly and physically attractive (i.e., remodeling of J. Howard Williams Student Housing and proposing a continuing education center), and by enlarging the new student recruiting organization to meet the needs of students who were actively interested in seminary education at one of the six Southern Baptist seminaries. The trustees were pleased with the direction suggested by the president and pledged their support.

"Youth Works 96" Annual Youth Lab

Based on the new computer lingo of "Windows 95," the 28th annual Youth Lab was titled "Youth Works 96." The annual meeting took place April 12-14, 1996. With an expectation of over 375 participants from 10 states and some international youth consultants, the conference had sessions that assisted in keeping youth ministers and church leaders abreast of the latest methods and trends in youth ministry.

Workshops this year were designed to address the special ministry needs facing youth in 1996. Some of the workshops spoke to Teens at Risk, Understanding African-American Youth, Youth Ministry with Asian Youth, Relating to Parents of Teenagers, and Teaching Youth to Minister to their Peers.

Two student leaders of "Youth Works 96"—Doug Diggs, a marriage and family counseling student from Little Rock, Arkansas; and Brooke Dozier, a religious education major from Dallas, Texas—directed the 28th annual lab. Dozier was a teenager in high school when the youth minister at her Dallas church was a student in the seminary and captain of Youth Lab. She always felt she was a byproduct of the Youth Lab. "I am really excited about reaching countless other young people and pointing them to Christ," she said.[57]

President Hemphill led the Friday evening worship service by speaking about leadership. In his message, he referred to Samson as a case study of failed leadership. Noting why Samson failed, Hemphill said,

> (1) He had no clear sense of purpose; (2) he abused the gifts that were his; (3) he tried to do it by himself; (4) he had a

lack of discipline; (5) he compromised his convictions; and (6) he took spiritual things too lightly. When people avoid the problems that plagued Samson, they can become true leaders that are needed when a great Christian movement is possible."[58]

Other leaders for "Youth Works 96" included Tan Flippin of the Baptist Sunday School Board and Sandi Black, counselor for the Christian Counseling Center in Arlington. Featured musicians included David Crain, a well-known youth worship leader from Grand Saline, Texas; Chris White, a seminary student and music evangelist; and Rosemary Hoover, "edutainer" and youth issue expert from Missouri. "The Company," Southwestern's drama group, developed and presented the theme interpretation around computer signage and lingo for "Youth Works 96."

BREAS 1996

Over 125 Baptist ministers of education and other educational ministry leaders from across the southwestern United States attended the BREAS annual meeting, October 28-30, 1996. Professional leaders from across the Southern Baptist Convention and from other evangelical seminaries, colleges, and universities led conferences to enhance and enlarge the educational ministry of the educational leaders who attended.

A leading Christian educator, Bob Agee, president of Oklahoma Baptist University, keynoted the conference and encouraged the attendees to "be the leader you were called to be." Identifying the life of the minister of education or administration in a church is like looking at a full rack of hats: one for each role the educational minister must put on and take off many times during the week as the educational minister of a local church.

Agee cited a recent Gallup poll that revealed that 70 percent of Americans claim to have church membership with only 13 percent—one-eighth of America—showing any kind of faith relationship with Jesus Christ. Agee asked, "What can be done to be effective ministers?"[59]

Agee said further,

Every born-again believer is called to ministry. It is God's intent for every believer to be a priest and to accept equal responsibility in evangelism. Christianity was never intended to be clergy-oriented. Christians are to minister in houses, businesses, assembly lines ... anywhere the unsaved live. To rally a congregation to evangelism, a religious educator must be more than an educator; he must also be a leader. There is a vast difference between your task as an educator and that of a leader. Leaders learn to be an effective part of a team. There is no place in the church for competing egos and personalities—concentrate on team-building and covering one another's weaknesses. God intends our work as leaders to be prioritized, and we must be agents of change. The religious educator needs to fill the role of a military leader during war—willing to lead the team wherever necessary to win the war. A church is like an army, it lives by conquest. When conquest ceases, mutiny begins."

School of Religious Education Gets a New Name

The trustees entered into three important aspects in the life of the School of Religious Education during the fall 1997 meeting, October 20-21. All three major changes had relationship to the 21st Century Task Force activity.

The Committee on Theological Education in the 21st Century was tasked with looking into all phases of theological education as they would be developing in the 21st century and making recommendations for implementation of the information found in the study as it applied to all facets of theological education. The trustees endorsed the work of the seminary's 21st Century Task Force and moved to accommodate the School of Religious Education's request for a name change and two new degrees in religious education.

The School of Religious Education's new mission/vision statement read: "To develop spiritual leaders who will fulfill the Great Commission by equipping and mobilizing people to worship, evangelize, disciple and minister through the educational ministries of the church."[60] Five core values were identified: "loving relationships, godly character, professional excellence, biblical ministry and lifelong learning."[61] With the mission/vision statement came a request to change the name of the school to the "School of Educational Ministries," which would highlight the emphasis in the vision statement to minister through the educational ministries of the church.

In response to the name change, two new degrees were approved: a Doctor of Educational Ministries and a Master of Arts in Christian School Education. Daryl Eldridge, dean of the School of Educational Ministries, made the case with the trustees that there was no religious education equivalent to the Doctor of Ministry degree in theology. In a recent survey, over 150 prospective students showed interest in a practical doctoral degree in religious education such as the Doctor of Educational Ministries and would apply for such a degree if it were offered. Eldridge said, "Talbot Theological Seminary in California and Trinity Evangelical Theological Seminary in Illinois will partner in the program, and Southwestern is seeking 'the right match' with an evangelical seminary in the East."[62] The new doctoral degree was 32 hours and included studies in four academic areas: Christian formation, organizational development, educational process, and research evaluation and design. The first classes were offered in the fall of 1998.

The second degree was the Master of Arts in Christian School Education, which was developed in response to the growing need in the exploding ministries of private Christian schools. Eldridge said, "In Texas alone, we are told that a new Christian school is opening every day, and if we are going to have an impact in this vital area of education, we need to offer training that is currently unavailable."[63] The 46-hour degree included teacher or administrator certification prerequisite, 20 hours of Bible and theology, 18 hours of Christian school education, and 8 hours of research. The classes offered met in one-week formats during the summer school semesters so that public school teachers were available to take the courses.

E.F. "Preacher" Hallock Chair of Student Ministries Inaugurated

Hemphill said, "If we lose this college generation, we lose America." So began the inauguration ceremony for the E.F. "Preacher" Hallock Chair of Student Ministries on January 23, 1997. Hemphill continued, "This chair is about touching colleges and universities. What's so special is that it is not just a vision to win America—Southwestern Seminary has a strategy to apply to that task."[64]

Many family members and friends of the longtime pastor of the First Baptist Church, Norman, Oklahoma, were in attendance at the inaugural ceremony. Tim Nickell, one of the leaders of the endowment thrust and the volunteer campaign director of the effort to fund the chair, said,

> It has taken 10 years to get to this point. This story has a history with a future. The Hallock Chair was born from the heart of God. Oklahoma, in the late 1980s, was in a period of economic chaos. But the idea to fund a chair at Southwestern to honor "Preacher" Hallock—one that could help train men and women to minister to college students—struck a chord.[65]

Mrs. Vera Hallock gave the first dollar toward the endowment and faithfully prayed for the project. From all over Oklahoma, people sent contributions wrapped in stories of how Hallock had ministered to them while they were students at the University of Oklahoma. More than $650,000 of such donations activated the endowment, with an ongoing goal to eventually reach $1 million.

Phil Briggs, professor of youth education, was installed as the first occupant of the endowed chair. Briggs was one of a thousand teenagers influenced by Hallock's class at Falls Creek Encampment in Oklahoma, and he still had a copy of the book *Deepening the Spiritual Life*, written by Hallock and used at Falls Creek to teach young people.

In his inaugural address, Briggs recalled that Hallock had a very specific approach to God—he was a man of God who listened to God and prayed to God. Briggs continued,

> "Preacher" Hallock often said, "If I had to choose between prayer and Bible study, I would stay with reading the Scriptures, 'cause it is more important that I hear what God says to me than what I can say to God." Someday we will all realize that 10 million people will find it difficult to agree intellectually. If all our preachers would major in Bible reading—with the first emphasis on finding the mind of God as they read and walk with God in this experience of reading—we would come to a ground of unity far superior to that of doctrine alone. But without the experience of God through the Book, theology and doctrine are barren.[66]

J.M. Price Chair of Religious Education Inaugurated

J.M. Price was packaging the message of God long before there were any of the modern translations of the Bible in the hearts and minds of those in his new Department of Religious Education on the plains of Texas. Price wrote in his most notable book, *Jesus the Teacher*, published in 1940, "The best binding for the Gospel is not Morocco but human skin."[67] This conviction continued with him during his 41 years as the founder and first director of the School of Religious Education.

On October 28, 1997, Price's legacy was honored with the inauguration of the J.M. Price Chair of Religious Education. Price, Kentucky-born and Southern Seminary-educated, was a serious soldier of the marching orders given by Christ to take the Gospel to the world. His greatest religious educational desire was to equip and empower the laity to become Sunday School teachers and to invest themselves in working in the Kingdom of God.

Price was named after the great evangelist John Milburn, who was leading a revival meeting when his mother made her profession of faith.

Price had two mottoes during his early school life. He wrote one on the schoolhouse wall—"I resolve to be diligent, for by diligence the mouse bit through the cable." The second are words from the hymn "I Would Be True": "I would be true, for there are those who trust me."[68]

William A. (Budd) Smith, professor of foundations of education, was elected to the faculty in 1979, also a Kentuckian, and named as the first occupant of the J.M. Price Chair of Religious Education. Smith also served as director of the Oxford Program, an international cultural/learning experience designed to expose Southwestern students to church and Baptist history in one of the most prestigious settings in the academic world.

As a student, Smith received the prestigious J.M. Price Award, given to a first-year student judged by the faculty to have qualities for making an outstanding contribution to the field of religious education. Smith shared Price's love for the local church and served in various capacities including youth ministry, deaf ministry, and as minister of education. Several members of the Price family were present for the ceremony, including his son, Jim Price, who gave the invocation clad in his father's academic regalia from Southern Seminary.

Dying Wish Completes Price Chair Funding

In 1943, Windy Rich hitchhiked to Fort Worth, arriving with a single suitcase and $100 dollars in his pocket saved from his summer job, to pursue a ministry call to become a minister of education. Price became his teacher, inspiration, mentor, and friend. In 1997, Rich flew to Fort Worth to celebrate the inauguration of an academic chair in Price's honor and to give the prayer of blessing on the present-day students benefitting from Price's legacy. His challenge gift of $500,000 established the endowment to activate the chair.

Rich said, "My whole life is centered here at Southwestern," citing the values and knowledge he gained during his two-year Master of Religious Education degree program. His wife, Ethelene Holt Rich, was also a graduate of Southwestern and shared the same love and, with an unusual gesture, set the gift in motion in a literal act of dying.

Ethelene was fighting a losing battle with cancer. When the disease came back in strength, it was clear she would not recover. She decided the cost of an ineffective hospitalization could be better invested in religious education at Southwestern Seminary.[69] She died in June 1991. Two years later, Rich made the $250,000 challenge gift, and over the next four years, more than 200 former students joined him to meet and exceed the challenge.

Rich, former students, and faculty stood before he prayed in order to say, "We are an extension of this teaching minister, and we anticipate the glorious future of Southwestern training religious education ministers and empowering the laity to hear, feel, and heed that still, small voice to couch God's truths in the language of our generation."[70] Because of this selfless gift from Ethelene Rich and the challenge gift by Windy Rich and others, the trustees voted at their March 10, 1997, meeting to activate the monies given for the Price Chair as active endowment with the presidential recommendation to inaugurate the chair in the fall of 1997.[71]

Heacock, Former Dean, Dies

Joe Davis Heacock, who for 40 years learned, taught, and led at Southwestern, passed away on November 2, 1997, at 91 years of age. Dean emeritus of the School of Religious Education (now the School of Educational Ministries) and professor of education administration, Heacock was remembered by his students who later became his colleagues.

Bob Brackney, professor of social work and ministry-based evangelism, said of Heacock, "We have lost a great educator and a great Christian gentleman. He had a genuine care for students and set parameters in which the school still operates today. He led with an example that showed he not only taught from the books, but also from a deep personal knowledge of service to others in the name of Christ."[72]

Phil Briggs, the Hallock Chair of Baptist Student Ministry and professor of youth education, said, "He was my teacher, my colleague, and my dean. We have had the passing of a real icon in our field. He perpetuated the tradition of J.M. Price by being a visionary in religious education."[73]

William Caldwell, professor of administration and church administration, said, "Heacock was a man who first taught his students and then came to us as respected colleagues. There was never condescension on his part. We became confidants, and he was comfortable asking us for advice. I will greatly miss my good friend."[74]

Jack Terry, former dean and now vice president for Institutional Advancement, recalled,

> Joe Davis Heacock became my mentor while a student. Because of family and church responsibilities, I could not spend much time on the campus as many other students who were not working in local churches. Dean Heacock sought me out on many occasions and asked me to share with him what I was doing in my church in Fort Worth. He would always encourage me to stay with the local church and keep on working while in school because he felt the best place to learn educational ministry and administration was working in a local church. He forged my great love for the educational ministry in the local church and the thrill of watching the Sunday School and other facets of the educational organization grow. He caused me to become a "church-man" for many years before I came back to study and later to teach.[75]

Heacock was a churchman and served many local churches in Alabama and Oklahoma. He worked at the Baptist Sunday School Board for two years as an educational consultant. His ministry in Fort Worth was serving many of the local congregations as an interim educational director. His home church in Fort Worth was the University Baptist Church, where he had the privilege of mentoring Harry Piland, who later became the director of Sunday School work for the Baptist Sunday School Board of the Southern Baptist Convention.

Heacock's name was synonymous with church educational ministry, where he served with excellence for over 60 years. All of the faculty of the School of Educational Ministries will miss our mentor, colleague, and, most of all, our friend.

Trustees Enthusiastic About Southwestern's Future

Excited trustees announced the reception of a $20.2 million pledge given to the "Touch the World, Impact Eternity" campaign for the construction of a leadership development center that would provide continuing education for every facet of theological ministry. The trustees at their March 9-11, 1998, meeting heard a progress report on the $100 million fundraising campaign (of which the leadership development center was a central part), approved the renaming of the continuing education center, approved the formation of a faculty council, and elected nine new faculty members. They also requested the seminary administration develop a strategy to improve faculty salaries and identify cost-saving measures to make the plan work. Hemphill said, "This was a very positive, affirming trustee meeting. The trustees were upbeat and visionary."[76]

A personal gift of $5 million was given by Harold Riley, national chairman of the "Touch the World, Impact Eternity" campaign, for the construction of the continuing education center. This one gift was believed to be the largest in the school's history. Relating to the gift given by Riley, the trustees approved the seminary's request to name the continuing education center the Ralph Smith Leadership Development Center in honor of Riley's pastor, Ralph Smith of Hyde Park Baptist Church, Austin, Texas. They also approved Riley's request to name Phase 1 of the leadership development center in honor of his father, Ray Riley, a graduate of the seminary, and to name Phase 2 in honor of Jack MacGorman, Riley's father's favorite professor while a student at the seminary.

Phase 1 was planned as a residence facility with single bedrooms and suites to accommodate those attending leadership conferences. Phase 2 was planned as a large lecture hall for large group presentations and several medium and smaller conference rooms where breakout sessions to the large group presentations could be housed.

A new organizational structure, the faculty council of Southwestern Seminary, was a representative and advisory body elected by the faculty to discuss matters of importance to the faculty as a whole and to make recommendations to the trustees, administration, accrediting agencies, and other constituencies. The council would serve as a forum for representatives of the faculty to have full discussion of any and all matters within the approval of the administrative structures, policies, and procedures, but would not have decision-making authority and could not interfere with or intrude in administrative affairs.

> The purpose of the faculty council shall be to facilitate communication, cooperation, and collegiality among faculty members and among the faculty, administration, trustees, and students with special attention to the policies affecting the faculty, the academic program, and the future development of the seminary; to exercise initiative and provide leadership in academic programs and faculty development so as to contribute to the overall advancement of the seminary; and to encourage faculty input and dialogue regarding the welfare of the seminary as a whole.[77]

Faculty Elected to the School of Educational Ministries

Three new faculty members were elected at the March 9-11, 1998, trustee meeting. Robert DeVargas was elected as instructor of foundations of education/communication arts. DeVargas had previously served with the Baptist General Convention of Texas, multiple local churches, and as campus evangelism coordinator at Texas Tech University. From 1996-1998, he served as a teaching fellow at Southwestern.

Robert R. Mathis was elected as professor of administration/director of institutional research and assessment. Mathis began his educational career as a public school teacher and later served in local churches and as a personnel administration specialist for the U.S. Army. He had most recently served as director of research doctoral programs and John T. Sisemore professor of Christian education at New Orleans Baptist Theological Seminary.

The final elected faculty member was David Penley, as instructor of social work and ministry-based evangelism. Like many of his fellow professors, Penley came to Southwestern with extensive experience of serving local churches, most recently as community minister/minister of education at College Avenue Baptist Church, Fort Worth, Texas.

Trustees received encouraging news about the increased enrollment for a fourth year. The fall semester of 1997 posted a total of 3,166 enrolled, with 1,808 in the School of Theology; 1,089 in the School of Educational Ministries; and 199 in the School of Church Music. The 1997 enrollment of 3,166 compared to 3,077 in the fall of 1996. The prospects for the fall of 1998 looked even brighter, with the possibility of over 3,200 to be enrolled.

Judy Morris, director of admissions, reported a new approach to the new students who visited the campus. She said,

> In addition to two nights lodging, class visits, and admission presentations, prospects are treated to lunch with professors. We have one of the only admission programs that offers an informal time to meet and talk with professors. It has proven true for Southwestern that direct faculty contact is the one key of not only getting students here but keeping them here.[78]

The School of Educational Ministries went one step further in fine-tuning this relationship by assigning incoming students during the 1998 spring semester to a "faculty friend." These advisers tracked students throughout their seminary experience, remembering birthdays, calling during illnesses, and ministering during troubling times. Eldridge said, "In all studies done on student retention, two of the top four factors include relationships with faculty outside the classroom and relationships with peers."[79]

President Hemphill said to the trustees, "We are excited about the continued growth of our seminary. God is mobilizing a great spiritual army for the coming great awakening. Our increase proves the confidence Southern Baptists place in Southwestern's ability to train effective ministers for His service. We pledge to be good stewards of that trust."[80]

30th Anniversary Youth Ministry Lab – "Home Run, '98"

Major league baseball was just about three weeks into the new '98 season, and the spring lab celebrated its 30th anniversary with a tremendous line-up of professional players. The three-day conference, April 17-19, fielded a team of over three dozen conference leaders with additional keynote speakers. This spring's Youth Lab roster included professionals such as Richard Ross, youth specialist for the Baptist Sunday School Board; Chuck Garman, also a youth specialist with the Baptist Sunday School Board; Bob Fowler, a pastor from Las Vegas, Nevada; Rosemary Hoover, a musician and parenting specialist from Independence, Missouri; and Don Mattingly, coordinator of youth programs at Baylor University (and who shared his name with then-New York Yankee second baseman). The music for the lab was directed by Paul Guffey, a musician from First Baptist Church, Oviedo, Florida.

The theme for the Youth Lab was "Home Run '98: Spring Training for Ministry." Session topics included technology, discipline, and race and gender issues. Interspersed between the sessions were major gatherings where Fowler preached about the role of the pastor in youth ministry, Gartman talked about starting peer ministry groups, Ross addressed the group on starting Bible clubs and leading teams, Guffy spoke on how to lead youth worship, and Mattingly spoke on how to do family Bible study that included youth participation. Everyone involved this year hit a "home run" for sure.

197th Commencement, a Graduation First (1999)

May 15, 1999, was a global emphasis day when a Cuban-American woman, an African-American woman, and the school's first Croatian student received degrees. This commencement was the 197th commencement since the beginning of the school in 1908. During this graduation,

378 degrees were conferred, including 267 master's degrees, 27 diploma studies degrees, one certificate of master's studies for a layperson, and one degree through the seminary extension program.

Marinko Kimmer, the seminary's first graduate from war-torn Croatia, completed his journey that began in Croatia in a Catholic Jesuit seminary and continued into the evangelical ministry at Southwestern. Kimmer graduated with his master's in communications degree from the School of Educational Ministries and planned to return to his native Croatia to work in Christian schools.

Esther Diaz-Bolet received her Ph.D. from the School of Educational Ministries and became the first Cuban woman to receive a doctorate from the seminary. Bolet moved with her family from Cuba in 1960. She earned the M.A.R.E. degree in 1989 and had served as an adjunct professor of administration. She also served as an adjunct professor at Tarrant County Junior College. She was blessed with a scholarship from the Hispanic Theological Initiative.

Casandra Jones became the first African-American woman to earn a Ph.D. from the School of Educational Ministries. She received her M.A.R.E. degree from Southwestern and a B.A. degree from Spelman College. She served as the national music director of the National Baptist Convention, USA, the largest black Baptist denomination.

But the global reach of the 1999 commencement did not end here. In the graduating class, there were 28 students who earned doctoral degrees, four of whom were missionaries to Malawi, Malaysia, Uganda, and Southeast Asia. Four other doctoral graduates were presently teaching in seminaries and universities across the United States.

Riley Leadership Development Center Under Construction

Phase 1 of the Riley Leadership Development Center was well into its construction phase, with completion projected for summer 1999. Phase 1, a residence center, had bedrooms and suites that housed participants attending continuing education conferences at Southwestern Seminary. Phase 2, which followed in construction immediately upon the completion of Phase 1, had a conference center format, with one large auditorium area that seated over 300 people at tables, a smaller conference room that seated about 100, and several medium conference rooms that were used for breakout sessions from the main auditorium.

Trustees Receive Encouraging Report from President Hemphill

Hemphill made an encouraging report to the trustees about the enrollment growth that was beginning to occur in all three schools and of their enthusiastic affirmation of the 21st century committee's activities. The report included the vision statement that Southwestern will be "a community of faith and learning which develops spiritual leaders with a passion for Christ and the Bible, a love for people, and skills to minister in a rapidly changing world."[81] Hemphill said that each of the three schools was enjoying steady growth in enrollment, with over 1,700 in the School of Theology, over 1,000 in the School of Educational Ministry, and over 200 in the School of Church Music. He reminded the trustees of the record enrollment of 188 international students and made a point to emphasize the fact that Southwestern Seminary had the only Islamic studies program among SBC seminaries, which was one of two such study programs in the entire United States.

The trustees elected Margaret Lawson, associate professor of foundations of education in the School of Educational Ministries. She came with local church experience and had already been serving at Southwestern, most recently as an adjunct teacher. Her courses included Principles of Teaching, Building Church Curriculum, Adult Education, and The Teaching Ministry of the Church.

Naylor Children's Center Receives National Accreditation

The Goldia and Robert Naylor Children's Center had been accredited by the nation's oldest and largest organization of early childhood educators and received three commendations from the group. The National Association for the Education of Younger Children (NAEYC) began its accrediting program in 1985 and not only accredited the center but also gave commendations concerning the administration, food services, and facilities.

Marcia McQuitty, faculty supervisor of the center, said the accreditation was the culmination of the dream of the former children's center director Jeroline Baker as well as Hazel Morris, who laid the groundwork for this achievement. Baker, who retired in 1991 and moved to Frankfurt, Kentucky, and Hazel Morris, associate professor of childhood education, noted that the accreditation is "a wonderful witness to our community."[82]

Baker remembered Ann Bradford, who began the program, talking about a building for the children's programs as early as 1956, when Baker was a student. She said, "Health and safety, staff, physical environment, administration, and developmentally appropriate teaching need to be taken into consideration between child, teacher, staff, and parents."[83] To honor Baker's contribution to the children's program, a scholarship had been established in her name to assist students who were pursuing a childhood education degree and were teaching in the center.

Photojournalism Conference Recognizes Award-Winning Photographers

A continuing education conference attracted several award-winning photographers and photo editors to the Southwestern campus,

March 16-18, 1999. Eight photography professionals whose work had appeared in magazines such as Time and National Geographic, as well as numerous major newspapers, made presentations at the conference. The speakers included Jim Mendenhall, picture editor of the Pittsburg Post-Gazette; Tom Kennedy, director of design and photography, Washington Post, Newsweek, Interactive; Mark Sandlin, travel photographer, Southern Living; Gary Fong, director of graphics technology, San Francisco Chronicle; and Hillery Smith Garrison, staff photographer for the Fort Worth Star-Telegram.

According to Continuing Education Director David Fite, "Most of the participants work in non-Christian settings and are attracted to the conference because of the quality of the conference and the Christian atmosphere."[84] The program provided an opportunity to present the Gospel throughout and ended with a worship service on Sunday morning.

During the conference, Canon and Nikon provided free clean-and-check service for participants' photographic equipment. Photographers had an opportunity to present some of their photographs during an "open-mic" time, with two minutes to show up to 10 slides of their work. Several who presented their work were commended by the professional photojournalists.

Ministry-Based Evangelism and Spring Practicum

From Billings, Montana, to Miami, Florida, 150 students from Southwestern Seminary took the Gospel to people in all walks of life in revivals, inner-city ministries, drama teams, and music ministry presentations during spring break. The result was over 900 decisions for Christ, including 206 professions of faith during the week.

In its 40th year, the Spring Evangelism Practicum sent 86 students to lead revivals in 102 churches in 26 states and three Caribbean Islands.[85] As part of this year's practicum, 37 students from David Penley's ministry-based evangelism class and John Babler's culture and family class headed to Florida to minister in Leesburg and Miami. The classes spent time assisting in a homeless ministry and working in a clothing exchange ministry in Leesburg. Another group worked in "Touching

Miami with Love," an after-school program in Overton, a neighborhood that is considered to be one of the most dangerous in Miami. They assisted in a music therapy class for children and in a residential center for adults. Another group worked with First Baptist Leesburg, which has more than 70 ministries, including a pregnancy center and a men's rescue mission. The merger of the two seminary class groups produced a great harvest of souls during the one-week experience.

Notes
1 *Southwestern News*, March-April, 1990, p. 6.
2 Ibid.
3 *Southwestern News*, May-June, 1990, p. 7.
4 Ibid., p. 12.
5 *Southwestern News*, January-February, 1990, p. 13.
6 Trustee Minutes, March 12-13, 1990, pp. 1-5.
7 Ibid., p. 7.
8 Trustee Minutes, September- October 15-17, 1990, p. 7.
9 *Southwestern News*, February, 1990, p. 4.
10 *Southwestern News*, July-August, 1990, p. 7.
11 *Southwestern News*, September, 1990, p. 7.
12 Trustee Minutes, March 11-12, 1991, p. 11.
13 Academic Affairs Committee Minutes, October 21, 1991, p. 1.
14 Trustee Minutes, October 21-22, 1991, pp. 9-10.
15 *Southwestern News*, September-October, 1991, p. 5.
16 *Southwestern News*, January-February, 1991, p. 7.
17 *Southwestern News*, September-October, 1991, p. 10.
18 *Southwestern News*, March-April, 1992, p. 2.
19 Trustee Minuets, March 9-10, 1992, pp. 12.
20 Ibid.
21 *Southwestern News*, November-December, 1992, p. 11.
22 *Southwestern News*, January-February, 1992, p. 10.
23 Ibid.
24 Trustee Minutes, March 1993, p. 4.
25 Ibid., p. 4-5.
26 *Southwestern News*, March-April, 1993, p. 5.

27 Ibid., p. 7.
28 Ibid.
29 Ibid.
30 *Southwestern News*, July-August, 1993, p. 6.
31 *Southwestern News*, May-June, 1993, p. 7.
32 *Celebrating 100 Years*, A Special 100 Year Celebration book, Southwestern Baptist Theological Seminary, 2008, p. 102.
33 *Southwestern News*, May-June, 1994, pp. 8-9.
34 Ibid., p. 4.
35 Ibid.
36 *Southwestern News*, March-April, 1994, p. 6.
37 *Southwestern News*, September- October, 1994, p. 14.
38 *Southwestern News*, November-December, 1994, p. 8.
39 *Southwestern News*, September –October, 1994, p. 10.
40 Ibid., p. 4.
41 *Southwestern News*, Summer, 1995, p. 18.
42 Ibid., p. 19.
43 *Southwestern News*, March/April, 1995, p. 5.
44 *Southwestern News*, Summer, 1995, p. 18.
45 Ibid.
46 *Southwestern News*, March/April, 1995, p. 11, 1995.
47 Ibid.
48 *Southwestern News*, Winter, 1996, p. 10
49 *Southwestern News*, Spring 1996, pp. 10-11.
50 Ibid.
51 Ibid.
52 *Southwestern News*, Fall, 1996, p. 19.
53 Ibid.
54 Ibid.
55 Trustee Minutes, March, 1996, p. 15.
56 Trustee Minutes, October, 1996, p, 10.
57 Ibid., p. 4-5.
58 Ibid.
59 *Southwestern News*, Fall, 1996, p. 11.

60 Trustee Minutes, Academic Affairs Committee, October, 1997, p. 1.
61 Ibid.
62 *Southwestern News*, Winter, 1997, p. 6.
63 Ibid.
64 Ibid., p. 6.
65 Ibid.
66 Ibid.
67 Price, J.M., *Jesus the Teacher*, Convention Press, (Nashville), p.
68 Baptist Hymnal, *I Would Be True*, Convention Press (Nashville) 1956, p. 315.
69 *Southwestern News*, Winter, 1997, p. 12.
70 Ibid.
71 Trustee Minutes, Business Affairs Committee, March, 1997, p. 2.
72 *Southwestern News*, Winter, 1997, p. 13.
73 Ibid.
74 Ibid.
75 Personal reference by Jack D. Terry, Jr., 2016.
76 *Southwestern News*, Summer, 1998, p. 4.
77 Trustee Minutes, March, 1998, p. 9.
78 *Southwestern News*, Spring, 1998, p. 12.
79 Ibid.
80 Ibid.
81 *Southwestern News*, Summer, 1999, p. 8.
82 *Southwestern News*, Spring, 1999, p, 1.
83 Ibid.
84 Ibid.
85 *Southwestern News*, Summer, 1999, p. 12.

Photos

Page 186 – Portrait of Daryl Eldridge.

Page 188 – The Terry family at the 75th anniversary dedication of the Terry portrait, 1990.

Page 190 – Jack Terry, Jeroline Baker, and Anne Bradford at the 75th anniversary dedication of the Anne Bradford Lobby in the Naylor

Children's Center, 1990.

Page 193 – Religious education deans Daryl Eldridge, Joe Davis Heacock, and Jack Terry.

Page 218 – Religious education faculty under Dean Eldridge.

Page 240 – Daryl Eldridge with children outside the Naylor Children's Center.

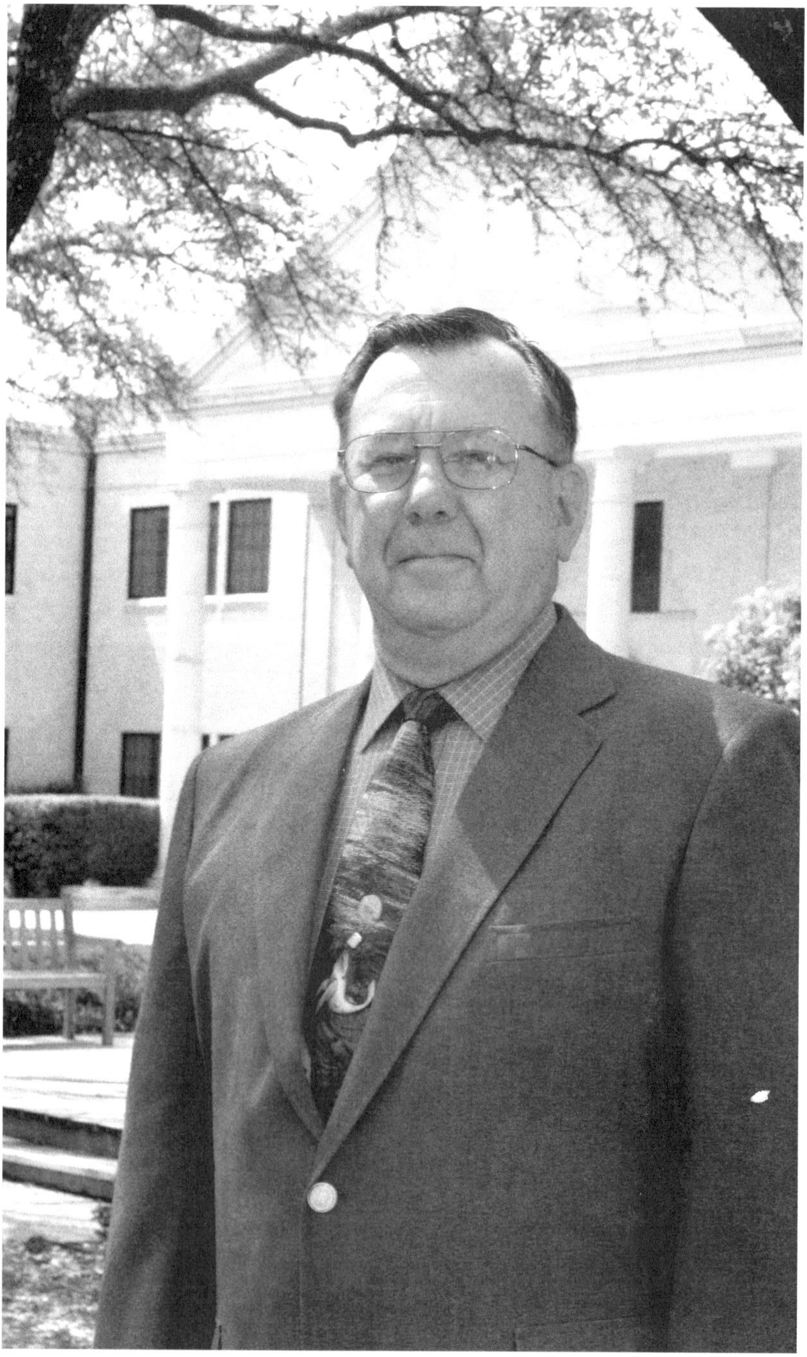

Chapter 5

The School of Educational Ministries in the 21st Century
2000-2009

The New Millennium Has Dawned

The ending of December 31, 1999, and the beginning of January 1, 2000, came on the world with less than a whimper. Prognostications and predictions covered the newspapers and television screens prior to the dawning of that day: catastrophic earthquakes, planetary chaos, interruption of satellite communication systems, tsunamis and oceanic floods, television and radio broadcasts eliminated or discontinued, the earth's ecosystem horribly interrupted and damaged, and mass confusion among all the people on the earth. Nothing of the sort happened. December 31, 1999, slipped into January 1, 2000, with little to no problem in any quarter. Life on the 1st was just as it had been on the 31st, and it continued just the same. It was a rehearsal of Shakespeare's *Macbeth*:

> Tomorrow, and tomorrow and tomorrow, creeps in this petty pace from day to day, to last syllable of recorded time and all our yesterdays have lighted fools the way to dusty death. Out, out brief candle! Life's but a walking shadow, a poor player that struts and frets his hour on the stage and then is heard no more. It is as tale told by an idiot, full of sound and fury, signifying nothing.[1]

The 20th century was but a prelude to the 21st, and as far as the School of Educational Ministries was concerned, it was just another day, given to us by God, for sharing the stimulating truths of the Kingdom of God with the most wonderful students in the entire world at Southwestern Baptist Theological Seminary.

Trustees Applaud 21st Century Committee

A report from the Theological Education in the 21st Century Committee under the leadership of chairman Daryl Eldridge was highly applauded by the trustees at the March 6-8, 2000, meeting. The committee's report highlighted major changes in the delivery system of education at Southwestern Seminary. Beginning with the fall semester of 2000, the changes were identified as:

- Implementing a new core curriculum emphasizing leadership, evangelism and missions, discipleship, and worship.
- Requiring all students to take interdisciplinary courses that address the four core areas.
- Placing all incoming students in eight-member spiritual formation groups that will meet with a faculty mentor throughout the first year.
- Changing from two- and four-hour courses to primarily three-hour courses.
- Offering courses from 7:00 a.m. until 11:00 p.m., and on Friday nights and Saturdays.
- Providing one-third of Southwestern's courses via the internet.[2]

Eldridge told the trustees that the changes would help prepare students more quickly for ministry in their chosen fields as well as improve the quality of their education. The trustees recommended that the new curriculum changes be implemented in the fall semester and that a report of improvements to the students' learning and ministry efficiency become an ongoing part of the annual academic report to the trustees.

Hemphill reported on a plan for the Houston and San Antonio extension campuses. A donor had offered property in San Antonio to accommodate the extension campus. Preliminary investigations were ongoing, with the South Texas Area planning committee to study the veracity of the gift and to determine if the property was in a location that would benefit the extension center in relation to the number of faculty members who flew to San Antonio each Monday to teach in the center. A thorough investigation gave the trustees information about the property, location, and necessary financial arrangements to make the property usable for a classroom instructional situation. Hemphill emphasized the financial needs that would accompany such a gift and that gifts were being sought in the San Antonio area.

Hemphill reminded the trustees that the Houston campus was the second off-campus plan, and there was no standalone theological seminary in the city of Houston, the largest city in Texas. The trustees endorsed a plan to turn the Houston campus into a "world-class theological institution supported by Southern Baptists of Southeastern Texas serving the unique ministry needs of that region."[3] In order for the campus to become an accredited unit of Southwestern, the following would have to take place: (1) develop a mature financial base, and (2) expand enrollment to an estimated 500 students. The plan needed to include constructing a $5 million, 30,000-square-foot building; hiring seven full-time faculty members; and developing a library for academic study and research. Estimated costs would be about $10 million, with about a $90,000 annual operating cost.

Vice President Jack Terry reported that cash gifts to the seminary exceeded $6 million for the second consecutive year. Austin business man Harold Riley gave the lead gift for the construction of the leadership center. He also initiated the Harold Riley/Southwestern Foundation. The foundation provided Southwestern an annual gift of $1 million for each of the next three years. "The gifts," Hemphill said, "will make Southwestern one of the highest-endowed seminaries in the world."[4]

Phase 1 of the Ray Riley Residence Center was dedicated on May 12, 2000. Phase 1 provided 39 residence rooms and suites available for anyone returning to the seminary to attend any of the continuing education conferences as well as other campus activities. A large piece of hanging art suspended from the ceiling welcomes everyone to the north entrance of the center. The original picture was painted by Christina Hemphill Bosch (the Hemphill's eldest daughter) and was titled "The Sower," depicting the parable of the sower in Matthew 13 and Luke 8. A large gathering lobby with an inviting seating arrangement was adjacent to the rotunda. The residence rooms in the center are as luxuriously furnished as any four-star hotel and available for any person who chooses to stay on the campus.

Enrollment was discussed with the president because of a slight decline after four straight years of 4-5 percent growth. Preliminary figures for the fall reported 3,213 students, about 90 fewer than the previous year. The School of Theology had 1,799 in the fall and 1,701 in the spring; the School of Educational Ministries had 1,060 in the fall and 985 in the spring; and the School of Church Music had 207 in the fall and 199 in the spring. Hemphill assured the trustees that plans were in place in the Office of Student Affairs to develop additional recruiters to visit prospective college and university Baptist Student Ministries and to visit on college campuses where interest in Southwestern Seminary and theological education was expressed.

During the October 16-18, 2000, meeting, the trustees elected three new faculty members in the School of Educational Ministries, and, in a last-minute surprise move, they also elected a fourth faculty member, Richard Ross from LifeWay in Nashville, Tennessee. Ross was elected as associate professor of youth education. Ross earned his M.R.E. (1974) and Ph.D. (1980) from Southwestern. He wrote or compiled 20 books on youth ministry, many of which are used as classroom texts in Southern Baptist universities and colleges. His most notable book, *True Love Waits*, was a program that encouraged young people to live a holy life, keep themselves pure, abstain from sexual immorality, and wait until marriage to give themselves to someone in an intimate encounter. Henry Webb, director of LifeWay's pastor-staff leadership department, said, "It is difficult to measure the tremendous impact Richard has made on the Kingdom during his 16 years at LifeWay."[5] *True Love Waits* was embraced by 100 denominations and national student organizations in the U.S. and in over 100 foreign countries.

William Michael McGuire was elected as associate professor of psychology and counseling. He previously served as an instructor/intern at Dallas Theological Seminary and adjunct professor at Criswell College and Dallas Baptist University. Dana Abernathy Wicker was elected assistant professor of psychology and counseling. She had previously served at Southwestern for two years as guest professor of psychology and counseling.

Esther Diaz-Bolet was the first Cuban-American elected to the faculty as assistant professor of administration. Her past experience included serving as corporate services instructor at Tarrant County Junior College and minister of adult education at the Templo Batista Emanuel Church, Fort Worth, Texas.

National Ministries Journal on the Internet

The School of Educational Ministries initiated a new journal for ministers of education, which represented a new breed of production delivery. The journal, "Equipping U," debuted in December 2000 on the seminary's website.[6] This electronic publication was directed primarily to educational ministers and featured articles from faculty, educational practitioners, and students.

The journal took advantage of the benefit of the internet to disseminate information in a timely fashion and in a non-print format that allowed the reader to interact with faculty, students, and other website visitors. Eldridge, dean of the School of Educational Ministries and managing editor of Equipping U, said, "There was a desire to see the wonderful experience on campus made available to a wider audience."[7]

The first issue's featured article was "Twenty-first Century Roles of the Senior Adult Minister" by Jim Walter, associate professor of adult education. The issue also included an abstract of a dissertation by James Michael Peters on juvenile delinquency among drug abusers, as well as a discussion on how churches decide on Bible study curriculum.

An educational ministries faculty member edited one issue of the magazine per year. The journal had an editorial board that served as a clearing house for topics, developed guidelines for submission of articles, and promoted the journal through the seminary's communications office.

Center for Christian Communication Invites Award-Winning Producer

The Center for Christian Communications, in conjunction with the Radio and Television Commission of the Southern Baptist Convention, invited Phil Cooke, an award-winning film, television, and video producer, to the campus, April 12, 2000. Cooke lectured at three seminars and spoke in chapel while on campus. His chapel address emphasized the fact that Christian television is too often marked by poor writing, poor acting, and poor producing. He said, "To communicate more effectively, Christians need to understand the audience and know what makes people tick by doing what Jesus did in showing up where people were, be it at parties, the temple square, or the marketplace."[8]

Cook said Christian communicators need to:
- Understand that the current generation retains 70 to 80 percent more information obtained through their eyes than through their ears.
- Understand the medium and how to best utilize it.
- Know society's traditions and beliefs through books, movies, and music, just as Paul was familiar with Greek literature and poetry.
- Use simple words to articulate an everyday language instead of church lingo that people outside the church do not understand.
- Use storytelling as the primary mode of communication in preaching and programming; learn to tell stories that will change people's lives.
- Expand their vision of Christian programming.
- Understand that Christian television is not a televised church service, just as a light bulb is not a candle plugged into a wall socket, nor is a television simply a radio with pictures.

Grappling with Youth Issues, 32nd Youth Lab

The theme for the 32nd annual Youth Lab, April 6-8, was "The Ultimate Wrestling Challenge" and addressed the battles that all youth ministers face. The lab was based on Ephesians 6:12 and reminded attendees that the youth minister's encounter was not against flesh and blood but against the powers of darkness the youth will encounter. Working with the theme, the conference featured exhibit matches by wrestlers from the Christian Wrestling Federation of Dallas. Included in the conference this year was a "Youth Track," a workshop for teenagers who desired to be more involved in their youth groups.

Gregg Matte of Breakaway Ministries in College Station, Texas, was the keynote speaker and told 303 youth ministers and teenagers,

> Teamwork is the key strategy youth ministers should use to fight the spiritual battles against the problems facing their youth. Youth ministers need to build a team of staff workers and students who have the same ministry vision and work toward a common goal. The biblical teams—such as David and his mighty men, Jesus and His disciples, and Paul and his associates—gave clear indication that there were not a lot of Lone Rangers in the Bible.[9]

Photojournalists Capturing the "'Light' - Life in Christ"

The annual Southwestern Photojournalism Conference, March 24-26, 2000, identified the kind of ministry that can be experienced when pictures are shaped by the light of Jesus Christ. Over 180 photojournalists from across the nation and as far away as Sweden and Germany participated in the conference, which encouraged them in their walks with Christ and in their chosen profession of photography. A keynote spokesman, Denise McGill, formerly with a Missouri newspaper and now a photojournalist missionary with the International Mission Board, said,

> For me, photography and my walk with God go really closely together. I was working harder to get my name on the front page than I was to show my city what God wanted them to see that day. I was so scared of my boss that I forgot that Jesus is the light of the world. Now, God is using me to shoot the movement of the work and ministry of Jesus Christ around the world.[10]

Other photojournalists included Dennis Fahringer, director of the photo school at the University of the Nations in Kona, Hawaii; Patrick Murphy-Racey, whose photo credits included Sports Illustrated and

ESPN magazine; and Jimi Lott, a photojournalist with the Seattle Times. Lott gave his testimony of a life of drug abuse and told how his life in Christ had helped him rise above his former life. Lott said, "Truth has been the battery power that my soul has run on."[11]

Trustees Approve $58 Million Master Plan (2001)

The trustees approved a $58 million master plan during their semi-annual meeting, October 17-19, 2001. The plan was presented at an earlier meeting in April, with approval sought at the meeting in October. The plan was a 10-year facilities master plan. Hemphill said, "It is not only far-reaching, it is also good stewardship."[12] The master plan called for:

- An elevated water storage tank on campus at a cost of about $2 million
- $14 million for new student housing
- $479,360 for a 6-foot-high steel, decorative picket fence to enclose the campus
- $18 million for the next three phases of the Ralph M. Smith Leadership Development complex
- $15 million to renovate five buildings on the campus
- $830,000 to improve handicap accessibility
- $3.77 million for new faculty/staff on-campus housing
- A building for an Institute for Biblical Research and classroom building[13]

The trustees also elected five faculty members in the School of Theology and granted faculty status to the new registrar and director of enrollment services, Douglas Jones. In addition, Bob Overton was given faculty status as the new director of the Houston campus.

Vice President Hubert Martin announced that Southwestern remained one of the highest endowed seminaries in the world. The value of the seminary's endowment had increased to $209 million, a substantial increase over its value five years ago.[14] Jack Terry, vice president for Institutional Advancement, told the trustees the seminary was having another strong year—giving was over $1 million ahead of last year's pace. He continued,

This has occurred in an atmosphere that has not been conducive to fundraising. For the third year in a row, cash gifts to the seminary exceeded $6 million in the fiscal year ending July 31, 2001. More than $34 million was raised on the first phase of Southwestern's "Touch the World, Impact Eternity" campaign. With the success of phase one and the completion of the facilities master plan, the campaign's overall goal has been raised to $125 million.[15]

The trustees received the 2001 fall and spring enrollment figures. The total enrollment on campus for the spring 2001 was 2,882, and the fall was 2,943—about a 3 percent decline in enrollment from the 2000 enrollment figures. The School of Theology in the spring of 2001 had 1,702 and in the fall, 1,788; the School of Educational Ministries in the spring had 1,000 and in the fall, 991; and the School of Church Music in the spring had 180 and in the fall, 164.

The new Doctor of Educational Ministries degree began with a kick-off in August 2001, with 47 students enrolled, one coming from as far as Japan. The degree was developed with specialty seminars, workshops, professional development, directed studies, project preparation, and a professional ministry project at the conclusion of students' course of study. The degree began officially on August 29, 2001.

Bill Caldwell, professor of administration and associate dean of the new program, was pleased with the initial number of students present. Caldwell said, "It's been real smooth. We had a lot of things to do this summer getting things into the registrar's office, but everything has started off great."[16]

Seminars were offered in a one-week format on the Fort Worth campus, and students in the Fort Worth area attended once-a-week or weekend study seminars. The seminary planned to offer more seminars in areas where several groups of students live as well as during leadership conferences and professional meetings attended by the enrollees.

The degree was intended for people in educational ministry positions who would have a difficult time coming to the campus for a regular semester of studies. The program was developed to keep alumni up-to-date on how the field of educational ministry was constantly changing. This was developed as a continuing education degree, but at the same time, it provided professional development as a plus to the practicing minister who enrolled.

Two Major Retirements

Hazel Morris had spent the last 30 years of her life teaching seminary students the correct way to educate children during their childhood years. Morris retired at the end of the summer as associate professor of childhood education. Born in Grey Hawk, Kentucky, poverty was prevalent in Morris' life, and she never gave a thought to attending college. Her uncle encouraged her to go to college, and even though she considered it could never happen, she found herself enrolled in Eastern Kentucky State College, where she completed her undergraduate degree in education in 1961. She said of her education, "We were poor, and I didn't really consider that a possibility because women didn't have many opportunities to go to college. Those who did became nurses or school teachers. So, I chose teaching, or it chose me because I had been teaching children in my church since I was 12 years of age."[17]

After college, Morris became a teacher and taught for five years at Mark Twain Elementary School in Miamisburg, Ohio. It was during that time that she began to feel God moving in her heart in a call to Christian ministry. At a camp one summer where she served as a counselor, she met a student from Southwestern who told her about her experiences at the seminary. Although Morris originally decided to attend Southern Seminary in Louisville, Kentucky, she met some Southwestern graduates at Ridgecrest Conference Center, and that meeting changed her mind. They told her about two wonderful children's work professors at Southwestern, Ann Bradford and Jeroline Baker (who was also from Kentucky), and that set the stage for her seminary education.

Morris completed her M.R.E. degree in two years and became the children's director at the First Baptist Church, Jackson, Mississippi, where she ministered for three years. Dean Joe Davis Heacock called her to ask if she would join the childhood faculty at Southwestern. She came to the seminary in the fall of 1971 and was a faithful teacher of childhood education for the next 30 years.

At her retirement dinner, Morris said, "I love teaching, and I love the subject that I teach, because I love children. Probably the best part for me, though, has been the students—childhood education majors who are serving around the convention today and some of them around the world."[18]

Lawrence Klempnauer, vice president for student services since 1980, retired at the end of 2000. Klempnauer, from Kansas City, Kansas, earned a B.A. degree in political science from the University of Kansas in 1955. He spent two years in the U.S. Army and was honorably discharged in 1957. He became a business man in Midland, Texas, and worked as a motel owner/operator.

In 1961, as a new student at Southwestern Seminary, he became minister of education at Sagamore Hill Baptist Church, Fort Worth. He completed his M.R.E. degree in 1964 and was called to Second Ponce De Leon Baptist Church, Atlanta, Georgia, from 1970 to 1977. He served as minister of education at Travis Avenue Baptist Church, Fort Worth, Texas, from 1977-1980.

After Russell Dilday, Klempnauer's pastor in Atlanta, became president at Southwestern Seminary, Klempnauer was brought to the seminary as director of church minister relations to develop a placement office called the Office of Minister Relations. The task was to work with students, graduating students, and former students searching for a ministry position. The office became a central point at Southwestern and served over 44,000 Southern Baptist churches as they became interested in employing Southwestern Seminary graduates. While on staff at Travis Avenue Baptist Church, Klempnauer served as adjunct instructor of administration in the School of Religious Education.

In addition to serving churches and the seminary, Klempnauer stayed busy writing for Baptist publications. His articles appeared in such periodicals as Adult Leadership, Church Training Magazine, and Outreach Magazine. In retirement, Klempnauer began working as the executive director of the Association of Christian Education. He continued his work with the Fort Worth Better Business Bureau, where he had served as one of the board of directors since 1995 and as chairman of the board of directors from 1998 to 2000.[19]

"Taking It To the Extreme" – Youth Lab 2001

With the advent of X-games, XFL, and extreme everything everywhere, youth ministers faced an unusual challenge in their ministry to teenagers. The wonderful caveat was that these same youth ministers had the unique privilege of developing a new generation of youth who have and demonstrate an extreme faith. Youth commitment in this present arena was unusually extreme, and ministers of youth needed to comprehend how to handle leading these youth to heights of extreme ministry. In another venue, this day and time called for youth ministers who used extreme measures to reach and disciple these teenagers.

The annual youth conference was held on April 5-7, 2001, and featured Gregg Matte of Breakaway Ministries. Other outstanding youth leaders included Richard Ross, author of *True Love Waits* and professor of youth/student ministries at Southwestern seminary; Johnny Derouen, youth minister at Travis Avenue Baptist Church; and Phil Newberry, youth minister at Bellevue Baptist Church, Memphis, Tennessee.

This spring lab offered youth ministers and volunteer youth leaders an opportunity to meet the challenge of reaching and producing Christians who have extreme faith. Jon Brooks, youth minister at First Baptist, Euless, Texas, said, "Christian teenagers need to be challenged. If we develop in our students a real ministry mindset, one in which they look outward not just inward, one that they look upward and not just outward, we're going to take them further in their walk with Christ than they ever will be. Jesus' model was not to serve Himself but to serve others. I think our students are ready for that challenge."[20]

For a second year, the lab offered a youth track especially for young people who were or wanted to become youth leaders. The lab gave practical help and resources to youth ministers, youth interns, volunteer youth workers, and teenagers. The whole idea was to take youth ministry a step further into extreme youth ministry and not ministry as usual.

Grand Opening of the Jack MacGorman Conference Center

The Jack MacGorman Conference Center, the continuing education building of the Ralph M. Smith Leadership Development Center, had its grand opening on September 10, 2001. The afternoon celebration featured Jack and Ruth MacGorman, Ralph M. Smith, Harold Riley, and President Hemphill dedicating the second phase of the center.

Phase 2 has a large gathering lobby just outside the James Leo Garrett Conference Room that can accommodate the guests who come for continuing education conferences. The lobby also has several comfortable seating areas with couches, chairs, and side tables. There are two large conference rooms that can accommodate 300 conferees at tables in the large one on the first floor and 150 conferees at tables in the smaller conference room on the second floor. Adjacent to the large conference room on the first floor are four breakout rooms that can be formed by moving sliding partitions to the left and the right of the larger room. There are four smaller, standalone conference rooms immediately down the outer hall or on either side of the larger room.

Upstairs, adjacent to the smaller conference room were several breakout rooms that can accommodate 25 to 50 people. All of the conference rooms can be used for a single conference or as breakout rooms for the larger conference rooms. The Jack MacGorman Conference Center is available for all seminary continuing education programs, conferences, and workshops as well as being made available to a larger context such as the city of Fort Worth and surrounding area for conferences, institutes, and workshops for business and professional meetings.

Perhaps the most spectacular feature in Phase 2 of the leadership development center was the large suspended art piece in the south entry rotunda. The artist, as in the lobby of Phase 1, was Christina Hemphill Bosch, Hemphill's eldest daughter. The suspended art piece depicts "The Heavenly Realm" (Revelation 5:6-13), a picture of the magnificent glories of the eternal throne of Almighty God. Magnificent glass colors of red, yellow, lime, green, orange, turquoise, magenta, scarlet light blue, royal blue, lavender, and deep purple adorn the art piece, all moving toward a hot yellow-white center representing the crown room of eternal God.

It is breathtaking to stand under the suspended art piece and look into all the various colors as they move symmetrically toward the apex, the hot yellow and whites. It is a visual buffet to stand under either of the two suspended art pieces (The Sower in the north rotunda and The Heavenly Realm in the south rotunda) and recall the Scripture passages as your eyes wander over the majestic shapes of the glass pieces and the accompanying colors that steal your eyes and move them to the apex of each art piece.

The Tragic Next Day

The celebration of the opening of the Jack MacGorman Continuing Education Conference Center was a defining moment in the hearts of the planners for continuing education on the Southwestern campus. However, the next morning, Tuesday, September 11, 2001, terrorists attacked the World Trade Center in New York as well as the Pentagon, with a fourth aircraft destined for the White House. The first aircraft struck the north tower of the World Trade Center at 8:46 a.m., with the second aircraft striking the south tower at 9:03 a.m. A third plane struck the Pentagon at 9:37 a.m., breaching to the third ring and causing extensive damage over five rings of the building. A fourth plane took off at 8:47 a.m. with the expectation of striking the White House, but because of some brave Americans on board who fought with the terrorists, the plane crashed at Stony Creek Township near Shanksville, Pennsylvania, at 10:30 a.m. A total of 3,039 died in the Trade Centers and 125 in the Pentagon.

Seminary Celebrates 202nd Commencement

Two months following the September 11 attacks, the first degree in Islamic studies was awarded by Southwestern Seminary at the December 15, 2001, commencement to Gregory Self, who enrolled in the program after it was approved earlier that year. Professor Samuel Shahid, who directed the Islamic studies program at Southwestern, also directs the evangelistic organization Good News for the Crescent World and worked closely with Self, who currently worships with an Arab Christian congregation in the Dallas-Fort Worth area.

Shahid said, "The outlook for the Islamic studies program is positive. Many church planters and missionaries serving in the Middle East are coming to Southwestern to gain a better understanding of Islam, and 20 more students are enrolled in the program with many more needed."[21] Along with the first Islamic studies degree, the School of Theology graduated 146; the School of Educational Ministries, 134; and the School of Church Music, 20.

Trustees Busy in April 2002 Meeting

The trustees elected eight faculty members, including two women to the theology and educational ministries faculties. Hemphill said, "Southwestern may have the greatest faculty in our history. These new faculty appointments only add to the diversity and quality of our faculty. There is really no comparable faculty anywhere in the nation."[22]

The trustees had their first semi-annual meeting in the newly dedicated Jack MacGorman Leadership Development Center in the Ralph M. Smith Leadership Development Complex. Hemphill reported to the trustees that he was proud to recite a list of completed activities on the campus:

> The B.H. Carroll apartments have been renovated, the Naylor Student Center with Wild Bill's Café, the new Paul Moore television lounge (named in honor of Paula Hemphill's father), and just adjacent to it the new Miller Prayer Room with the beautiful stained glass window of praying hands below the throne of God and also the renovated prayer garden behind the Naylor Student Center. The newly dedicated Ralph M. Smith Development Complex, where we are meeting for this trustee meeting, is a topic of great interest for continuing education alumni and others who will use the facility for leadership workshops, institutes and continuing education courses.[23]

Several major reports were given to the trustees during the meeting. Hubert Martin, vice president for business affairs, reported that "for the first time our salaries are the top among sister seminaries. All of this has come over the last four years."[24] Jack Terry, vice president for Institutional Advancement, said, "Charitable giving rose 40 percent in the past year while most secular charities suffered declines after September 11. The gifts that we have received are a reflection on our president. People do not give money to leaders that they don't trust."[25]

Elected to the educational ministries faculty was Teresa (Terri) Hill Stovall as assistant professor of adult education and aging. Stovall completed her M.A.R.E. (1991), M.Div. (2012), and Ph.D. (2001) at Southwestern. She co-authored *Women Leading Women* and was a contributing author to *The Teaching Ministry of the Church* and *The Christian Homemaker's Handbook*. Stovall was and continues to be active in training women ministry leaders in the local church; she leads women's ministry training workshops at the state and denominational level; and she speaks at women's conferences.

The trustees were given information about a student enrollment decline even though there was an increased enrollment of international students. The international student enrollment increased from 138 to 250 in recent years, and was one way globalization of Southwestern was expressed in the student body. The enrollment of 3,004 in the spring of 2001 declined to 2,839 in the spring of 2002. Nevertheless, Hemphill expressed optimism to the trustees and told them, "Southwestern is strong because few other institutions blend the practical and theological the way Southwestern does. The seminary is particularly strong in the area of missions. We want theologians, church musicians, and Christian educators who have a heart for missions."[26]

Olympic Torch on Seminary Hill

A runner passed the Olympic flame to Cameron Smith in front of the B.H. Carroll Memorial Building on Seminary Hill, December 12, 2001, on the way to the XIX Winter Olympic games. The carrying of the Olympic flame, a famous activity leading up to the Winter Olympic Games in Salt Lake City on February 8-24, 2002, came up Seminary Drive on its way to Utah shortly after 9 a.m.

Smith, a graphic designer for the Salt Lake City organizing committee for the Olympic Winter Games and a Fort Worth native, came back to town to carry the torch. A small but enthusiastic crowd of seminary staff and students greeted the Olympic torch runner and cheered as the flame was passed to Cameron Smith for the continuation of the run.[27]

The location of the occasion of the passing of the flame was in the front of Southwestern Baptist Theological Seminary, on Seminary Drive, where the flame of the Gospel of Christ had passed from generation to generation of students who became pastors, missionaries, educators, and church musicians. These students, in turn, passed the "flame of the Gospel of the Lord Jesus Christ" from person to person all over the known world. It was a thrilling symbolic day for Southwestern Seminary to celebrate its heritage of passing the flame.

"Fire Fall" Isaiah 64:1

God can use today's youth to bring revival to this nation and the world—the emphasis of the 34th Youth Ministry Lab, April 5-6, 2002. The keynote speaker, J.R. Vassar, encouraged the youth leaders present to understand that God's movement may not be what they expect. He said, "It is not always sensational, but it is significant. Don't overlook the significant because you are just looking for the sensational. Every individual is important, and it is necessary for each youth leader to be in a serious relationship with God and leading youth to that serious relationship as well. Every message should come from God, and don't speak for Him until you've heard from Him."[28]

The theme for the youth lab was "Fire Fall" from Isaiah 64:1—"Oh, that You would rend the heavens and come down, that the mountains might quake at Your presence." The focus was to call out this generation of youth to revival.

Richard Ross and Wes Black, professors of youth/student ministry at Southwestern, told the teenagers attending that throughout history God had started major revivals through teenagers. Ross challenged the attendees to "raise their spiritual sails by keeping a daily appointment with God and memorizing Scripture. One must be in an intimate relationship with God in order to hear and follow His call. Revival requires that God's people obey Him instantly and completely. We believe that God is up to something huge with you, and we want you to catch what God intends to do through you."[29]

Although Ross and Black served as advisors for the Youth Lab, the entire program was student-born and student-led. Subjects for the breakout conferences covered a wide range of spiritual activities, from evangelism to discipleship to personal purity. Individual sessions were led by a number of practicing youth ministers, professors, and representatives from Southern Baptist Agencies such as LifeWay Christian Resources, the North American Mission Board, and any number of student discipleship ministries.

Youth Lab 2002 had 640 registered youth ministers and leaders, with 160 youth participating. The emphasis was to inspire, encourage, stretch, and expand the teenagers' walk with God through Bible study, personal prayer time, and witnessing to other youth in all settings where youth gathered.

President Hemphill Resigns, April 8, 2003

Kenneth Hemphill was elected as the seventh president on July 28, 1994, and was a healing agent with the trustees, faculty, students, donors, the Fort Worth community, and beyond. Due to the trauma that preceded Hemphill's administration, there was a need for a great deal of "the balm of Gilead" to be applied to the larger constituency that demanded some kind of normalcy to a bruised campus, faculty, and student body. Hemphill filled that need and brought with him the aura of peace and consolation so desperately needed.

On July 28, 1994, the trustees unanimously elected Hemphill as the seventh president of Southwestern Seminary, and he was inaugurated on May 1, 1995. Hemphill's focus from the beginning was on student and faculty needs. He encouraged staff and faculty to be sensitive to the needs of students, but more than that, he put action with his words. During his administration, he majored on student housing, renovating both the J. Howard Williams Student Village and the B.H. Carroll apartments. He led the seminary to move a "beloved faculty parking lot" behind the B.H. Carroll Memorial Building and the Naylor Student

Center to create a Prayer Plaza that included a small waterfall trickling down a stream under a foot bridge into a large Koi Fish pond.

In the Prayer Plaza are several bronze pieces of art by created by Max Griener, Jr. (Jesus the fisherman, Jesus washing Peter's feet, and a large globe representing the Great Commission and the theme of the seminary, "As Ye Go, Preach!"), all emphasizing President Hemphill's chosen slogan for the seminary during his administration, "Touch the World, Impact Eternity." In the middle of the prayer garden is a large gazebo, and on two sides of the grassy area and gazebo are several prayer benches for students to sit, converse, and pray for their needs and the needs of the world.

The prayer garden was to encourage students and the community who walk by the seminary to stop, rest, pray, and be refreshed in the vine-covered bench areas. Along the sidewalk perimeter of the campus, decorative light poles lined the walks with Scripture passages on bronze plaques placed on granite stone sharing the biblical plan of salvation in both English and Spanish. Many of the people who walk the perimeter of the campus are of Spanish descent. The Scripture Walk stemmed from Hemphill's earnest desire that people walking the campus would be presented the Gospel and would find an opportunity to trust Christ as personal Savior.

Hemphill recommended several programs that would assist the institution academically and financially. Working with Jack Terry, vice president for Institutional Advancement, he initiated a $100 million fundraising campaign that raised over $125 million by the end of his administration. Academically, he led the School of Church Music to develop a Ph.D. in church music, the first of its kind to be offered at any Southern Baptist seminary.

During his last year as president, Hemphill was the impetus that directed the seminary to show its support for the Baptist Faith and Message 2000. He initiated a beautiful archival volume that has all the names of all elected faculty members from 1908 to 2000. Beginning in 2000, all new faculty members signed their names in this archival volume to show their agreement with this Baptist confessional. Each faculty member sits in B.H. Carroll's office chair at his desk as his/her name is entered into the historic volume. Hemphill said, "I am reminded of Dr. Carroll's deathbed request that we keep the seminary lashed to the cross."[30] The 1963 Baptist Faith and Message confessional was the version that the seminary held to prior to the 2000 confessional.

April 8, 2003, was a somber day as Hemphill announced his resignation as president, nine years after he had committed himself to the direction of the institution in 1994. His announcement was made to the student body during a chapel service in Truett Auditorium and to the board of trustees that afternoon.[31] He told the student body that he felt called to take on a new challenge serving as the national strategist for the SBC's Empowering Kingdom Growth initiative that began in August 2003.

As part of their business agenda, the trustees made a motion to establish a presidential search committee to begin the search for the replacement of President Hemphill. Trustees appointed Denny Autrey to chair the committee.[32]

At the same trustee meeting, April 7-9, 2003, the trustees continued to do the business of the seminary by electing Elias Moitinho as assistant professor of psychology and counseling in the School of Educational Ministries. He was one of four faculty members elected (one in the School of Educational Ministries and three in the School of Theology). Moitinho was born in Sao Paulo, Brazil. He graduated from the South Brazil Baptist Theological Seminary in 1988, and then from Southwestern Seminary with his master's in religious education and marriage and family counseling in 1995 and his Ph.D. in 2000. He came with church experience in both Brazil and Texas.

Eldridge Resigns Deanship

Daryl Eldridge, dean of the School of Educational Ministries, resigned effective July 25, 2003. Eldridge, who had been a professor since 1984 and dean since 1996, was leaving Southwestern to pursue the establishment of an international university with its home base in Springfield, Missouri, Eldridge's hometown. Eldridge now provides presidential leadership for Rockbridge Seminary, which offers an educational opportunity for church ministers via the internet. Eldridge was looking for an educational opportunity to participate in the development of the church and considers this to be the endeavor of a lifetime. He expressed appreciation that he had been privileged to be a part of Southwestern Seminary for 19 years and said the School of Educational Ministry "is the finest Christian education school in the world."[33]

Outstanding Achievements by Educational Ministry Faculty

Margaret (Mops) Lawson, a native of Rhodesia (now Zimbabwe), became a U.S. citizen after living 19 years in this country. She took her oath of citizenship and was congratulated by the faculty of the School of Educational Ministries on November 14, 2002. Dean Eldridge said, "You've been a part of our hearts for a long time, and we are delighted you are part of our country. This has been a long journey, and the process has taken many years and now we are overjoyed that it has come to this conclusion."[34]

Lawson was serving in educational ministry as coordinator for Christian education with the Baptist Union of South Africa when she decided to come to Southwestern Seminary to study. Budd Smith, professor of foundations of education, said, "When Mops came to us as a student, several of us realized that God had given us a unique gift. We encouraged her to enter the doctoral program, recognizing that God was going to do something special with her life."[35] She earned the Master of Arts in Religious Education in 1986 and the Ph.D. in 1994. Lawson was elected as a faculty member in 1999 after serving as director of the curriculum lab in the School of Educational Ministries and teaching adjunctively in the foundations of education division. One of her fondest dreams was to travel back to her native Zimbabwe, which her new U.S. passport would allow her to do.

Wesley Black, professor of youth/student education, was elected president of the Association of Youth Ministry Educators (AYME). AYME is a professional organization for professors who teach youth ministry in colleges, universities, and seminaries. Black served as the president of the organization as it celebrated its 10th anniversary in 2003. Approximately 100 professors of youth and student ministry are currently involved in the membership. Black said,

Like most organizations, AYME is designed for networking and developing the professional. Our annual convention meets every year for three days. We have speakers who speak on some facet of adolescence research with teenagers and different elements of Christian ministry. We have breakout conferences of sharing research that most members have been doing either in their schools with their students or on their own. This is one of the few organizations in the country designed for professionals who teach youth ministry.[36]

Southern Baptists have a number of conferences, institutes, and workshops annually at the state and associational level specifically for teenagers, lay youth workers, or church staff youth workers (i.e., Southwestern's Youth Lab), but very few were designed for the teaching of youth professionals. AYME would be of interest to any student studying youth/student ministry who may feel God is calling him to teach youth/student ministry at a college, university, or seminary level in the future. Some doctoral candidates from Southwestern Seminary and other Southern Baptist seminaries are members of AYME with the hope of teaching youth/student ministry at a college or seminary.

Black had recently established a new internet site called "Student Leadership Training Network" for those interested in going further in the study of youth/student ministry. The site is a live, interactive leadership training site for adults who work with youth and can be used as a tool to gain more insights into that ministry.

Black and Richard Ross, professor of youth/student ministry at Southwestern Seminary, led a discovery study group to the Baptist World Alliance (BWA) World Youth Congress in Hong Kong, July 13-16, 2003. The study group members functioned as a small group of study leaders at the BWA World Youth Congress and in many other ways. The group was composed of students, youth ministers, youth/student professors, and denominational employees whose task is shaping the Southern Baptist youth/student ministry. External to participating in the BWA World Youth Congress, the group spent five days around

Beijing visiting the Great Wall, Ming Tombs, and the Forbidden City. As a part of the trip, the group members spent quality time with career missionaries and indigenous leaders and learned how God is marshaling Chinese students to become a mighty force for His Kingdom.

Esther Diaz-Bolet, assistant professor of administration in the School of Educational Ministries, was elected president of the *Asociacion para la Educacion Theologica Hispana* (AETH) at its meeting in Austin, Texas, in August 2003. AETH is an organization devoted to the advancement of theological education among Hispanic Americans in the United States, Puerto Rico, and Canada. The organization was founded in 1991 and has over 800 members with affiliation in over 60 theological institutions.

Serving with Diaz-Bolet on the executive council was a well-known Hispanic Christian writer, Justo Gonzalez. Gonzalez would be familiar to many seminary students as the author of *The Story of Christianity (2 vols.)* and *A History of Christian Thought (3 vols.)*. Gonzales said, "I am certain Dr. Bolet's selection [as president] will be a great benefit to AETH. I also hope that it will be a benefit to Southwestern in making a wealth of wisdom in the Latino community more available to the school."[37]

Gonzalez was the first president of AETH. Every summer, the organization administers a fully accredited, two-week conference for students to meet with top Hispanic educators for intensive study.

Two-Week Childhood Education Certification for Lay Workers

A new program developed by Marcia McQuitty, associate professor of childhood education, provided training for laypeople serving in church leadership positions in weekday, preschool, and children's ministry programs in the local church; this program was being explored by using the Leadership Development Center as the classroom for this continuing education experiment.[38] McQuitty said, "In Texas and related conventions, a shortage of seminary-trained ministers exists in the field of childhood education. Pastors and ministers of education, when unable to find a seminary-trained person to fill a need, will turn to laypersons in the congregation asking for their help."[39] Many of these people cannot take time off to attend a seminary but are still in need of training. In order to help counteract that problem, Southwestern Seminary offers a certification course on weekends once a month to meet the needs of these untrained lay leaders. The weekend course allows the attendees to receive training plus an academic credential in their specific area of ministry.

McQuitty said, "Sixteen different certificate courses will be offered over a two-year period at the seminary. Participants may select the courses in which they are interested and which meet their ministry needs."[40] At the conclusion of 12 courses, each participant received a certificate in weekday/childhood education from Southwestern Seminary. Should the layperson decide to enroll in the seminary and take courses in childhood education, then the 12 seminary credit hours would be counted toward the completion of a Master of Arts in Christian Education. Many of these lay leaders have other professions and are desirous of learning more about the education of children and may choose the weekend childhood education certification study program as an addition to their childhood education task in the local church.

2003 Youth Lab "A Call to Consecration, Joshua 3:5"

Truett Auditorium was decorated to resemble the Jewish temple in Jerusalem, and the *Shofar* was used to call the 775 attendees to "Consecrate themselves to the Lord" as they worshiped during the opening session of the 35th annual Youth Ministry Lab based on Joshua 3:5—"Consecrate yourselves, for tomorrow the Lord will do wonders among you." The *Shofar* (a ram's horn), the instrument that called the people of God to come worship in Solomon's temple in Jerusalem, called the participants together to worship and became the central theme around which the 35th Youth Lab was organized.

The Company, Southwestern's drama team, brought life to the consecration theme as they reenacted a scene from the book of Joshua where the children of Israel prepared to move into the Promised Land. Additional contemporary scenes were acted out, emphasizing personal sins so common to youth and their ministers.

Matt Chandler called attention to the might and majesty of God as written in Isaiah 6. His message emphasized the unrest and uncertainty of the world in which we live such as the war in Iraq and the SARS virus in Southeast Asia. Chandler said he saw "a lack of confidence in the might and sovereignty of God. God's glory will be fully displayed in the future, and worship will no longer be optional. God will force knees to bow. He will show Himself, and that will be enough."[41]

Forty-four speakers addressed 82 topics during the Youth Lab. James Darby, pastor of the First Baptist Church, Blue Springs, Mississippi, asked this challenging question, "How many of us are really here to see God? If God gets all over you this weekend, can you handle it?"[42]

The Youth Lab had grown expeditiously in the last four years. The attendance in 2000 was 350 youth ministers, volunteer youth workers, and youth. In 2001, the attendance was 425; in 2002, 630; and in 2003, 775. Ross and Black hoped for 1,000 in attendance at the 2004 Youth Lab next spring.

Called Meeting of the Trustees

A called meeting of the board of trustees of Southwestern Seminary was held on the seminary campus in Fort Worth on June 24, 2003. Chairman David Allen called the meeting to order. Allen called on presidential search committee chairman Denny Autrey to present a recommendation from that committee. Autrey presented the following recommendation:

> After diligent prayer and a careful search for God's man to lead Southwestern Baptist Theological Seminary, the Presidential Search Committee unanimously recommend to the board of trustees that Dr. L. Paige Patterson be elected as the eighth president effective August 1, 2003.

Chairman Allen called on Secretary of the Board R.E. Smith to take a roll call vote with the trustees present to vote "yes" or "no" when their respective names were called. Secretary Smith reported that the vote was unanimous for the 33 trustees present. Allen then announced that Leighton Paige Patterson had been elected by unanimous vote of the board of trustees to become the eighth president of Southwestern Seminary.[43] Dr. Patterson responded to the board:

> Mr. Chairman and trustees, it is, of course, a signal honor for anyone to be chosen to a position like this. I come to the position with a keen sense of what is expected and a keen awareness of the fact that no one, least of all I, have the ability to do what must be done except for the intervention of God. I had already made my mind up as I had told Dr. Autrey that if called I would accept. So Dorothy and I are happy today to accept the opportunity to serve with you here.[44]

Allen called on presidential search committee and Chairman Autrey to present a second recommendation: "Upon the election of Dr. Patterson, the committee recommends that Dr. Dorothy Patterson be elected to the status of full professor without pay, but to include faculty benefits effective August 1, 2003."[45] The motion carried unanimously. The meeting adjourned immediately and was followed by a press conference.

Paige Patterson, Eighth President of Southwestern Seminary

Leighton Paige Patterson was born to Thomas Armour and Roberta Patterson on October 10, 1942, in Fort Worth, Texas, where the elder Patterson was completing his doctoral degree under the direction of the renowned professor of theology W.T. Conner. After graduation, T.A. Patterson moved his family to Beaumont, Texas, where he became pastor of the First Baptist Church. Paige Patterson made a profession of his faith in Christ as Savior during a revival meeting at First Baptist Church, Beaumont, Texas, sobbing his way to Christ as he fell into his father's waiting arms and was ushered into his Heavenly Father's redemptive grace in Christ Jesus. Joining him in receiving Christ that evening was a young girl he knew in school, Dorothy Kelley. She was his childhood sweetheart and future bride.

On the Wednesday following his conversion, Patterson informed his father that he had also committed his life to missions. He was baptized and began his ministry pilgrimage, going with his father on salvation visits to lost individuals and also care ministry visits to members of First Baptist Church, Beaumont. He was influenced by his father, who encouraged him to read L.R. Scarborough's *With Christ After the Lost* and B.H. Carroll's *Interpretation of the English Bible*. At 16 years of age, Patterson accompanied his parents on a 13-country world missionary journey, preaching alongside his father as they toured.

Patterson graduated from Beaumont High School, Hardin-Simmons University (B.A.), and New Orleans Baptist Theological Seminary (Th.M. and Ph.D.). During his college years, he served churches in Rotan and Abilene, Texas, and during his seminary years, he served as pastor of Bethany Baptist Church, New Orleans, Louisiana, and organized a coffee house ministry with street evangelist Leo Humphrey for outcasts, prostitutes, and addicts in the French Quarter in New Orleans. After seminary, he became pastor of the First Baptist Church, Fayetteville, Arkansas, where within five years he baptized 239 people, planted seven churches, and saw 50 youth commit their lives to ministry.[46]

W.A. Criswell called Patterson in 1975 as president of Criswell Bible Institute (now Criswell College) and as associate pastor at First Baptist Church in Dallas. Beginning with eight full-time students, Patterson turned the miniscule college into a thriving, prominent, conservative theological institution within 17 years.

Patterson served on the International Council on Biblical Inerrancy. This council, with its highly respected array of scholars, produced the historic Chicago Statement on Biblical Inerrancy. Not only did he move to have biblical inerrancy accepted in the evangelistic community of the convention, he also took the fight to the Southern Baptist Convention floor with the able assistance of Judge Paul Pressler and others. They would become the architects of what came to be known as the "Conservative Resurgence" in the SBC. Taking the heat from certain attacks to come, Pressler and Patterson stood in the fire to allow the grassroots movement to return the convention to fidelity in the inerrant Scriptures.[47]

In 1992, Patterson left Criswell College to serve as president of Southeastern Baptist Theological Seminary. When he arrived, there were 555 enrolled. Between 1992 and 1996, the enrollment increased 115 percent, with 2,000 students enrolled in the spring of 2000.[48]

During his tenure at Southeastern, Patterson was elected in 1998 as president of the Southern Baptist Convention—one of only three seminary presidents to hold both offices at the same time. In 1999, the convention voted for Patterson to appoint a committee to review the Baptist Faith and Message. The work on the project was completed and became known as the Baptist Faith and Message 2000. This confessional statement capped the Conservative Resurgence in the Southern Baptist Convention and is now used by boards, agencies, and institutions of the SBC.

Patterson has come full circle over four decades of dedicating his life to educating pastors, missionaries, church educators, church musicians, women ministry leaders, and other leaders for Southern Baptist ministry. Returning to the city of his birth, Fort Worth, Texas, he became the second person in Baptist history to serve as president of two Southern Baptist seminaries. Patterson is the consummate evangelical scholar with a heart on fire for evangelism, while at the same time publishing scholarly works, from commentaries to systematic theology.

Southwestern Seminary changed expeditiously under Patterson's leadership. The nature of the students changed in relation to his philosophy of ministry. Patterson said,

> Two kinds of seminaries are available for students worldwide. There are those that are essentially committed to training occupation troops. No criticism can be offered against these schools since occupation troops are necessary. But, any modern army must have and train its Special Operations Forces, and that is the assignment of Southwestern Seminary.[49]

Patterson Makes First Faculty Appointments (2004)

The spring trustee meeting, April 5-7, 2004, received several recommendations for new faculty in the School of Theology and one in the School of Educational Ministries. During his inauguration speech the previous fall, 2003, Patterson outlined his vision for faculty hires:

> We shall attempt in our program of Christian education to have a cutting-edge program that will instruct people in how best to effectively teach the Bible, Christian witnessing, Baptist history, and Baptist missions. We shall, by the grace of God, teach the clear, unadulterated, exciting exposition of God's Word as the appropriate and desperately needed method of preaching in our day.[50]

The new faculty member in the School of Educational Ministries was Octavio Javier Esqueda from the University of Guadalajara in Mexico. The appointment of Esqueda marked the addition of another faculty member able to use his bilingual skills in English and Spanish to equip the culturally diverse student population of the future. Craig Blaising, executive vice president and provost, said, "Esqueda is one of the brightest young scholars in the field of Christian education today.

He brings to this discipline a strong foundation in biblical exposition, a Christ-centered love for people, and a unique insight into the issues of Christian higher education, especially in the Hispanic culture."[51]

The trustees received recommendations from President Patterson for the establishment of three new schools and a new dean for the School of Educational Ministries.[52] The recommendations were as follows:

- That the trustees approve the designation of the Havard School for Theological Studies, Houston, TX, as a School of the Southwestern Baptist Theological Seminary.
- That the trustees approve in principle the establishment of a School of Evangelism on the Fort Worth campus.
- That the trustees approve in principle the establishment of a College on the Fort Worth campus for the purpose of offering baccalaureate degrees.
- That the trustees elect Dr. Robert Welch as Dean of the School of Educational Ministries.[53]

The trustees also added the three schools to "Article 1 - The Seminary" in the Seminary Bylaws. Article 1 then read,

- Academic Organization: To fulfill its purpose and carry on its academic work, the Seminary is organized into schools as follows:
  - The School of Theology
  - The School of Educational Ministries
  - The School of Church Music
  - The School of Evangelism and Missions
  - The J. Dalton Havard School for Theological Studies, Park Place Campus, Houston, TX.
  - Southwestern Baptist Theological College

During the fall trustee meeting, October 18-20, 2004, Johnny L. Derouen was elected associate professor of student ministries and chair of the human growth and development division. Derouen had extensive experience in local churches, and he had previously spoken at Southwestern's Youth Ministry Lab.

The trustees approved the three recommendations from the April 5-7, 2004, meeting that established the School of Evangelism and Missions;

constituted the J. Dalton Havard School for Theological Studies, Park Place Campus, Houston, Texas, as an official school of Southwestern Seminary; and established Southwestern Baptist Theological College as the official college of Southwestern Baptist Theological Seminary. These three recommendations passed unanimously. Each new school became a major entity of the Southwestern Seminary family of schools.

Two Educational Ministry Professors Retire

In the very year that the new youth professor Johnny Derouen joined the faculty, Philip Briggs, professor of youth ministries and the Edgar F. "Preacher" Hallock Chair of Student Ministries, retired after 33 years of service at Southwestern Seminary. Robert Welch, dean of the School of Educational Ministries, said, "Briggs is a student's professor. His care and concern for students are not paralleled on this campus."⁵⁴

Briggs said, "I am retiring, but not quitting. In my opinion, there is no retirement in ministry. I will continue to teach and serve in churches as opportunities are available. Writing will consume some of my time."⁵⁵ Briggs has been recognized by multiple academic professional organizations as well as many Southern Baptist educational organizations.

Tommy Bridges retired after 27 years serving students at Southwestern Seminary in the School of Educational Ministries. Bridges was professor of administration and taught in Spanish-speaking seminaries and colleges in South America and Mexico. He taught at all of Southwestern's extension centers in Houston, Shawnee, and San Antonio. Bridges said, "The most memorable moments have been seeing students answer the call to international mission. My prayer is that the students at Southwestern will be faithful to God's call and continue to prepare themselves for the Kingdom of God."[56]

Bridges' plan for the future was to teach a course or two at Southwestern when needed, spend more time volunteering as a deacon at his church, and continue his international teaching ministry in Peru, Russia, and South America. Because of the tremendous impact Bridges had over the years on the Tom Cox Association Baptist Theological Seminary in Trujillo, Peru, on May 31, 2016, the seminary's board of trustees honored Bridges with an honorary Doctor of Ministry degree.

Three New Schools Added to Southwestern's Arsenal (2005)

One year into the administration of President Patterson, the trustees were busy implementing the new plans and procedures introduced in the 2004 meetings. During the April 4-6, 2005, trustee meeting, Patterson commented on the historic nature that this meeting would take on with the involvement of the three new schools, the election of a large number of faculty members, and the historic master plan that moved the center of the seminary campus from Seminary Drive and the B.H. Carroll Memorial Building to the Naylor Student Center. All new construction would be south of the Naylor Center. The acceptance of the master plan as a framework for the development of future campus construction plans was historic. Specifically, this plan met the immediate campus construction needs for student housing, a chapel, and a School of Evangelism and Missions.[57]

A major part of this new movement was the addition of a library in the president's home, now named Pecan Manor. First Lady Dorothy Patterson expressed appreciation to a long-time friend of Southwestern, Carliss Phillips, as well as to Barbara and Jack Terry for the gift and time invested in the addition of the new library at Pecan Manor.[58] The new library displayed over 30,000 volumes contained in the Pattersons' collective libraries. Phillips also made possible the addition of hospitality space with a second dining room.

The curriculum for the College at Southwestern (originally identified as the Southwestern Baptist Theological College and later officially named Scarborough College) was approved by the trustees. The curriculum offered studies in Early Western Civilization, Church and Empires, World Religions, Renaissance and Reformation, Baptist History and Heritage, Enlightenment and Romantic Period, The Arts Perspective on Life, The 19th Century, The Early 20th Century, Introduction to Social Science, Late 20th Century to the Present, Developments in Natural Science, Greek or Latin, Biblical and Theological Studies, and Physical Education. Each IDE (History of Ideas) had "breakout sessions" to focus on specific studies such as Mathematics, Science, Literature, Philosophy, Political Science, and other essentials of a General Education.

The approval for a new extension center at the *Bibelseminar* in Bonn, Germany, for the purpose of offering a Master of Arts in Theology was established. Associated with this recommendation was another naming of several faculty members to academic chairs. In particular, two in the School of Educational Ministries were named to chairs: Richard Ross was named to the J.M. Price Chair of Religious Education, and newly elected faculty member Max Barnett was named to the Edgar F. "Preacher" Hallock Chair of Baptist Student Work.

Max Barnett was elected professor of collegiate ministry training. Barnett graduated from Southwestern Seminary with his M.Div. (1965) and from Midwestern Baptist Theological Seminary with his D.Min. (2004). He was the Baptist student director of three college campuses in Dallas, Texas, while finishing his degree at Southwestern, and a year and a half later moved to Norman, Oklahoma, to serve as the Baptist student director at the University of Oklahoma for 37 years. Barnett developed collegiate ministry classes at Southwestern and Midwestern Seminaries, teaching during January and May I Terms. Recently, the International Mission Board reported that there are more IMB missionaries from the University of Oklahoma than any other state school in America.

During the last session of the April 2005 trustee meeting, Jack Terry announced his planned retirement as vice president for Institutional Advancement, effective December 31, 2005. President Patterson said,

> During Terry's tenure as dean of the School of Religious Education, he was responsible for directing over $6 million in donations and since becoming vice president, the Office of Institutional Advancement has generated over $48 million in cash and $18 million in pledges under his leadership. He and Barbara are significant donors personally, becoming members of the President's Club in 1979, the second year of its inception.[59]

In a final action, Ted Stone, trustee from North Carolina, made a motion that the School of Evangelism and Missions be named the Roy Fish School of Evangelism and Missions in honor of longtime evangelism professor Roy Fish. The motion was seconded and unanimously passed.

Houston Extension Celebrates 30 Years

The Houston extension center celebrated its 30th year in 2005. It was founded in 1975 and has been moved to several locations, beginning with sharing a building with Houston Baptist University only to discover that the university needed the entire building. Southwestern sold its portion of the building to the university. Homeless, the extension began exploring various Baptist churches in the Houston area to little avail. The initiative of seven Baptist associations to locate a Southwestern Seminary extension center in the Houston area in 1975 culminated with the shared building at Houston Baptist University and worked well for 25 years, but now the need was to relocate. For years, the closest Baptist seminary was 250 miles away, in Fort Worth, and the need for seminary education in Houston was immense. Houston was a virtual mission field. Union Baptist Association was the nation's largest Baptist association. According the Harford Institute for Religious Research, "29 of 111 mega-churches in Texas are located in the Houston metropolitan area, and 13 are Southern Baptist."[60]

God moved in the heart of the pastor and members of Park Place Baptist Church in Houston to deed their property, worth $5.3 million, to Southwestern Seminary in February 2002. Accrediting agencies affirmed that everything was in place to enable the trustees to elevate the Houston center to the status of a theological school, a free-standing and degree-granting institution under the authority of Southwestern Seminary.[61] The director of the center, Denny Autrey, was named dean to give direction to the newly accredited J. Dalton Havard School for Theological Studies in Houston.

During the 2005-2006 academic year, 230 students enrolled at the Houston campus. The 30th year looked bright for this newly accredited theological institution because now the international world that is Houston, Texas—with immigrants from virtually every corner of the globe living in metropolitan Houston and its surrounding cities and communities—had access to a world-class theological education right in its own backyard.

Women's Studies Program Certifies 25

A historic event was celebrated during a chapel service on November 4, 2005, when 25 women received their certification from the Women's Studies Program. Terri Stovall, director of Women's Programs and assistant professor of adult education and aging, said, "It is the vision for Southwestern to be the premier institution of theological education for women. This includes seminary studies in the student wives program and our Leadership Certificate in Women's Ministry."[62]

There are two study areas available for women to pursue. The Certificate in Ministry is designed for the student wife on the Fort Worth campus. The leadership certificate is targeted for the woman who is responsible for the women's ministry in her local church. Two diploma programs are also available for women who have not earned a baccalaureate degree. The woman who has an earned baccalaureate degree can pursue the Master of Arts in Christian Education, which equips those who will be serving in ministry to women or working with women in some way in the local church, association, or at the denominational level.

Stovall noted, "In two years, Southwestern has gone from having two women's ministry courses to having seven women's ministry courses in the School of Educational Ministry."[63] Southwestern would offer the certificate program on the Houston campus beginning in 2005, and plans were in the making for the courses to be offered online.

This – In This – By This Generation

Youth Ministry Lab, April 8-9, 2005, set the bar for attendance in all the 36 years that the lab had met on the Southwestern campus. More than 1,200 youth ministers, parents of youth, and youth group leaders from 300 churches attended. Evangelist Louie Giglio (M.Div., 1985) inspired the participants to step out of their life stories and into God's story for them. He told the conferees,

> Paul could have been the guy who had it all if not for his radical meeting with God. He would have been the star of his own small story, but would not be known today. The Apostle Paul was radically re-aimed and resized by God, and God invited Paul into His story, and that invitation is still on the table today for you and me. But, this generation needs young men and women who actively live out the reality that Jesus is relevant for today. Young people need those who can lead them to the power that is in the resurrection of Jesus Christ. Leave your story behind and join God's story because there is stuff He is doing in your town that you don't even know about, and it is huge. God is good, and He is on the move.[64]

According to Richard Ross, the reason for the largest attendance in the history of the Youth Lab was related to the planning team's intensive pre-conference prayer strategy. He said,

Perhaps the largest conference attendance in Youth Lab history is related to what may have been the most expansive conference prayer strategy in the seminary's history. On two Friday nights, prior to the week of meetings, the Lab committees prayed from 10:00 p.m. until sunrise the next morning. Twice they prayed—walked the campus, praying over every room and in many cases over every chair. For a semester, students have prayed weekly at 7:00 a.m. for God to come in power during the Youth Lab. Virtually everyone who attended was prayed over by those wearing prayer bracelets.[65]

A Year of New Beginnings

Many things *new* seemed to be the theme at the spring trustee meeting, April 3-6, 2006, where plans were discussed for a new chapel, a new building to house the Fish School of Evangelism and Missions and the College at Southwestern, a new name and a new dean for the San Antonio extension center, a new vice president for Institutional Advancement, a new dean of Extension Education, three new School of Theology professors, and two new School of Educational Ministries professors. During the president's report to the trustees, the architectural plans for the new chapel were introduced. Patterson said, "The funding would not come as the result of Cooperative Program funds, increase in student tuition, reduction in salaries, or an organized capital campaign. If it is done, it will be done on the basis of private donations."[66] Vice President for Business Affairs Greg Kingry told the trustees that "the chapel would have 106,000 square feet and would seat 3,500 on a main floor, two side balconies, and one rear balcony. Plans for the Roy Fish School of Evangelism and Missions and the College at Southwestern were also in the process of being formulated."[67]

Rudy Gonzalez, former vice president for Student Services, was named the new dean of the extension center in San Antonio. President Patterson recommended that the trustees name the center in San Antonio the William R. Marshall Center for Theological Studies, in honor of William R. Marshall, who was the director and a development officer for the extension center in San Antonio for more than 20 years.[68] The recommendation was unanimously approved. The appointment of Gonzalez as the dean of the Marshall Center was part of the strategy of the trustees to elevate the seminary's San Antonio extension center to the level of a fully accredited degree-granting school, as was done in Houston in 2003 to the Havard School. Gonzalez's presence as the dean would intensify the training of ministers in Central and South Texas, especially in reaching out to the Hispanic community there and in Mexico.

Mike Hughes was elected as the new vice president for Institutional Advancement. Hughes was a businessman in Abilene, Texas, and was called into the ministry. He sold his car dealership and came to Southwestern as a student. While a student, he served as director of Business Services for the seminary in 2004 and had been acting vice president since January 1, 2006.

Seven new faculty members were elected during the spring 2006 meeting. One faculty member was elected in the School of Educational Ministries: Robert Vaughan, as associate professor of administration. Vaughan graduated from Oklahoma Baptist University (1981) and Southwestern Seminary (M.A.C.E., 1985; Ph.D., 1990). Vaughn served the First Baptist Church, Fort Smith, Arkansas, as associate pastor for seven years and was the administrator of their Christian school.

National Child Spirituality Conference

Six doctoral students in the School of Educational Ministry who were studying childhood education participated in a national childhood education conference presenting doctoral-level research papers on the spiritual life of young children and their parents. Marcia McQuitty, associate professor of childhood education, provided the six students an opportunity to present their research findings at a national Children's Spirituality Conference that convened at Concordia University in River Forest, Illinois, June 2-7, 2006. The doctoral students had assisted McQuitty in presenting qualitative research prepared for a childhood education seminar, Parenting and Faith Development, the previous fall.

The Children's Spirituality Conference provided opportunities for the students to interact with well-known authors and theologians from various traditions, share insights, and engage in meaningful theological discussions. Plenary session speakers included John Westerhoff, author of the book *Will Our Children Have Faith*, and Patrick McDonald, international director and founder of *Viva Network*. Doctoral students presented research on several different subjects dealing with young children and Christian faith. Kelly King's topic was "Santa and Salvation: The Coexistence of Fantasy and Faith in the Mind of a Child"; Joshua Hong's topic was "Young Children's Abstract God Concepts and Parental Influence"; Karen Kennemur's topic was "Prayer and Children: What Do They Understand?"; Sung-Won Kim's topic was "Parenting Styles and Spiritual Development"; Yunhee Lim's topic was "Children's Spirituality: Transcendence and Empathy"; and Heuikwang Shin's topic was "Christian Faith and Sixth Graders' Awareness of Physical Changes, Relationships with Opposite Sex and Their Understanding of the Biblical View About Their Body Change."

Serving on the conference team with McQuitty were professors from Wheaton, Concordia, Asbury Theological Seminary, and John Brown University, and all were pleased about the overall experience with other professionals in the area of childhood education. McQuitty returned from the conference with a stronger desire for master's and doctoral courses to be more theological in their discussions relating to children's ministers. She said, "This conference confirmed my belief that each student of childhood education must be thoroughly grounded in the knowledge of the Scriptures."[69]

Waller and Caldwell Retire

Gary Waller, professor of administration and director of extension learning, retired after 22 years of service as a faculty member in the School of Educational Ministries. Waller was elected to the educational faculty in 1984 after several years of adjunctive teaching in the administration department. During his tenure, he developed a Christian school administration course in 1988. In 1990, the School of Educational

Ministries added a Master of Arts in Christian Education (M.A.C.E.) in Christian School Administration, which Waller administered.

Waller developed several doctoral courses in higher education administration and chaired the committee that recommended the change of the Ed.D. to the Ph.D. Waller later became the dean of distance learning and led the seminary in establishing the online course study program. Waller said, "It has been such a blessing and honor being able to teach with some of those I took classes from and those that have come along since. I will always remember my mentors being accepting of me when I came on board as a faculty member and their encouragement."[70]

William G. Caldwell, professor of administration and church business administration, was elected to the faculty in 1976. During his doctoral studies at Southwestern, Caldwell served as a teaching fellow for Lee McCoy, senior professor of church and education administration. In 1981, Caldwell led the School of Religious Education to develop a Church Business Administration Certification program in conjunction with the Church Administration Department of the Baptist Sunday School Board. Southwestern Seminary was the first Baptist seminary to offer Certification in Church Business Administration. Caldwell assisted in establishing the National Association of Church Business Administrators and became the lead instructor for the certification program. Following his retirement, Caldwell would continue serving churches in church business administration and educational ministries.

Terry Retires as Vice President of Institutional Advancement

Jack Terry announced his retirement for the end of the year during the fall trustee meeting, October 18-19, 2006. He continued serving in a semi-retirement position beginning December 31, 2006. He remained as the chairman of Southwestern's Centennial Celebration Committee, which was then preparing for a grand 100-year anniversary festival in 2008. President Patterson lauded Terry's contributions as a teacher, dean, administrator, and vice president. He said,

> There is not an anthill in the U.S. where Jack is not on a personal, first-name basis with some of the ants, and

has tried to get them to contribute to Southwestern. If there was a Mount Rushmore here on campus, I think there would be three faces on it: B.H. Carroll, L.R. Scarborough, and Jack Terry. We can never pay back all the generosity and contributions to this institution during his 37 years of service."[71]

When Terry was the dean of the School of Religious Education (now the School of Educational Ministries), he raised over $8 million for the seminary, and when he moved into the vice president's role, he continued fundraising for several major buildings. He raised the funds to construct the Ray I. Riley Alumni Center and the Jack MacGorman Conference Center, the home of Southwestern's Center for Leadership Development. He continued raising funds for the construction of the projected 3,500-seat chapel, which would be a critical building to the growth of the Fort Worth campus. It was essential that the construction of the new chapel get underway by the seminary's centennial celebration in 2008.

Terry was honored by the city of Fort Worth as one of its outstanding mentors. Greg Tomlin, director of public relations at Southwestern, said,

> Terry has exhibited the qualities of a good leader in his various roles at the seminary. When you look at Jack Terry's life, you see all of these churches he has had his hand in from East Texas to Kaiserslautern, Germany. Each one of them has benefited from his ministry, even when he was serving at Southwestern in some capacity. He is a true church leader, a gifted communicator, and a trusted friend.[72]

Reunion: Bringing a Generation Back to God

The 38th annual Youth Lab experienced more than 270 young people who were excited to be at school. They gathered at the Rosemont Middle School, across the street from the Southwestern Seminary campus, for a "Reality Evangelism" experience that set aside the entire day to train them how to witness at school. This day of evangelism training was part of the plan for youth from across the nation who had gathered as part of the Youth Lab, which was totally organized and effectuated by students at Southwestern Seminary. This year's lab had an enrollment of 1,320 youth ministers, volunteers with youth, and youth leaders who came for this year's conference. The theme was "Reunion: Bringing a Generation Back To God."

The Reality Evangelism was new to the participants and the leaders of Youth Lab. Chad Childress, director of student evangelism with the North American Mission Board, had never used this method of training anywhere else, and it was an excellent, transferrable method of sharing Christ with classmates in school. Childress taught the youth three principles of evangelism: (1) build a relationship intentionally; (2) love people; and (3) proclaim the Gospel to others.[73]

After the training, the youth moved over to Rosemont Middle School to do a mock walkthrough of an average day going to the classrooms, cafeteria, and campus clubs and engaging those who were acting as non-believers with the three principles they had just learned. The students were incredibly engaged in the experience and ready to get home to their own campuses in the fall to put into practice what they had learned in the mock involvement. Jenni Kennemur, a freshman at South Grand Prairie High School and daughter of doctoral candidate Karen Kennemur, said, "It was good! Usually, when you go to a youth conference, someone just talks to you about how to witness and share with your friends. But this time, it was realistic and challenging. We got to actually do something, not just listen. By practicing, it helped give us confidence in going back to school and sharing Christ with our friends."[74]

Wes Black, professor of youth/student ministry at Southwestern, recounted, as with last year, the orchestration of intense prayer before the conference began by praying for hours and prayer-walking the Southwestern campus as well as Rosemont Middle School. The prayer strategy was as intense this year as last, and the results were overwhelming.

Roy Fish, professor of evangelism at Southwestern, spoke to a session telling the participants that prayer is essential for bringing a generation of youth back to God through the Gospel. He reminded the youth that the Great Awakening that spread across the United States during the mid-19th century began with an emphasis of prayer by laypeople. Newspapers reported what was going on in terms of it being a "prayer revival." Fish asked, "You want to bring a generation to God? That's the starting place. That's the place in which it is kept going: the prayer room."

Dean of Women's Programs

Rapid growth in the women's programs at Southwestern Seminary demanded a strong person in the leadership role of that emerging ministry in local churches and denominational agencies. The expanding offerings at the master's level and particularly at the doctoral level called for a person to guide, direct, develop, and intensify the curriculum in the women's studies programs. At the April 2-4, 2007, meeting, the trustees elected Terri Stovall as dean of Women's Programs and associate professor of women's ministries. Stovall had taught adult education and church administration in the School of Educational Ministries and had been the director of the women's programs since 2002.

In 2005, 25 women were certified in the Women's Studies Program under the direction of Stovall. This program was primarily for wives of seminary students who could earn from Southwestern Seminary a bona fide certificate that would qualify them to work in the church with their respective pastor-husbands in developing and leading women's ministries in their churches. This program had such growth that it became important enough to have its own dean and its own curriculum. Several of the women who earned the certification in 2005 continued in the School of Educational Ministries working on a M.A.C.E. degree in women's studies.

Van McClain, chairman of the trustees, said, "We are pleased with what has happened in the area of women's studies. It is very important. Dr. Stovall has done very well directing women's programs, and we are happy she has taken on this increased responsibility."[75]

During the 2007 trustee meeting, 10 new faculty members and two administrators were elected to various schools and positions. Elected to a faculty position in the School of Educational Ministries was Paul Stutz, assistant professor of administration and recreation. Stutz had experience in multiple local churches and had most recently served as adjunct professor of church recreation (1990-1995) and director of the RAC (1995-2007) at Southwestern Seminary.

Nathan Christian (Chris) Shirley was elected as assistant professor of adult ministry. Shirley served as associate director of camps for boys and girls at Ridgecrest, North Carolina; Minister of Family Life, Calvary Baptist Church, Ashville, North Carolina; and associate pastor for Christian development, Wedgewood Baptist Church, Fort Worth, Texas. He had written multiple resources for LifeWay Christian Resources, including *Straight Talk Bible Studies*, *Youth Vacation Bible School Resources*, and *Evangelical Dictionary of Christian Education*.

Major campus building recommendations were made during the October 15-17, 2007, trustee meeting that changed the face of the seminary campus for the future. Plans were progressing rapidly for the construction of a new chapel adjacent to the president's residence, Pecan Manor, with a recommendation for a location alongside and behind Pecan Manor for the construction of a Homemaking House. Construction would not begin on the Homemaking House until the design and complete funding were secured. This construction would provide facilities to accommodate the homemaking degree program recently developed at the seminary. A second recommendation was to move forward with the development of plans for the construction of four quad apartment units, and that construction would not begin until after final plans had been provided for and approved by the Foundation Board.[76]

Terry Chair of Religious Education Inaugurated

The Southwestern Baptist Theological Seminary faculty wore full regalia at a chapel service honoring the inauguration of the Jack D. and Barbara Terry Chair of Religious Education, September 11, 2007. Terry, vice president emeritus and special assistant to the president for development, used Ephesians 4:1, 11-12 as the basis for the chapel message for empowering the saints for the work of ministry to the edification of the church. The passage is an ancient first-century church growth formula that can be used in today's modern churches. Terry used this formula in four churches where he was minister of education and administration, and each of the churches grew expeditiously during his ministry.

Carliss Phillips and his wife Lois, longtime friends of Southwestern Seminary and personal friends of Jack and Barbara Terry, endowed the chair through their estate in 2005. Carliss was an active businessman, mayor, and community leader in Quitman, Texas. The couple were outstanding church leaders in First Baptist Church, Quitman, with Carliss serving as the Sunday School superintendent, a deacon, and the chair of multiple committees in the church. At Southwestern Seminary, the Phillipses were the recipients of the B.H. Carroll Award; served on the Southwestern Advisory Council; established multiple funds for Women's Programs; and provided scholarships for the College at Southwestern, the seminary main campus, and the San Antonio extension campus.

One cannot think of Jack Terry without including his wife, Barbara, who served by his side through 60-plus years of marriage. Terry will tell you that Barbara is the guiding light that has inspired, challenged, and encouraged him to think beyond the present into the future and to prepare effectively to meet that future. Her loving spirit of ministry for many people the Terrys have served over their ministry years is the true center of their life and the absolute principle of God's movement in their ministry. According to Terry, "Without her love and inspiration, I would have been just another husband, but with her loving motivation,

God used us to do some astounding things in His Kingdom for which we are most grateful."

Craig Blaising, executive vice president and provost, said, "In finding someone to occupy the chair, we had to find someone who has the same infectious, joyous personality as Jack Terry, which is difficult. Of all the professors in the School of Educational Ministries, the one who best fits that description would have to be Dr. Wes Black."[77] Black was elected to the faculty of Southwestern Seminary in 1983. He served as a youth consultant for the Southern Baptist Sunday School Board from 1981-1983 and in several Texas and Oklahoma churches as youth minister for 15 years. Black had been active in the Association of Youth Ministry, serving as chairman of their board and receiving the Award of Excellence in 1998. Black published several works, including *Parenting by Grace*.

Youth Lab and Tornado Come in Together

We do not have a large number of tornadoes in the Fort Worth area, but when we do, we have a dandy. Such was a tornado-spawning storm on the evening of April 13, 2007, that spewed its venom over Haltom City, a suburb of northeast Fort Worth, causing a good deal of damage, injuries, and a fatality. The storm caused the participants of the 39th annual Youth Lab to literally "Go underground," which was the theme of the lab—"Underground Church, through Reality Missions Experience."

Just after the opening worship service began, the tornado sirens near the seminary began to howl. Quickly, the Youth Lab staff ushered the conferees to the basement below Truett Auditorium to a large safe area. The scene brought to mind the number of Christians and churches meeting in catacombs and underground facilities to participate in worship. Joel Engle, the worship leader for the lab walked among the youth ministers, volunteer youth leaders, and teenagers who were huddled against the walls in the basement to lead them in worship and praise. Others hunkered in groups, praying and singing songs in the semi-darkness of the basement. After the tornado threat had passed and the sirens sounded the "all clear," Gregg Matte told the group that "there is nothing like a good tornado to wake up the people of God."[78]

This year, the Youth Lab moved from the seminary to the 75-acre Mainstay Farm near Burleson to participate in the reality of the underground church in areas that are not conducive to the Christian Gospel. With the assistance of the seminary's World Missions Center, Youth Lab leadership, volunteers, and local churches composed of predominately international membership coordinated mock villages and multicultural experiences where the teens could learn to shape the Gospel across cultures and religions. The stations visited represented nations such as China, Thailand, Botswana, and Nigeria.

Johnny Derouen, event coordinator and associate professor of youth/student ministry, said, "Our prayer was that God would step in and use this experience to give them a heart for the nations and for some response to God's call for short- or long-term missions."[79] Wes Black, Youth Lab co-organizer, reported, "There were 1,312 participants at this year's lab representing 321 churches from 24 states. Three teenagers made professions of faith, 22 participants recommitted their lives to Christ, 66 committed their lives to be missionaries, and 69 responded to a call to vocational ministry in the church."[80]

Youth Education Professor Dies

Harold T. Dill, founder of the Youth Ministry Lab in 1968 and retired professor of youth education, died October 8, 2007. Dill graduated from Southwestern Seminary with an M.R.E. (1941) and a D.R.E. (1954). He was the minister of education at several churches before joining the School of Religious Education faculty in 1959 as professor of youth education, serving until 1984.

Dill was greatly loved by his students and admired by his colleagues. He was a genuine Christian, a scholar, held high integrity as a classroom professor, and expected and received exceptional work from those who were privileged to sit under him as a teacher. We will miss this devoted Christian professor.

Centennial Celebration Rocks Seminary Campus

The Centennial Convocation, January 17, 2008, marked the beginning of a new academic year and the addition of a new piece of academic regalia. It seemed only fitting, since Southwestern was celebrating its 100th birthday, that a bit of *Texas Cowboy* be added to the stoic 13th century medieval academic regalia. Craig Blaising, executive vice president and provost, reminded the faculty that many of the academic hat designs reflected what was popular at the time. "So as Southwestern celebrates its centennial, we felt it was appropriate to wear a hat that reflects the time and location of this great school: a beaver felt western black hat in keeping with formal academic tradition."[81]

After welcoming both the new and returning students, trustees, and guests, Blaising introduced a special guest. The room darkened to blackness, then a spotlight blazed on a framed portrait of the founder and first president, B.H. Carroll. What appeared to be a narrative soon resulted in a dramatic presentation as a graduate student, Matt Brandt, dressed to resemble the man in the portrait, burst through the frame onto the stage. The content of the dramatic presentation was B.H. Carroll proposing to move the seminary from Baylor University to Fort Worth.

The communication department of the School of Educational Ministries was responsible for all dramatic presentations during the centennial year. This signaled the beginning of many more dramatic presentations of the history of the seminary as well as a year-long celebration beginning with Founder's Day, March 13-14, 2008—a two-day celebration culminating with a seminary homecoming for all alumni, students, and friends.

A Simple Beginning, March 14, 1908

Receiving unanimous approval from the Baptist General Convention of Texas on November 9, 1907, B.H. Carroll returned to his hotel in San Antonio with his own charter and board of trustees for the new seminary, Southwestern Seminary at Waco, Texas. The charter was officially filed with the secretary of state on March 14, 1908. The charter name was shown as Southwestern Baptist Theological Seminary.[82] Now,

School of Educational Ministries in the 21st Century

100 years later, the fledgling seminary on a piece of paper in the hands of the giant pastor, educator, and theologian B.H. Carroll had become the largest theological seminary in the world and would be celebrating that Centennial Celebration on March 13-14, 2008—Founder's Day.

The campus was completely inundated with Southern Baptist Convention leaders, seminary presidents, special city leaders from Fort Worth and surrounding suburbs, local pastors and their church fellowships, alumni from across the nation and from many mission fields, students and their families as well as guests from all over Texas. The day was celebrated in grand Texas style with a centennial chapel service in Truett Auditorium, featuring an inspiring speech from a very special guest, alumni gatherings planned in each of the three schools, and a campus-wide Texas-sized BBQ lunch with all the trimmings. The gathering of all those who were present to form a large human "100" on the quadrangle would cap off the day's celebrative spirit, and a spectacular fireworks display honoring the seminary's 100 years would close out the evening.

A beautiful cloudless spring sky allowed the Founder's Day chapel to be held on the lawn of the seminary. President Patterson recognized alumni, welcomed students and guests, and read letters of congratulations from David Dockery, president of Union University and a distinguished alumnus, and from alumnus Jeff Iorg, president of Golden Gate Theological Seminary in California. Alumnus Danny Akin, president of Southeastern Baptist Theological Seminary, thanked Southwestern for setting the pace for evangelism for Southern Baptists. He said,

> In the day and age in which we live, wedding a healthy, robust theology to a Great Commission passion is my prayer for Southern Baptists, that is my prayer for all of our seminaries, and, in particular, the one that has set the pace for so long, that is my prayer and my heartbeat for Southwestern Seminary.[83]

Alumnus O.S. Hawkins, president of GuideStone Financial Resources, recognized that Southwestern, by its influence, has trained more pastors, religious educators, music ministers, and missionaries than any other seminary. He praised the seminary for staying true to the heritage of its founder, B.H. Carroll. As Hawkins concluded his statements, a Master of Divinity student, Andy Smith, stepped forward portraying B.H. Carroll and said what might have been said by the giant of a man, mirroring the 100 years and with a challenge to launch the seminary forward. He said,

> I urge you as a brother, founder, and fellow servant to stand fast upon the inerrant Word of God, keeping the seminary lashed to our Savior's cross, that all men might know Him. May God bless Southwestern Seminary, the president, the faculty, and the students to always remain true to the Lord Jesus Christ.[84]

President Patterson displayed the *Library of Centennial Classics*, 10 blue hardback books with the centennial stamp on the front of each. These books were written by some of the most prodigious minds in the 100-year history of Southwestern Seminary: B.H. Carroll, L.R. Scarborough, Albert Newman, H.L. Dana, William T. Conner, T.B. Maston, J.M. Price, and Robert Baker. Most of these books were out of print and were resurrected for the centennial library. This library was made available to all who attended.

Kenneth Hemphill, the seventh president of Southwestern Seminary and the national strategist for the Southern Baptist Convention's Empowering Kingdom Growth, delivered the Founder's Day address. Using the passage John 17, Hemphill encouraged those assembled to keep "being sanctified" while in the world. Noting that graduates leave Southwestern to literally go around the world to serve the Master, he said emphatically, "Wherever it may lead, as a pastor of small churches or mega-churches, or spending their last days in the grasp of a captor, continue to advance God's Kingdom by His power and for His glory."[85]

After lunch, alumni were invited to Truett Auditorium for a time of singing and testimonies from several alumni. James Leo Garrett, distinguished professor emeritus in the School of Theology and noted Baptist historian, represented the alumni from its founding to 1965. He briefly discussed the progress of the seminary over the first 60-plus years. David Allen, dean of the School of Theology, represented the alumni from 1966-1986 and described his pilgrimage as a student, trustee, and finally as professor and now a dean. Bart Barber, pastor of First Baptist Church in Farmersville, Texas, represented the alumni from 1987 to present and told the group,

> I am convinced we are living on the eve of a great Baptist renaissance that is going to breathe vitality and confidence into our churches as the New Testament Gospel is proclaimed and we plant new churches throughout the world. Because of this and because of you and so many other reasons, I am proud to be a Southwesterner.[86]

Following this gathering, the alumni attended separate alumni receptions held in each school, where "birthday cake" and punch were served with an opportunity to meet with past and present faculty and friends. When these individual celebrations were over, all were encouraged to move quickly to the quadrangle in front of the B.H. Carroll Memorial Building, where they formed a large number "100" for an aerial photograph memorializing the 100th Centennial Celebration.

As the sun began to set on the beautiful spring evening, 2,100-plus centennial participants sat down under the beautiful Burkett pecan trees on the west side of the campus or under one of a number of pavilions with tables and chairs to enjoy a sumptuous old-fashioned Texas BBQ. A feast fit for a Texas cattle baron, to be sure.

As dinner ended, the crowd was invited to Truett Auditorium once again to hear a presentation by the School of Church Music. The evening began with music from *New Sound*, a new vocal ensemble; Don Wyrtzen, professor of piano, playing original compositions and old favorites; and a Southern Gospel Quartet sharing many of the hymns and Gospel songs that were prevalent in the early years of Texas Baptist church music. Joe Hardin, professor of church music and jazz, led in a contemporary worship period utilizing the small jazz group in contemporary church music.

The culmination of a very long day moved the group back to the quadrangle where the large "100" had been photographed to enjoy a remarkable fireworks display in the cool breeze of the Texas spring evening. As the colorful explosions burst above the B.H. Carroll Memorial Building in the clear night sky, the final impression for all attending was to shine the Gospel of Jesus Christ all over the world just as the fireworks spread light all over the beautiful spring Texas sky.

Trustee Meetings Sandwiched Between Centennial Events

Getting Southwestern Seminary trustees on campus twice a year is a logistical activity within itself, but to have them on campus several times during the Centennial Celebration Year was yet another challenge. However, seminary business had to go on, and although the trustees were on campus several times during the centennial year for other activities, the bi-annual meeting is a bylaw must. During the spring meeting, April 7-9, 2008, three new professors were elected, one professor was tenured, and four professors were promoted in rank. One major activity during the meeting was the announcement of groundbreaking for the Horner Homemaking House, an instructional facility. All the necessary funds for the construction of the facility had been secured, and groundbreaking would be announced in the immediate future.

A new recommendation about the new student housing was shared with the trustees. Whereas the original plan was to have four quad units, totaling 16 apartments, the new design would be three units with six apartments each, totaling 18 apartments. Current projections had the units completed by January 2009.[87]

During the October 20-22, 2008, trustee meeting, Patterson informed the trustees about the five consistent enrollment growth years from 2004-2008; the official totals were from 3,551 to 3,581, with this year's enrollment being the highest in five years. On the main campus, the unofficial total was 2,671 in comparison with 2,567 in 2004. The number of total graduates in all four schools in 2004 was 190, and in 2008 the number was 244, supporting a five-year growth pattern.[88]

A recommendation was made that an immediate study be undertaken to study needed improvements for the older J. Howard Williams Student Village apartments and to determine if some needed to be razed and others remodeled.[89] A final resolution was prepared by the trustees to support Dr. and Mrs. Patterson against recent public attacks. The board prepared a 25-statement resolution about the Pattersons' integrity, openness, accomplishments, and conservative theological position, ending with a resolution stating,

> The board of trustees of Southwestern Baptist Theological Seminary, October 20-22, expresses sincere gratitude for the first five years of service of Paige Patterson as president, and be it further resolved that the board expresses their commitment to prayer and hope to God for many more years of service from Paige and Dorothy Patterson.[90]

40th Annual Centennial Youth Lab

The 40th annual Youth Lab, "Overwhelmed, Humbled in His Presence," welcomed over 1,200 youth ministers, volunteer youth leaders, and teenagers from across the United States. The spring lab event became a premier national training event for student ministry. The keynote speaker for this year's lab was Francis Chan, who identified the biggest challenges in youth ministry today:

> We tend to teach students not to do bad sins, which paints such a small picture of God. They need to be overwhelmed by Him. Our theology and our reality are so far apart that it sets us up for ridicule. If you become overwhelmed with who God is, awed by His presence, you are going to get excited to see God reveal His presence in your high schools and in your churches.[91]

One of the highlights of this year's lab, led by students Jeff Black and Clay Thomas, master of arts students in the School of Educational Ministries, was the Reality Revival Experience on Saturday. During the Reality Revival Experience, the conferees were given a glimpse of what components were present in all the past revival upheavals, such as the "haystack prayer meeting" that led to revival celebrations at the beginning of the 20th century. The session led the students to internalize how God could move with overwhelming power in their own individual lives and do things in their churches, schools, and communities that could not be done by a Christian working in the flesh. The participants needed to understand that they were the source of revival in their time, and that they could be the generation that could change the world. They also grasped the reality that such a revival needed to start with each individual actively participating in personal daily prayer, Bible study, Scriptural reflection, and daily worship of God, who can overwhelm all of us with His supernatural power.

100 Days of Evangelism

Engraved in a cornerstone on Fort Worth Hall, 1910, by B.H. Carroll were the words, "As You Go, Preach." This phrase became the impetus for a centennial plan for 100 days of evangelism by the administration, faculty, and students of Southwestern. Plans were already in motion to "Take the Hill," an evangelistic opportunity for every student to move beyond the campus into a one-mile radius of the seminary and present the Gospel to people in every home within that mile. A continual reminder by the seminary's administration to "Do the work of the evangelist" had permeated a movement far beyond the "Hill" into other opportunities for evangelism.

In celebration of Southwestern's centennial, the professors set the example in the first 50 days in the spring and 50 days in the fall of the 100 Days of Evangelism to encourage students to get out and evangelize in their areas of influence, wherever that may be. As reported in the summer 2008 issue of Southwestern News, School of Educational Ministries professor John Babler "has taken the opportunity to become a leader in the Texas Alliance Raceway Ministries (TxARM) that is part of the Motor Racing Outreach. Some may call Babler a professor, but many at the Raceway call him an evangelist."[92]

Babler became involved with TxARM when his son, Hudson, was 10 years of age and a huge racing fan. (During the centennial year, Hudson was a junior in the College at Southwestern preparing for a life of vocational ministry.) Babler had invited other professors to volunteer during the two annual races in the spring and fall to help evangelize the people who frequented the NASCAR races. In years past, ministry at the raceway focused on the children with bounce houses and other children's activities, but now under Babler's leadership, evangelism had taken on new meaning as the ministers moved among the community campsites at the racetrack sharing the Gospel from RV to RV and inviting the occupants to evangelistically driven musical concerts and five church services.

Caleb Higgins, a student in the College at Southwestern who grew up a NASCAR fan, realized the evangelistic opportunity available after attending his first race in 2006, "since NASCAR is one of the only sports that still allows public prayer in Jesus' name," he said. Higgins realized the fans may be open to Christ since they hear His name before every race, even televising the prayer. "The sad fact is that most of them don't have a personal relationship with Christ," Higgins said. "But if you just show them you care for them, they will listen."[93]

Cameron Moore, who had been a raceway chaplain in Dallas and Austin, said, "Many fans are trying to use NASCAR to fill the spiritual void in their lives. When you look around you at the raceway, the fans have all of their physical needs met. They have food, shelter, and friends, but they still know there is something in their lives that is missing."[94] Babler met Moore at a NASCAR race at the TxARM Raceway and introduced him to Southwestern. Moore began classes at Southwestern in May 2008 to pursue his master's degree.

Babler reminded the centennial participants at a meeting during celebration week of the tremendous evangelistic opportunities at the TxARM Raceway when the crowd would be about 80,000—a large community of RVs at different campsites. Even the smallest event at TxARM is still the largest sporting event in North Texas.[95]

Centennial Celebration Focuses on Women's Studies

The Women's Studies program at Southwestern Seminary is a vital part of the School of Theology and the School of Educational Ministries and invites all student wives to participate in one of many accredited opportunities. The Student Wives Certificate (13 credit hours) prepares a pastor's wife to stand alongside her husband in a church and minister to the women of the church in which they will serve. The Leadership Certificate in Women's Ministry (12 credit hours) equips a laywoman or professional church staff woman to lead a women's ministry in a local church in a professional manner with quality instruction and training.

The Bachelor of Arts in Humanities in the College at Southwestern with a homemaking concentration (131 credit hours) provides a woman an earned college degree with theological and educational training for ministry. This degree prepares the woman for her role in the home of nurturing and caring for her family while at the same time preparing her for ministry as a staff person in a local church, on the mission field, or as the helpmate of her husband in ministry.

The Master of Divinity in Women's Studies (91 credit hours) provides a study opportunity in theological education through a program that focuses on womanhood in the home, the church, and the community. The Master of Divinity in Women's Ministry (91 credit hours) prepares a woman through the study of significant theological courses including languages, systematic theology, evangelism, missions, and the like to practice and lead a ministry to women in the local church, the mission field (foreign or home), and denominational positions that minister to women.

The Master of Arts in Christian Education, Women's Ministry Concentration (64 credit hours), prepares a woman to minister in a local church, Christian private school, mission field, or denominational leadership position with women. The Doctor of Philosophy (44 credit hours) prepares women for highly specialized ministries with women in colleges, universities, and seminaries as professionals in the field of Women's Ministry. Dean of Women's Programs Terri Stovall says,

The breadth and focus of these women's programs provide women the breadth and depth needed to be fully grounded both biblically and theologically. These women not only receive superior theological training that all Southwestern students receive but also focused study to combat evangelical feminism in our culture and to teach God's truth to women in many different contexts.[96]

NACBN Honors Dean Welch

The National Association of Church Business Administrators (NACBA), at its annual meeting in Nashville, Tennessee, inducted Robert Welch into its Church Management Hall of Fame as the "Significant Contributor to Church Management," 2008. Welch, who retired as dean of the School of Educational Ministries in July 2008, was presented this honor for his leadership in church business administration.

For the last 20 years, Welch had served as a seminar instructor for the NACBA certification program, which was held on Southwestern's campus each summer. His textbook, *The Church Organization Manual*, has been the standard for the certification program since 1992. Welch had directed the proceeds from the book to be placed in the NACBA's scholarship program and to subsidize the certification training centers. Welch's *Church Administration: Excellence and Efficiency in Ministry* is recommended by the NACBA as a textbook for classes in Southwestern's School of Educational Ministries. The royalties from the book are used to fund scholarships for disabled students at Southwestern.[97]

Welch had served as a professor of administration in the School of Educational Ministries since 1991 and had served as dean since 2003, when Daryl Eldridge resigned. Prior to his service at Southwestern Seminary, Welch served in the U.S. Navy for 22 years and retired with the rank of commander. After retirement, he returned to Norman, Oklahoma, where he served previously as a professor in the Military Science ROTC department, to serve as the church business administrator of Trinity Baptist Church.

Director of Homemaking Concentration Elected

Laura Zettler was elected as director of the Homemaking Concentration in the Women's Studies Program. President Patterson said, "I believe Laura Zettler is exactly what Southwestern needs to enter the next phase of the homemaking program. She brings the academic credentials, coupled with college teaching experience. These basic qualifications are enhanced with a heart of service and ministry."[98] Zettler completed her bachelor's and master's degrees at the University of Alabama in consumer economics. She did her doctoral studies in family and consumer economics at the University of Missouri. Terri Stovall, dean of Women's Studies, and First Lady Dorothy Patterson visited with Zettler about the Lord's vision for the Homemaking Program that He had placed on their hearts and concluded that she was a perfect fit for the next phase of the Homemaking Concentration program.

Wesley Black, Acting Dean, School of Educational Ministries

Robert Welch retired as dean of the School of Educational Ministries in July 2008 and was replaced by Acting Dean Wesley Black, professor of youth/student ministry, during the trustee meeting, November 20-22, 2008. Black had been a faculty member since 1983 and had also served as the associate dean for the research/doctoral program.

During his tenure as a professor, Black had the privilege of learning from the example of three deans (Terry, Eldridge, and Welch) about the leadership and administration of the School of Educational Ministries. Black said of his new interim position: "I feel the interim positions I have led in churches will help me continue the work that someone else has started, while moving forward with new tasks and challenges that lie ahead."[99] Black would serve as interim dean until the trustees met to appoint a new dean at their April 2009 meeting.

Chair of Biblical Counseling Inaugurated

The Hope for the Heart Chair of Biblical Counseling was inaugurated and installed on November 12, 2008. The faculty, in full academic regalia, were present during the chapel hour of the inauguration, giving impetus to the importance of academic chairs as part of an institution's heritage. Elias Moitinho, assistant professor of psychology and counseling was elected by the trustees to occupy the chair. Moitinho has taught at seminaries in Cuba, Mexico, and Spain.

Hope for the Heart, a biblical counseling ministry that includes an engaging radio broadcast that is aired daily in the United States and in over 26 different countries, funded the chair. Its founder, June Hunt, is the author of *Counseling Through the Bible* and *Biblical Counseling Keys*. During the inauguration ceremony, Hunt said that her organization endowed the Chair of Biblical Counseling to aid Southwestern in training men and women to provide the healing Word to a hurting world. Explaining the evangelistic opportunities presented in counseling sessions, Hunt said, "This is, in many places throughout the world, how we will reach people for Christ.[100]

Sarah Horner Homemaking House Dedication

The April 6-8, 2009, semi-annual meeting of the trustees was the venue that ushered in the newly completed Horner House, the homemaking house that had been under construction since approval by the trustees in the fall meeting, with groundbreaking on August 13, 2008. The Horner House, named for Andy and Joan Horner, founder and CEO of Premiere designs, was dedicated on April 8, 2009.

The homemaking program, primarily part of the College at Southwestern, and the accredited women's program certificate for women will use the facilities of the Horner House expeditiously. The gracious gift by Baily Draper, son of Dr. and Mrs. Jimmy Draper, was the construction of the house by his company at his cost. His friend, Jon Bolton, also a committed believer, provided the architectural drawings of the house free of charge. The house was completed in record time.

The uniqueness of this educational building is resident in its multipurpose rooms such as an oversized kitchen for teaching nutrition and meal preparation; the textile/sewing room for making and caring for clothing; and the living/dining area for entertaining and table preparation for dinners, teas, and receptions using all the necessary tableware in its proper order. The Horner House is an answer to prayer for the Women's

Programs at Southwestern, both for the college and the master's-level programs in the schools of educational ministries and theology.

The trustees received a recommendation for a new concentration in Christian School Education in the Master of Arts in Christian School Education in the School of Educational Ministries. The new concentration was specifically designed for students interested in administration or teaching opportunities in Christian private schools. The courses in the concentration prepared the individual for an administrative position or teaching position. The courses include Philosophy of Christian School Education, Christian School Curriculum, Christian School Administration, Methods and Instructional Strategies, and Christian School Legal Issues and Finances.[101]

Elected to the School of Educational Ministries faculty at this meeting was Karen Kennemur, assistant professor of children's ministry. Kennemur had experience in several local churches and most recently served as director of the curriculum center in Southwestern's School of Educational Ministries as well as graduate assistant and adjunct professor of children's ministry.

New Dean for the School of Educational Ministries

Waylan Owens was elected as an associate professor of pastoral ministries in the School of Theology at Southwestern Seminary in 2008. President Patterson named him dean of the School of Educational Ministries, effective August 1, 2009.

Patterson, in an announcement to the seminary faculty, staff, and students, thanked Wes Black for his service as interim dean in the School of Educational Ministries. (Black would continue in his role as associate dean for the research/doctoral program and professor of youth/student ministry.) In the announcement, Patterson recognized Owens for his keen ability to manage the deanship of the School of Educational Ministries. He said, "Owens has a thorough knowledge of accreditation, a full understanding of church life in America today, and a grasp of the new directions that must be taken in the area of Christian education in the days that lie ahead."[102]

Owens served in various capacities at Southeastern Seminary during Patterson's tenure as president there. He was the vice president for planning and communication, associate professor of pastoral ministries, and special assistant to the president while Patterson served as president of the Southern Baptist Convention. Owens earned his B.A. from West Florida University, Pensacola, Florida (1983), and his M.Div. (1987) and Ph.D. (1992) from New Orleans Baptist Theological Seminary. He previously served as a middle school math and science teacher in public and private schools in Florida, Louisiana, and Mississippi; and he pastored churches in Mississippi, Alaska, and North Carolina.

Construction for 3,500-Seat Chapel Approved

The trustees recommended the authorization of the seminary administration to obtain the services of a construction management company as an owner's representative and general contractor for the purpose of completing the construction of the Riley Chapel not to exceed $30.2 million.[103] The board also approved the ceremonial groundbreaking to be held during the fall board meeting, October 21, 2009, in the afternoon at the conclusion of the meeting. The board unanimously approved the authorization of the administration to proceed with securing the company to construct the chapel.

Harold Riley, insurance executive from Austin, Texas, and the son of a Southwestern alumnus, said, "I have great admiration, I have great appreciation, and I have great thankfulness that God called my father into the ministry. I saw the life we lived and the struggles that we had getting through the different schools, with seminary being one of them. But, God always provided."[104] The impact of the seminary on his father's life and the love his father had for Jack MacGorman moved Riley and his wife Dottie to give a substantial lead gift for the purpose of building the chapel.

The great need was to have a worship center adequate for graduation and other large gatherings. The new chapel would have 3,500 seats and be one of the largest indoor event facilities in Fort Worth. Presently, Truett Auditorium, which seats a little over 1,200, was too small for the large graduation ceremonies, and Travis Avenue Baptist Church needed to be secured to accommodate the large graduation crowds. With the new chapel, that problem was solved.

In another recommendation from the academic affairs committee, President Patterson recommended a name change for the School of Educational Ministries. The recommendation was to name the school the Jack D. Terry, Jr. School of Church and Family Ministries, effective immediately.[105] Patterson said,

> Changing the school's name to the Terry School of Church and Family Ministries will encourage a family-oriented approach to ministry and reflect the variety of programs within the school. It also honors a man who has given many highly productive years to Southwestern. Jack Terry has given an unbelievable 40 years to Southwestern Seminary. He has taught as a professor, served as the dean of the School of Religious Education and as vice president of Institutional Advancement, raising significant funds and building long-lasting relationships that continue to benefit the seminary today and into the future."[106]

Terry presently serves as vice president emeritus and special assistant to the president for development as well as a senior professor of foundations of education in the School of Educational Ministries.

41st Youth Lab – "Desperate for God's Spirit"

The 41st Youth Lab looked inside to find the theme for this year's gathering, "Desperate for God's Spirit." David Platt, pastor of the Church at Brook Hills in Birmingham, Alabama, was the keynote speaker, calling the youth ministers, volunteer youth leaders, and the highest attendance in the 41 years of Youth Ministry Lab's history back to a spiritual life in the Word and in Christ. Platt told the 1,300-plus participants,

> I am part of a religious system that has created a whole host of means and methods for doing church and ministry

that, in the end, require little if any help at all from the Holy Spirit of God. We have made a deadly mistake in our day, by mistaking the presence of physical bodies for the existence of spiritual life. You can draw a crowd with anything. Moses saw the depth of the call that God had given to him to do, and he saw his own resources and he saw he didn't have what it takes to accomplish his call.[107]

During breakout sessions, Kevin DeYoung, co-author of *Why We're Not Emergent (By Two Guys Who Should Be)*, told the student audience that one of the critical misconceptions of youth ministry is that reading Scripture is old-fashioned, like reading fables. He challenged the conferees to read two things regularly: Scripture and theology. He said, "I think we are starving for it."[108]

New Seminary Seal and Logo

An institutional seal is the official mark for documents coming from the president's office, the seminary's cabinet, and the board of trustees. It is stamped on diplomas awarded by the school. The seal marks Southwestern's mission and history and remains proud of its Texas heritage. The parts of the seal have intrinsic meanings such as the rope around the entire circle heralding its "cowboy" roots. Texas' Lone Star in the middle bespeaks of the rugged Texas of the Old West. The seminary moved from Waco to Fort Worth because of its stockyards and its attachment to the Chisholm Trail coming down from Kansas. Situated six miles south of downtown and between "Hell's Half Acre" and the main city, students preached the Gospel to the patrons of the bars and brothels. B.H. Carroll was a Texas Ranger and L.R. Scarborough was reared on a ranch in West Texas where he was skilled at riding horses, handling a six-shooter, and roping steers.

In the upper top of the seal is the Latin phrase *pro ecclesia* (for the church), which reminds us that our task is to educate men and women to perform ministry in the church. Finally, the watchword that thrusts men and women into the world to spread the Gospel: "Preach the Word, Reach the World." The waves of grain sweeping up the sides of the seal are to remind us of the urgency of the necessity for the sowing of the Gospel.

The logo, a picture of an open Bible and the circumference of the earth, is reminiscent of Matthew 28:19-20: "Go therefore and make disciples of all the nations, baptizing them in the name of the Father and the Son and the Holy Spirit, teaching them to observe all that I commanded you; and lo, I am with you always, even to the end of the age."

Loyal Servant Passes Away

William R. Marshall—namesake of Southwestern's extension center in San Antonio; radio and television personality; and public school teacher, principal, and superintendent in Bexar County—passed away October 23, 2008. Marshall was an advocate for Southwestern in South Texas and for San Antonio in particular. He served in his local church as a Sunday School teacher, deacon, and committeeman. He was a member of the executive board of the Baptist General Convention of Texas, the San Antonio Baptist Association, and the board of trustees for the Hispanic Baptist Theological Seminary. As a member of the board of the Hispanic Baptist Theological Seminary, he assisted the fledgling seminary that offered only undergraduate degrees to later become an international seminary offering master's-level education.

Marshall became the director of the San Antonio extension center in the mid-1980s and served with distinction until his retirement, at which time Southwestern Seminary named the San Antonio extension center the William R. Marshall Center for Theological Studies in San Antonio. A native of San Antonio, Marshall was fervent about enhancing theological education in the city, especially for Hispanic pastors and for Christian education in the local church. He was the impetus that motivated many pastors and ministers of education in South Texas churches who could not travel to Fort Worth for seminary education to attend the seminary in San Antonio and complete a large portion of their seminary education before going to the Fort Worth campus for the remainder of their studies.

Because of his enthusiastic leadership, the extension center in San Antonio grew large enough to have major theological offerings with a dean on site. This gentleman, who loved the Lord and whose favorite expression was "Bless your heart!," led the South Texas extension center to its highest enrollment to date. Although he retired in 2000, he continued to work with Rudy Gonzalez, dean of the San Antonio Center, until the time of his death. All Southern Baptists of Bexar County and San Antonio in particular will miss this giant of a man whose greatest love was for his fellow man, especially the Hispanic church leaders and Southwestern Baptist Theological Seminary.

Notes

1 Black, Walter J. *The Complete Works of William Shakespeare*, Published for the Classic Club, New York: 1937, p. 1124.
2 *Southwestern News*, Winter, 2000, p. 21.
3 Ibid.
4 Ibid.
5 *Southwestern News*, Fall, 2000, p. 23.
6 *Southwestern News*, Spring, 2000, p. 19.
7 Ibid.
8 *Southwestern News*, Summer, 2000, p. 23
9 Ibid., p. 22.
10 Ibid.
11 Ibid.
12 *Southwestern News*, Winter 2001, p. 12.
13 Ibid.
14 Ibid.
15 Ibid.
16 Ibid., p. 13.
17 *Southwestern News*, Summer, 2001, p. 33.
18 Ibid.
19 *Southwestern News*, Spring, 2001, p. 20.
20 Ibid., p. 21.
21 *Southwestern News*, Spring, 2002, p. 22.
22 *Southwestern News*, Summer, 2002, p. 26.
23 Ibid., p. 4.

24 Ibid., p. 27.
25 Ibid.
26 Ibid., p. 27.
27 Ibid.
28 *Southwestern News*, Summer, 2002, p. 31.
29 Ibid.
30 *Celebrating 100 Years*, Southwestern Baptist Theological Seminary, 2008, p. 115.
31 Trustee Minutes, April 7-9, 2003, p. 9.
32 Trustee Minutes, April 7-9, 2003, p. 15.
33 Ibid., p. 21.
34 *Southwestern News*, Spring, 2003, p. 28.
35 Ibid.
36 Ibid., p. 29.
37 *Southwestern News*, Winter, 2003, p. 37.
38 Trustee Report, April 7-9, 2003, p. 10.
39 Ibid.
40 Ibid.
41 *Southwestern News*, Summer, 2003, p. 31.
42 Ibid.
43 Minutes of the Called Meeting board of trustees, June 24, 2003, pp. 1-2.
44 Ibid.
45 Ibid.
46 *Celebrating 100 Years*, Southwestern Baptist Theological Seminary, 2008, p. 124.
47 Ibid., p. 125.
48 Ibid.
49 Ibid., p. 127.
50 *Southwestern News*, Spring, 2004, p. 28.
51 Ibid.
52 Trustee Minutes, April 5-7, 2004, p. 4.
53 Ibid., p. 6.
54 *Southwestern News*, Summer, 2004, p. 52.
55 Ibid.

56 Ibid.
57 Trustee Minutes, April 4-6, 2005, p. 13
58 Ibid., p. 5.
59 Trustee Minutes, April, 5-6, 2004, p. 22.
60 *Southwestern News*, Fall, 2005, p. 44.
61 Ibid.
62 *Southwestern News*, Winter, 2005, p. 35.
63 Ibid.
64 *Southwestern News*, Summer, 2005, p. 32.
65 Ibid.
66 Trustee Minutes, April 3-5, 2006, p. 4.
67 *Southwestern News*, Summer, 2006, p. 39.
68 Trustee Minutes, April 3-5, 2006, p. 12.
69 Ibid. p. 44
70 Ibid.
71 *Southwestern News*, Winter, 2006, p. 38.
72 Ibid.
73 *Southwestern News*, Summer, 2006, p. 36.
74 Ibid.
75 *Southwestern News*, Summer, 2007, p. 48.
76 Trustee Minutes, October 15-17, 2007, p. 8-9.
77 *Southwestern News*, Fall, 2007, p. 41.
78 *Southwestern News*, Summer, 2007, p. 37.
79 Ibid.
80 Ibid.
81 *Southwestern News*, Summer, 2008, p. 41.
82 Baker, Robert, *Tell the Generations Following*, Broadman Press, Nashville, TN, 1983, p 136.
83 *Southwestern News*, Summer, 2008, p. 40.
84 Ibid.
85 Ibid.
86 Ibid.
87 Trustee Minutes, Consent Agenda, April 7-9, 2008, p. 3.
88 Historic Enrollment data (1993-1015), Southwestern Seminary Office of the Registrar, June, 2015.

89 Trustee Minutes, October 20-22, 2008, p. 10.
90 Ibid., pp. 6-7.
91 *Southwestern News*, Summer, 2008, p. 5.
92 Ibid., pp. 30-33.
93 Ibid.
94 Ibid.
95 Ibid.
96 *Southwestern News*, Fall, 2008, p. 8-9.
97 Ibid., p. 4
98 Ibid., p. 3.
99 *Southwestern News*, Winter, 2009, p. 35.
100 Ibid.
101 Trustee Minutes, April 6-8, 2009, p. 6.
102 *Southwestern News*, Fall, 2009, p. 38.
103 Trustee Minutes, October 19-21, 2009, p. 7.
104 *Southwestern News*, Fall, 2009, p. 38.
105 Ibid., p. 39.
106 Ibid.
107 *Southwestern News*, Summer, 2009, p. 32.
108 Ibid.

Photos

Page 246 – Portrait of Robert Welch.

Page 275 – Religious education deans Jack Terry, Robert Welch, and Daryl Eldridge.

Page 277 – Robert Welch with professor Phil Briggs at the dedication of the Phillip H. Briggs Collection in Roberts Library.

Page 288 – A typical scene from Southwestern's annual Youth Ministry Lab in Truett Auditorium.

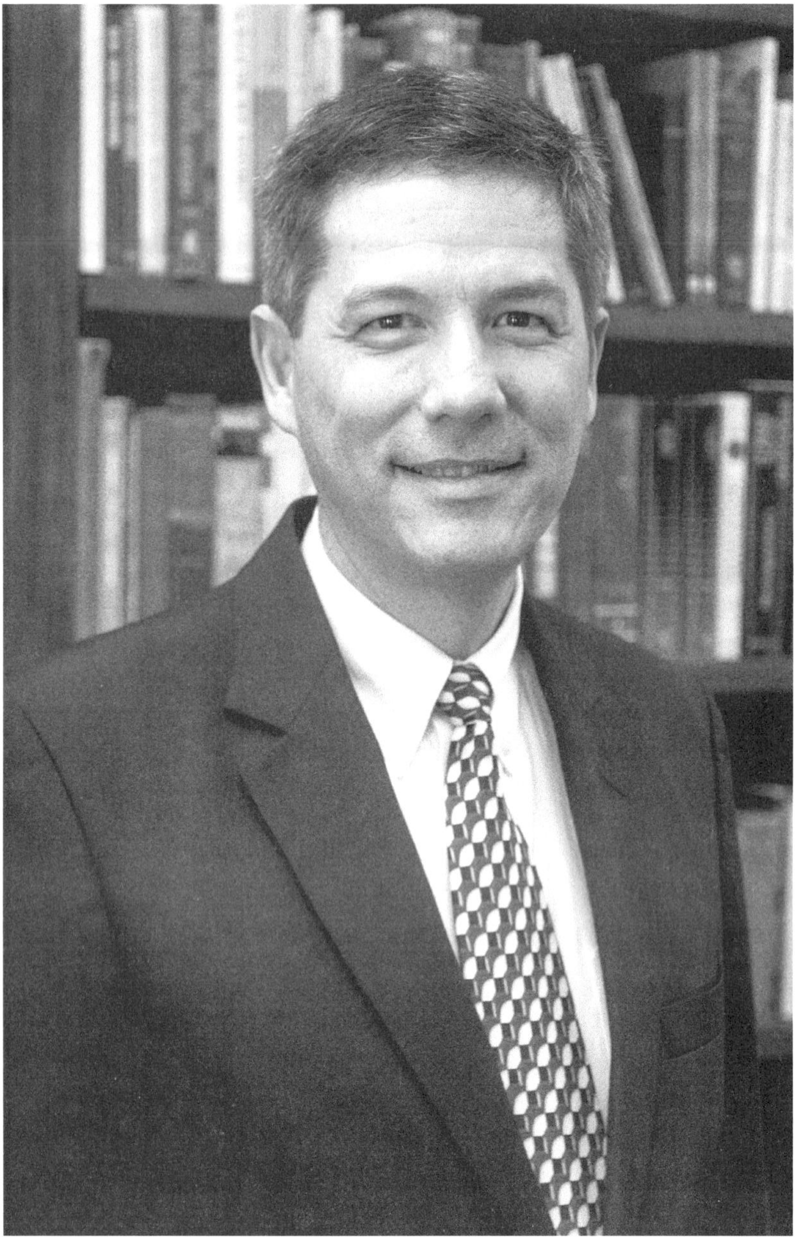

Chapter 6

The Evolution of A School
2010-2015

School of Educational Ministries Has a New Name

In 2009, the School of Educational Ministries, by a vote of the trustees, was named the Jack D. Terry, Jr. School of Church and Family Ministries to better reflect the mission of the school and to honor one of its longtime faculty members and deans. Patterson, in his recommendation for the name change, said to the board, "The changing face of church life in America and in the churches of the Southern Baptist Convention has revealed an alarming loss of emphasis on the preparation of families in the local church to accomplish tasks assigned by our Lord."[1] He continued,

> The School of Church and Family Ministries stands as the largest and oldest religious education school in the world. For nearly a century, the school has pioneered new programs, curriculum advances, and innovative strategies in the field of Christian education. Unparalleled in the areas of interactive learning, field experiences, and internships, the school remains a top supplier of professors and educators across the denomination as well as in schools, colleges, universities, and seminaries around the world.[2]

Chapel Construction Progressing

The new chapel construction progressed rapidly toward completion. Within six months of its groundbreaking, an almost completed edifice was growing daily on the location of the groundbreaking ceremony. Harold Riley, who spoke at the groundbreaking and gave his testimony of how his father, a West Texas roughneck, was called to ministry and how their family struggled during his father's studies at Southwestern, had once again stepped up with a lead gift for the chapel. Riley and his wife Dottie gave the lead gift for the Ray I. Riley Center, just to the east of the chapel construction, and blessed the seminary with another lead gift for the chapel. Just as they named the adjacent center for his father, Ray I. Riley, they chose to name the second building phase, the chapel, for his father's favorite professor, Jack MacGorman, professor of Greek and New Testament. The 3,500-seat chapel would serve as the worship center for daily chapel services and for other venues such as graduation twice a year, musical presentations like the School of Church Music's annual Gala, civic gatherings, and special events. One such special event, just on the horizon, was the "Dead Sea Scrolls and Biblical Exposition" that encompassed most of the chapel facility for a six-month period of time.

A special feature in the construction of the chapel was the large baptismal pool at the main entrance to the building from the campus. This baptismal pool was not only to enhance the beauty and ambiance of the building as a continuous flowing fountain but would also have a very practical purpose. Every student pastor needs to learn how to baptize a believer correctly. Pastoral ministry classes that teach baptism use the baptismal pool in a very practical way to teach the correct method.

As a major addition to each of the lobbies, on the first and second floors are several library rooms constructed specifically to house special library collections and personal effects of outstanding ministers and laymen in the Southern Baptist Convention. There would also be two prayer rooms, one on either end of the second floor lobby. On the east side, there would be a prayer tower and prayer room named for Dottie Riley, wife of Harold Riley. On the west side, there would be a prayer room named for Don Miller, an outstanding pastor and instructor in the ministry of prayer, and his wife Libby. At the rear end of the second floor lobby is a large gathering room for relaxation and refreshment during the intermissions at special events named in honor of Minette and Huber Drumwright, former professor of Greek and New Testament and dean of the School of Theology and executive director of the Arkansas Baptist Convention.

Special study rooms were embedded in the hallway adjacent to the Drumwright Room for chapel speakers to rest and pray as they prepared for their chapel messages. The chapel was a magnificent addition to the landscape of the campus, and its imposing structure highlighted the ministry of the Word of God on the Southwestern Seminary campus.

Trustees Evaluate Two Major Program Necessities

During the two semi-annual meetings, the board of trustees was given several recommendations concerning major program necessities. Pieces of Scriptural antiquity, the Dead Sea Scrolls, were presented. Many scholars argue that the Dead Sea Scrolls discovery was the greatest archaeological discovery of the 20th century.

Trustee Gary Loveless, founder of Square Mile Energy in Houston, Texas, provided the lead gift for the purchase of the fragments from a private collection in Europe. President Patterson told the trustees that he was grateful for the three fragments that included Exodus 23, Leviticus 18, and Daniel 6, which are still owned by Southwestern. Patterson said, "I am particularly grateful for having Daniel fragments. Daniel is one of the most attacked books in the Bible. It was clear that these fragments were copies of copies of copies so that it established the certainty that Daniel was written when it claims to have been written."[3] Included in the construction plans for the chapel was a state-of-the-art library to house the Dead Sea Scrolls fragments as well as other ancient artifacts.

A report was made to the trustees by the academic affairs committee concerning the progress taking place with the unified Southwestern counseling program model. The program proposal being studied by the academic administration committee was to combine the two counseling programs—the biblical counseling program and the marriage and family counseling program—into a single, unified counseling program. This changed the nature of the marriage and family counseling program considerably and placed strong emphasis on a biblical counseling model design as the major counseling program focus on the campus.[4]

Patterson disapproves of clinical psychology because of its humanistic philosophical approach, as well as the leading psychological proponents (Freud in particular) who led the charge. Patterson was not pleased with the involvement the State of Texas had as the licensing agent for seminary clinical psychology graduates. He felt strongly that a state-licensed counselor was more than acceptable in the private sector but was not needed on a local church staff. He was convinced a biblical approach to counseling was more realistic and stood stronger in line with the Word of God. A major emphasis in biblical counseling became the direction of the Department of Biblical Counseling, offering a new degree, Master of Arts in Biblical Counseling (M.A.B.C.).

First Family Ministry Conference

The seminary hosted the first Family Ministry Conference on February 26-27, 2010. The conference was developed to assist and encourage all ministers to consider seriously the role of the family in the spiritual development of the family within the mission and ministry of their churches. The recognition of the lack of participation on the part of the parents in the spiritual lives of their children had brought religious educators to ask solemn questions about the spiritual effectiveness of programs in the church for the various age-level groups. Richard Ross, professor of youth/student ministry, said:

The family exists primarily for the glory and adoration of God. Spouses are responsible to encourage each other to love God, and parents have the responsibility of raising their kids to love God. They should also encourage their children to allow Christ to live through them. Scripture exhorts parents to tell their children about God's truth. If this does not happen, however, the truth can be lost. In the absence of faith at home, do we really think church programs can make up the difference?[5]

Major speakers at the first Family Ministry Conference included Waylan Owens, dean of the Terry School of Church and Family Ministries; Brian Haynes, associate pastor at Kingsland Baptist Church, Katy, Texas; Steve Hunter, executive director of counseling ministries at Hope for the Heart, Dallas, Texas; and Ken Lasater of the Southern Baptists of Texas Convention (SBTC).

42nd Youth Ministry Lab, Empowering Prayer

The second largest group on record gathered for the 42nd Youth Ministry Lab with 1,310 attendees to confront the empowering power of concerted prayer. During the lab, April 9-10, 2010, a 24-hour prayer room was available with Youth Ministry Lab leadership welcoming the students and youth ministers for intercessory prayer and contemplation.

The entire weekend before the lab, Youth Lab student volunteers were awoken at all hours of the night by text messages from other Youth Lab leaders as part of an unbroken 36-hour prayer chain. Pulling themselves out of bed, they prayed for an hour for the participants, the speakers, and the empowering of God's Holy Spirit to come down on the meeting.

One of the speakers, Southwestern alumnus Wes Hamilton, said, "Success is good, but it has the potential to dull one's appetite for giving God glory and pursuing Him, which results in hypocrisy as the life and message of a minister cease to match up."[6] J.R. Vassar, pastor of Apostle's Church in New York City, led a plenary session on the importance of Holy Spirit-driven leadership. Seminary professors David Allen, Malcolm Yarnell, and Paige Patterson participated in an open forum confronting difficult Bible questions such as the security of the believer, eschatology, whether there was a literal seven-day creation, etc.

The youth ministers, volunteer youth leaders, and the youth attending were encouraged to learn hermeneutics in order to understand that it is necessary to learn how to study the Bible in order to know how to teach others to study the Bible. The lab was a spiritual dynamo of Holy Spirit-filled empowering of the youth and youth leadership who attended.

The Teaching Legacy of Lottie Moon

A cargo container arrived on the Southwestern campus from China on December 16, 2010, containing the Chinese home and personal belongings of Southern Baptist Missionary to China Lottie Moon. Plans were made to preserve the legacy of Lottie Moon by displaying her home and belongings to a Southern Baptist community that has given missions offerings in her name since 1916. Most Southern Baptists have participated in the Lottie Moon Christmas Offering for Foreign Missions at one time or another. In the cargo container were some of Moon's furniture, chairs, a stove, bricks, roof tiles, and other materials from her home in P'ingtu, China. The crates—carrying 35,000 pounds of materials—also contained antiquities from 19th-century P'ingtu City that will help Baptists understand the Chinese culture and the people to whom Moon devoted her life.[7]

The furnishings were in a four-room house with dirt floors, clay shingles, and thatched roof that rented for $24 a year. Moon lived, cooked, and entertained guests in three rooms, and she rested and prayed in the fourth. Her bed was a Chinese kang—a traditional bed made of mud bricks and covered with a thatched straw mat.

Expressions of thanks were given to Paul Kim, pastor of Berkland Baptist Church, Cambridge, Massachusetts; and Louie Lu, president of Yangtze International, Inc., whose efforts purchased and delivered the home by boat, train, and automobile.[8] A prominent location to showcase the Lottie Moon legacy treasures permanently was discussed by the president and the trustees.

Time Capsule Marks 100 Years

October 19, 2010, marked 100 years of ministry education for Southwestern Baptist Theological Seminary in Fort Worth, Texas. In 1910, the seminary moved from its place of origin, Baylor University, to its new home in Fort Worth, Texas. The seminary opened its doors for the first student on October 3, 1910. A century had passed.

The celebration for this 100-year anniversary was highlighted when the city of Fort Worth proclaimed October 19, 2010, "Southwestern Seminary Day" and presented a framed proclamation in the chapel service. At that chapel service, a 60-year-old time capsule containing treasures from Southwestern's past was opened. The container was placed in the cornerstone of the B.H. Carroll Memorial Building on January 24, 1950, and was re-set on December 6, 1955, when the building was expanded. Three books were in the container—B.H. Carroll's *Jesus the Christ*; a signed copy of L.R. Scarborough's *With Christ After the Lost*; and E.D. Head's *The Bible Book by Book*. Other treasures were two Bibles, one from E.D. Head and the other from J. Howard Williams; sermon notes from George W. Truett, for whom the auditorium was named; a statement of faith and Christian stewardship booklet written by William Fleming, for whom the east wing of the building was named; seminary catalogues and orders of services from 1950-1955 chapels, convocations, and celebrations; and a list of trustees and Fort Worth City Councilmen from 1955.[9] Barry Driver, dean of libraries said, "There is nothing new in the materials, but it gives us a window into seminary life on the Hill 55-60 years ago as well as a picture of liturgical life, the scholarly life, even the exemplars of the writing that was done at that time."[10]

New Student Housing Approved

One of the most pressing needs on the seminary campus was the need for additional larger housing for married students. The trustees, at their April 6-8, 2011, meeting, approved plans for the construction of married student housing, Phases 1 and 2. Phase 1 was immediately across the street from the main entrance of the campus on Seminary Drive, in an open field adjacent to the current student housing. This large area is bordered by James Avenue on the east and Seminary Drive on the south and is a prominent enhancement to the corner, which had been an open field. Phase 2 replaced the oldest section of the current student housing immediately across the street from the main campus facing the B.H. Carroll Memorial building, constructed in 1958.

The completion of Phase 1 consisted of 12 buildings that have 26 two-bedroom units and 36 three-bedroom units for a total of 252 new units. The construction of the new three-bedroom units provided opportunity for families with children to have a larger apartment. Another amenity was the common area to the west of the new apartments with a large playground, pavilion, and picnic area.

Accreditation Reaffirmed

Southwestern is accredited by three major accrediting agencies: Southern Association of Colleges and Schools (SACS), National Association of Schools of Music (NASM), and the Association of Theological Schools (ATS). On June 27, 2011, Southwestern Seminary received a letter of reaffirmation following evaluation. A comprehensive assessment committee of the ATS reaffirmed Southwestern Seminary's accreditation for the customary 10 years, with the next evaluation coming in 2021. Patterson told the good news to employees in a campus email expressing his appreciation for all who aided in the preparation for the board's site visit and the faculty for their constant excellence.[11]

Trustees Elect New Faculty

Faculty acquisitions during the spring meeting enhanced the Terry School of Church and Family Ministries with the election of two new faculty members. Frank Catanzaro was elected as associate professor of adult education and counseling as well as associate dean for the Doctor of Educational Ministry program. Catanzaro's ministry experience included minister of music positions, associate pastorates, and a tenure as associate professor of counseling at Southeastern Seminary.

Patricia L. Nason was elected as professor of foundations of education and director of the Master of Arts in Christian School Education program. Her prior teaching experience included: lecturer at Texas

A&M University; assistant professor at University of North Carolina; associate professor at Stephen F. Austin State University; and professor of science education and department chair at the Institute for Creation Research Graduate School.

During the October 20-22, 2010, meeting, the trustees approved the recommendation by the president and the academic affairs committee for a Master of Arts in Biblical Counseling degree. The degree is the culmination of the study for a unified Southwestern counseling program model that was recommended to the trustees at the October 2009 meeting. This new biblical counseling degree replaced the former counseling degree, Master of Arts in Marriage and Family Counseling (M.A.M.F.C.). (Students enrolled in the M.A.M.F.C. degree are allowed to complete the degree or transfer courses over to the new biblical counseling degree.)

The new master's degree is 66 hours and was designed by the Southwestern counseling faculty. Waylan Owens, dean of the Terry School of Church and Family Ministries, said, "We are committed to preparing counselors who will apply the words of the Bible to the point of God's work in a person's life, seeking first of all a right relationship with Christ for every person we serve, primarily in the context of the local church."[12]

The degree included courses in Old Testament and New Testament studies, systematic theology, and hermeneutics, which form the basic biblical basis for counseling. The counseling courses included in the degree plan examined the history of counseling, psychology, and psychotherapy while at the same time providing a biblical approach for counseling in such matters as: sexuality, gender, marriage, family, and grief. As a major facet of the counseling program, the students conducted their counseling sessions through the Walsh Counseling Center while being observed, critiqued, assessed, and evaluated by the biblical counseling faculty.

In regard to this new biblical counseling degree, John Babler, professor of biblical counseling and chairman of the Department of Biblical Counseling, made several observations about the need for the biblical counseling degree. He observed,

> Many years ago the church became very comfortable with outsourcing counseling. In fact, for years, the primary teaching in seminary for pastors and others was the defer-and-refer mentality: defer to the professionals and refer to the professionals.... Because of that, I think the church has been absent from being able to minister freely the love of Christ to people in crisis and challenging situations.[13]

Another professor in the biblical counseling department, David Penley, said,

> The church and the Word of God lie at the heart of Southwestern's counseling program. The emphasis upon the church also complements the vision of the Terry School for Church and Family Ministries as reflected in its name. The ministry of counseling naturally enhances Christ's mission for the whole church, namely, evangelism and discipleship.[14]

Elias Moitinho, assistant professor of psychology and counseling, said,

> God calls counselors to interpret and apply God's Word on a one-on-one or small-group basis much as He calls us to proclaim the Scripture to a congregation. Counseling has to be Bible-driven, it must go beyond merely symptom relief, and it must aim at spiritual transformation, to get people to conform to the likeness of Christ.[15]

The new counseling degree was intended to re-emphasize the church's ministry of counseling. As reflected in its name, Southwestern Seminary's Master of Arts in Biblical Counseling upholds the centrality of Scripture in the practice and ministry of counseling and must be used effectively and employed consistently in all counseling encounters and situations.

Professors Recognized for Articles on Childhood Evangelism and Baptism

The Associated Christian Press (ACP) and the Evangelical Press Association (EPA) recognized several writers from Southwestern Seminary for articles published in 2010. The Associated Christian Press gave the award to The Alabama Baptist for "Baptizing Children." The series of articles was written by Southwestern president Paige Patterson; Malcolm B. Yarnell, associate professor of systematic theology; Karen Kennemur, assistant professor of childhood education ministry; Kelly King, assistant professor of childhood education; Joy Cullen, adjunct faculty member; and Waylan Owens, dean of the Terry School of Church and Family Ministries.[16] Owens' article, "Preparing a Child's Heart to Respond to Christ," won first place among evangelism articles in EPA's Higher Goals Awards, and competed with work in nationally known magazines such as Christianity Today.

Beloved Professor Passes Away

J. Leon Marsh, distinguished professor of foundations of education, passed away on December 12, 2011. Marsh taught from 1956 to 1986 when he retired to his boyhood hometown of Arab, Alabama. Marsh was a favorite of J.M. Price, who mentored him in his own distinctive teaching discipline, philosophy and history of education and educational psychology.

Prior to his 30 years at Southwestern, Marsh taught at Hardin-Simmons University in the Department of Religious Education and Bible and served as dean of men. Marsh had an unusual ability to mentor young students at Southwestern even as Price mentored him. Jack Terry, former dean of the Terry School, said,

> I recall when I matriculated at Southwestern Seminary for the first time in 1956. "Doc," as we affectionately called him, asked me where my father was. At that time, my father was an electrical supervisor on a Foster-Wheeler construction job in Bogota, Colombia. Marsh told me that day he would be my "Dad" while I was in the seminary. He did just that, and we bonded.
>
> When I graduated, Marsh wanted me to do doctoral study, but I was tired of school and wanted to do ministry in my church, First Baptist Church, Lake Jackson, Texas. A year later, "Doc" wrote me a letter and told me I had been accepted in the doctoral program and to get myself back to Fort Worth and go to work on my doctoral degree. He even recommended me to a church, North Richland Hills Baptist Church, where I served for the four years of my doctoral studies. When I was about to graduate, "Doc" recommended me to Hardin-Simmons University to teach Bible and religious education, the same place and courses he had taught there. Three years later he convinced President Robert Naylor that he needed to separate his teaching load and that he knew a teacher skilled in philosophy and history of education and principles of teaching at

Hardin-Simmons University who would come to Southwestern to teach those subjects. President Naylor did, and I did come back to Southwestern. Now my mentor became my colleague for 17 years.[17]

Marsh mentored many young men who were elected to the faculty at Southwestern Seminary, including William A. (Budd) Smith, Rick Yount, Daryl Eldridge, and Charles Ashby. All of us will miss our teacher, mentor, and friend. But, in our own ministries at Southwestern Seminary and beyond, we have attempted to be the kind of "Dad," mentor, and friend that J. Leon Marsh was to all of us. We all love you, "Doc," and will see you in the morning.

Two Major Events Engulf the Campus for Much of 2012

The year ended with an academic activity as a major event in a new venue, the Jack MacGorman Chapel. The first graduation took place in the new facility on December 16, 2011. The chapel was under construction very soon after the trustees approved the recommendation, and a major lead gift propelled its beginning in early 2010. Its massive footprint was outlined in concrete to the east of Pecan Manor. The enormous steel girders began to creep into the clear Texas sky and presented a form of the shape of what it was to become. Gigantic numerical figures began to mount up: 17 million pounds of concrete; 2.2 million pounds of steel; 414,000 bricks; 54 square feet of plaster; 17,400 square feet of glass; 20,000 roof tiles; 2,400 light fixtures; 130 miles of electrical, data, and A/V wire; plus one-quarter of a million man-hours with no lost time incidents.[18] Once the exterior of the building was completed in spring 2011, crews worked day and night to complete the interior task and enhanced the outside with landscaping in the O'Neal Prayer Garden between Pecan Manor and MacGorman Chapel.

On December 1, 2011, the chapel was officially dedicated with a day-long celebration. The lead donors, Harold and Dottie Riley, participated with President Patterson, Board Chairman Hance Dilbeck, and honorees Jack and Ruth MacGorman in the ribbon-cutting. That day hosted the first chapel in the new worship center, a baptism in the baptismal pool in the foyer, and a free concert in the evening. During the afternoon, multiple libraries, prayer rooms, lobbies, and special features of the chapel were highlighted.

Patterson presided over the dedication of the Leta Phillips Library, which houses the Dead Sea Scrolls and was named in honor of Gary Loveless' grandmother. Gary and Stephanie Loveless provided the lead gift for the Dead Sea Scrolls.

Orville Rogers, missionary pilot in service to the Lord, presided over his library named for him and his wife, Esther Beth. The Dottie Riley Prayer Tower, located on the east end of the second floor lobby, contains prayer kneelers and a place to make prayer requests. The tower rises above the prayer room 100 feet into the sky, pointing its pinnacle to the heavens where prayers are received in the throne room of God. On the west end of the second floor lobby is the prayer room honoring Don Miller, the founder of Bible Based Ministries, a ministry of prayer conferences, and his wife Libby.

Jim Richards, executive director of the Southern Baptists of Texas Convention, officiated the dedication of the SBTC Baptismal Pool, which is the astounding feature at the entrance of the chapel. A beautiful prayer garden, located between the chapel and Pecan Manor, memorializes the parents of Don and Elizabeth O'Neal. Seasonal blooming plants can always be found in the garden, which is designed for enhanced prayer and contemplation. The plants are all identified by colorful plaques commissioned from an Armenian potter in Jerusalem.

The first floor W.A. Criswell Lobby honors the long-time pastor of the First Baptist Church, Dallas, and links future preachers with the legacy of his pulpit ministry. Also on the first floor is the Wicker-Reed Lobby, funded by David and Carolyn Wicker and named for their parents, Dave and Helen Wicker and R. Alton and Helen Reed.

On the second floor is the Lockman Foundation Lobby, funded by and named in honor of the Lockman Foundation, which translates and distributes the New American Standard Bible. Another lobby on the second floor, honoring Andy and Joan Horner, graces the other side of the foyer and enriches the concept of the homemaking program located in the Horner House just south of Pecan Manor.

Finally, toward the rear of the west side lobby is the Huber L. Drumwright Hospitality Suite. This suite features a full kitchen and reception area used for hosting private gatherings during choral or dramatic presentation intermissions.

Graduation on Campus Again

For a long spell, 34 years in fact, the Southwestern Seminary graduating classes both spring and fall were too large to be held on the campus in the very small Truett Auditorium. Graciously, for those 34 years, Travis Avenue Baptist Church allowed Southwestern to hold its graduation exercises in their beautiful colonial appointed worship center. Truett Auditorium would accommodate less than 1,400 persons, and for 34 years, the graduation classes had as many as 3,000 attend the two commencements. The last graduation ceremony at Travis Avenue Baptist Church was on May 6, 2011. Finally, that cycle was broken with the December 16, 2011, graduation ceremony, only 15 days after the dedication of this magnificent worship facility. This historic landmark graduation came 100 years after the first graduation ceremony in the city of Fort Worth in 1910.

The first commencement ceremony in the MacGorman Chapel presented degrees and diplomas to students in the various bachelor's, master's, and doctoral degree programs. The School of Theology graduated 91; the Fish School of Evangelism and Missions, 23; the Terry School of Church and Family Ministries, 87; and the School of Church Music, eight.[19] Over the first 100 years, 42,000 students graduated from Southwestern Seminary, each trained to reach a lost and dying world for the Kingdom of God.

The Dead Sea Scrolls

The second major event that immersed the campus of Southwestern Seminary in its historical significance was the Dead Sea Scrolls and Bible Exposition, which began July 2, 2012, and continued through January 13, 2013. The history of Dorothy and Paige Patterson and the Dead Sea Scrolls reads like a modern-day mystery of intrigue and discovery.

In 1947, a Bedouin shepherd boy searching for a lost sheep in the caves around the ruins of the Qumran community of the second century B.C. threw a rock into a cave and heard breaking pottery rather than the bleating of a sheep. Crawling into the cave, he was startled to find a large room filled with clay vessels. Looking at the broken vessel, he saw what looked like writing on some kind of material. He brought some of the pieces of material back to his Bedouin tent and later attempted to sell them. An archaeologist saw the fragments and asked where he got them, and thus began the discovery of the Dead Sea Scrolls, the richest biblical treasure of second-century Scriptural texts discovered in the 20th century.

Patterson began his quest for the fragments in 1975 when he met the senior Kando, who had purchased the fragments from the Bedouin. In 2009, the son, William Kando, approached Patterson about purchasing the fragments. With financial assistance from Gary and Stephanie Loveless and others, the seminary acquired the fragments in 2010-2011.[20]

Southwestern Seminary had committed the new MacGorman Chapel as the staging area for a six-month exhibition of the fragments of the Dead Sea Scrolls that belong to Southwestern and other major educational institutions. When asked why Southwestern Seminary wanted to acquire the fragments, Patterson gave four reasons why they were so important to the seminary and to the archaeology program in particular. He said:

> First, the possession of these scrolls that are now owned by Southwestern Seminary gives our Old Testament students the opportunity to decipher ancient texts and to grasp the importance of the Dead Sea Scrolls. Students will actually have the opportunity to work closely with these fragments—an opportunity few students in the world would ever have.
>
> Second, putting these scrolls on exhibition for six months will bring thousands of people who will be in touch with the Bible and with the most ancient copies of biblical

texts. Many who attend will be Christian, but many who are not Christian will attend because of their interest in history and antiquity and want to see the scrolls. We are praying, as a result, many will come to know the Lord; in effect, the Dead Sea Scrolls Exhibition becomes a major evangelistic opportunity.

Third, we hope the children coming to the exhibition will not only learn about the Bible and the Dead Sea Scrolls but also have the opportunity to be challenged to think in new areas: riding a camel, entering a Bedouin tent like the one used by the lad who found the scrolls, visiting an artificially prepared dig site and participate in an archaeological excavation. Literally hundreds of pottery shards dating from antiquity have been planted. Each student digging will find and take home a piece of antiquity.

Finally, the Dead Sea Scrolls Exhibition will help us achieve one of our most important goals—permanent funding of our program of biblical archaeology. Southwestern purposes to provide a program of biblical archaeology that will produce professors who will stimulate the development of archaeological programs in other evangelical seminaries and colleges in America and, for that matter, around the world.[21]

An added feature to the exposition of the Dead Sea Scrolls was an authentic Bedouin goat hair tent put up on the lawn outside MacGorman Chapel. Abu Abdallah, a Jordanian Bedouin whose father is now sheik[22] and who will eventually become the head of the Ajrami Bedouin tribe, prepared Bedouin coffee. He roasted the coffee beans that he brought from Jordan over an open fire in metal kettles, ground the coffee, and served all who visited the tent an authentic cup of Bedouin coffee. Guests were invited to sip their coffee while sitting on cushions inside the tent. The Bedouin tent was put up inside the MacGorman Chapel lower lobby for the duration of the Dead Sea Scrolls and Bible Exposition.

Southwestern owns more Dead Sea scrolls than any academic institution outside Jordan and Israel, and during the six-month exposition, the campus displayed 16 scroll fragments, including Southwestern Seminary's collection as well as scroll fragments on loan from Israel, Jordan, and private collections.[23] Bruce McCoy, director of the Dead Sea Scrolls and Bible Exposition, said of the opportunity to see the scroll fragments,

> It is an opportunity to see historic documents—fragments of Holy Scripture—that they would have to go to Israel to see, and such fragments may not even be on display there if visitors did travel to Israel. I think people should come because of the high value, the fact that these are historic, they are rare, and they are fragments of the oldest manuscripts of the Hebrew Old Testament known in the world today.[24]

44th Annual Youth Lab

During the very busy 2012, other activities on the campus were relegated to more of a back-seat position on the campus calendar. This, however, did not stop the colossal Youth Ministry Lab, the 44th on the Southwestern campus.

As in other years, the Youth Ministry Lab drew over 1,000 youth ministers, volunteer youth leaders, and teenagers to the campus for a weekend of discovery, spiritual growth, and introspection of who and where they were as youth in this ever-shrinking world in which we live. The theme for the two-day conference was "In and not Of the World!" Outstanding notable Baptist leaders, along with the Southwestern faculty Wes Black, Johnny Derouen, and Richard Ross, led worship and breakout sessions and engaged the youth in the spiritual issues facing the 21st-century teenager.

The Evolution of A School

May Graduation Awards 206 Degrees and Diplomas

Just prior to the opening of the six-month Dead Sea Scrolls and Bible Exposition, MacGorman Chapel was the scene of the second graduation on campus in the past 34 years. During the May 4, 2012, commencement, 219 diplomas were awarded to 206 graduates, which included 22 bachelor's degrees, 170 master's degrees, and 14 professional and research doctoral degrees. The School of Theology awarded 99 degrees, the Fish School of Evangelism and Missions awarded 22 degrees, the Terry School of Church and Family Ministries awarded 90 degrees, and the School of Church Music awarded eight degrees.[25]

Of special interest at this commencement, Trey Thames was awarded the Master of Arts in Archaeology and Biblical Studies degree. Thames had taken the lead role in constructing the interactive, educational dig site on the campus in conjunction with Southwestern Seminary's Dead Sea Scrolls and Bible Exposition.[26]

J. Howard Williams Student Housing Never Looked So Good

As a former student, do you remember the flat-roofed, tiny one- or two-bedroom apartments, kitchen so small that you could bend over to remove an article from a cabinet on one side of the kitchen and blister yourself as you touched the oven on the other? You could hear your neighbors in the apartment next door through the thin walls, and there was little, if any, cool air coming from the small air-conditioning units. The multiple apartment units were light brown and blended well with the brown grass that was present most of the year or with the light tan dust where the grass refused to grow. This is what many remember of the 12 buildings of the J. Howard Williams Student Village in the 1960s through the '80s. As time drew on, other two-story condominium-type student apartments were constructed, and these were far better than the original 1958 models. They were much larger throughout, and the separation of the second floor bedrooms from the living room/dining and kitchen areas on the first floor where most of the studying took place was a great blessing to those who had to study and to other members of the family who wanted to sleep.

Enter 2013, and the 12 new anticipated Student Village apartments were completed and opened to seminary families. Student families, some with children and in need of the three-bedroom configuration, began moving in November 8, 2012, and continued through the month of December into Phase 1 of the student housing project. Phase 2 included the demolition of several of the 1958 flat-roofed units, making room for a larger common area with a pavilion, playground, and a picnicking area and the construction of the remaining new units. Completion of the project doubled the number of three-bedroom housing available and would bring the total number of on-campus apartments from 715 to 815. The total project was to be completed by the summer of 2013.

Students and Faculty Receive Diplomas at Fall 2012 Graduation

During the December 14, 2012, fall commencement, Terri Stovall, dean of women's programs, received a Master of Divinity degree, and Don Wyrtzen, professor of church music in the School of Music, received a Doctor of Ministry degree. Stovall, who already had her M.A.C.E. and Ph.D., wanted the M.Div. to be better prepared to train women for service in local churches, women's ministries, and missions around the world. Wyrtzen, a Dove Award-winning musician who is known worldwide for his more than 400 musical compositions and arrangements, wanted to be better trained theologically to instruct the younger church musicians in theology as well as in the dynamics of church music.

Graduating along with the two faculty members were 197 students receiving 13 undergraduate degrees, 156 master's degrees, and 32 doctoral degrees. The School of Theology awarded 85 degrees, the Fish School of Evangelism and Missions awarded 25 degrees, the Terry School of Church and Family Ministries awarded 71 degrees, and the School of Church Music awarded 12 degrees.[27] The high point of the commencement was the awarding of 32 doctoral degrees, which was the most President Patterson said he had personally witnessed. The international nature of Southwestern was demonstrated with the awarding of degrees to Yaroslav Pyzh, the president of the Ukrainian Baptist

Theological Seminary, and to Ralf Schowalter, a pastor in Rhaunen, Germany, and adjunct professor at Bibelseminar Bonn.

Trustees Approve Online Master's Degree

At their April 1-3, 2013, meeting, the board of trustees approved a completely online master's degree. The online Master of Theological Studies (MTS) and online Master of Arts in Christian Education degrees would become the shortest online master's degrees among Southern Baptist seminaries. The online degrees are taught by full-time faculty members rather than adjunct professors. Neither of these degrees is meant to replace the more comprehensive Master of Divinity or Master of Arts in Christian Education degrees, which provide further ministry training and still require a portion of credit hours to be completed on campus. The proposal was submitted to the accrediting agency ATS for approval and upon approval would be instituted immediately.

Patterson made a proposal to the board of trustees to eliminate tenure at Southwestern Seminary immediately. There were several reasons for the elimination of tenure, which formed the basis for the recommendation. The major reason dealt with the historical implications that are associated with church-sponsored academic institutions that have lost their historical faith perspectives because of faculty tenure. Patterson said:

> Tenure was created in America, virtually unique to the educational establishments. Attorneys, doctors, and pastors have no such invention. The primary purpose of tenure was to guarantee the freedom to teach in accordance with their desires and without undue obligation to the concerns of the founders and constituents of the institutions of higher education. As such, tenure was one of several devices that led to the loss of Harvard, Yale, Brown, Princeton, and a host of other church-sponsored universities from the wishes and convictions of their founders. Tenure has a long history of defending professors who are inept or failing in the discharge of their duties.[28]

A motion was made by Eddie Miller to eliminate tenure, with a second by Bart Barber, and it passed unanimously. No professor at Southwestern Seminary from that day forward will be eligible for tenure in any of the six schools. However, the trustees made a provision for elected faculty who had already been granted tenure. The provision states,

> Elected faculty who have been granted tenure by the board of trustees prior to the decision of the Board to cease the future extension of tenure effective following the Fall 2013 Board meeting shall retain the rights and privileges of tenured faculty at Southwestern Seminary according to Article VI in the Seminary bylaws last amended on April 11, 2012.[29]

Spring Graduation is a Family Affair

Several members of the graduating class were joined by their parents at the May 10, 2013, graduation ceremony. Diplomas were presented to 234 students, including 109 in the School of Theology, 20 in the Fish School of Evangelism and Missions, 76 in the Terry School of Church and Family Ministries, and 19 in the School of Church Music. Several received degrees from the College at Southwestern.

Assisting President Patterson in awarding the degrees were parents and professors whose children were in the graduating class. Senior Pastor Hayes Wicker and Senior Associate Pastor Doug Pigg each had a son in the class; Evan Wicker received a Master of Arts in Christian Education while Timothy Pigg received a Bachelor of Arts in Humanities from the College at Southwestern. John Babler, associate professor of biblical counseling, had two daughters, Rebecca Babler and Sarah Babler, each of whom received a Bachelor of Arts in Humanities from the College at Southwestern. Bill Apelian, chief publication officer of Bob Jones University in Greenville, South Carolina, and father-in-law of Ph.D. graduate Scott Aniol, offered the benediction. This was the third graduation ceremony on the campus in the newly constructed Jack MacGorman Chapel.

ATS Approves Online Master's Degrees

The online master's degrees that were approved by the trustees at the spring meeting were sent to ATS for academic approval. The approval notice was received by Executive Vice President and Provost Craig Blaising on August 8, 2013, that the Master of Divinity (M.Div.) and the Master of Arts in Christian Education (M.A.C.E.) could be completed online. The decision by the national accrediting agency removed residency restrictions on the seminary's two most prominent degrees.[30]

Southwestern had offered online courses since 2000, increasing and expanding the offerings over the years. The nature of this approval allowed a student to complete the entire degree online, whereas before the approval a student could only do a portion of each of the degrees online. The two degrees joined the Master of Theological Studies degree (MTS), an online 45-hour degree with a concentration in cross-cultural missions.

The approval by ATS provided an enormous opportunity for students to receive degrees from Southwestern Seminary without coming to the campus for any residency requirements. Pastors can now complete the M.Div. online without leaving their pastorates, and ministers of education, adults, youth, and children's ministry are able to remain in their church positions while completing a seminary degree. These degrees are designed, however, so that all hours can be moved into the regular M.Div. if the student desires to pursue a more extensive degree.

"The Frailty of Life" – 45th Youth Lab Emphasis

The theme "END." for the 45th Youth Ministry Lab expounded on the passage in James 4:14 that spells out this "frailty of life." Sarah Winburn and Jeremy Houf, co-captains of this year's lab, wanted to help the conferees understand this frailty as expressed in Scripture—"You are just a vapor that appears for a little while and then vanishes away." The emphasis was to awaken the next generation and equip the present youth with tools for the end of high school, for the end of this life, and for the end of this age.[31]

The David Gentiles Band led the worship periods with author Clayton King leading the main worship sessions. Unlike other labs, the breakout sessions had an international flavor, with sessions for Korean ministry, Hispanic ministry, and girl's ministry, as well as for student praise bands. With almost 1,000 in attendance, Youth Lab leaders were pleased to see 12 youth make professions of faith and 47 commit their lives to vocational ministry.

A major emphasis this year was a family ministry necessity that helps youth leaders develop practical ways to connect teenagers with their parents and then with the full congregation. The time has passed when teenagers are kept in a "youth group silo" skirted away from the imperative influence of their parents and other spiritual leaders of the congregation. It is time to reconnect the youth with the spiritual leadership of their parents and the spiritual leadership of congregational guides and pastoral leadership.

"True Love Waits" 20th Anniversary

Richard Ross, professor of youth/student ministry, returned to the church Tulip Grove Baptist Church, Old Hickory, Tennessee, where 20 years ago (February 1983), the first "True Love Waits" seminar occurred with 53 teenagers committing themselves to abstinence before marriage. In the past 20 years, literally millions of teenagers had accepted the challenge of abstinence before marriage. This commitment has strengthened hundreds of marriages. Ross returned to Tulip Grove Baptist Church to lead a True Love Waits-themed DiscipleNow event. Ross, co-founder of the movement with fellow LifeWay employee Jim Hester, watched as a second generation of teens pledged to protect their purity and practice abstinence before marriage. Ross recounted,

> In several cases, I was speaking to teenagers who are the teenage children of those who made the first promise. True Love Waits was not just for one generation of teens but every generation. Susan (Fitzgerald) Bohannon was

among the first group making a promise in early 1990. She is now married and is the mother of three. She told me, "True Love Waits is not just a movement that is relevant to only our culture, but [it is] an international, intergenerational, timeless movement."[32]

Ross made an interesting observation about the spiritual depth and direction of the 20 years of the program's existence. He said,

> In the past, True Love Waits young people have often made promises thinking, "Jesus wants me to do this because it will make my life better." But, I have detected a shift toward what they now say—"Not that I do this so my life will be better, but I choose purity for Christ's glory." The focus comes off "me" and the focus goes on Him. There is no moralism. "If I choose sexual purity for the glory of Christ, then that is just pure worship."[33]

At the end of the second 20-year DiscipleNow event at Tower Grove Baptist Church, 65 young people made promises to practice abstinence along with those of 20 years earlier.

Price Hall Renovation in Progress

Price Hall, the home of the Terry School of Church and Family Ministries, was in serious need of renovation. The lobby furnishings, both the lower and upper lobbies, were shabby and very uncomfortable. All the walls were in grave need of a fresh layer of paint. The carpet in the hallways and office suites was worn and tearing. The faculty lounge needed to be relocated and completely refurbished. The kitchen facilities needed to be near the faculty lounge. The office suites needed a major face-lift. The building in general was in need of a complete overhaul. Patterson and the trustees identified Price Hall, along with several other buildings that were earmarked for a renovation, but the major problem was funding. As early as 2006, drawings for a renovation of

Price Hall were sketched, and priority of renovation would come as soon as funding was available.

Jack Terry, vice president emeritus for Institutional Advancement and special assistant to the president for development, became associated with a family in North Central Oklahoma. Kenneth and Sue Fellers were active members of the First Baptist Church, Cherokee, Oklahoma. During a series of annual Bible studies Terry led for Pastor Tom Cooksey between 2006 and 2013, Terry had the privilege of sharing information about various ministries at Southwestern Seminary with the Fellers and helped them understand the tremendous impact Southwestern Seminary had been on the lost world since its inception in 1908.

The Fellers became very interested in the mission and ministry of Southwestern and began to ask Terry questions about becoming ministry partners with the seminary. Discovering their charitable involvement with Northwestern Oklahoma University, their alma mater, and Oklahoma State University, where their two children were educated, Terry began to talk with them about the possibility of establishing scholarships at Southwestern Seminary. A couple of years later, after a Bible study week, the Fellers gave Terry a check to establish an endowed scholarship. The following year, Kenny Fellers gave Terry another check to add to the first endowed scholarship.

At Terry's invitation, the Fellers, who were members of the President's Club because of their endowed scholarship gift, came to the seminary for the President's Club annual dinner and attended a Christmas musical presentation by the School of Church Music. While they were there, Terry invited the Fellers to visit Price Hall, now the home of the Terry School of Church and Family Ministries, just to see the building that housed his school. Seeing the dire need of renovation for Price Hall, the Fellers began to discuss with Terry what they could do to help renovate the building. Terry shared some of the plans that had been put on hold with them. After seeing the plans and hearing what needed to be done to the building, Sue and Kenny began praying about how they could be used in the renovation of Price Hall. They asked Terry to give them an estimate of what it would cost to completely renovate the building, including building a new office and library conference room that would bear his name.

Four major projects would be involved in the renovation of Price Hall:

(1) A large new commodious faculty lounge on the first floor located adjacent to a kitchen area where the faculty could have food preparation facilities and a comfortable lounge area for rest and relaxation between classes, which could also serve small luncheons and meetings of the faculty or other school committees. The area chosen was a large room, which had once been a banquet room, that could be divided to provide for a new large classroom, a small doctoral seminar room, and a large comfortable faculty lounge. The outdated kitchen area adjacent to the lounge could be refurbished into a new state-of-the-art food preparation facility.

(2) The two lobbies would be furnished with new chairs that would be student-friendly, with movable tablet arms for study and computer work. The electrical outlets needed to be updated for additional floor lighting and for charging computers while students were in the lobby studying. A pleasing fresh coat of paint was put on not only in the lobby areas but throughout the entire building including all classrooms, faculty offices, hallways, and restrooms. New ceiling lighting to brighten up the lobby and hallway areas was installed.

(3) An office suite needed to be totally renovated in order to provide the area needed for the new library/conference room. An outer administrative assistants area with new desks, bookshelves, side chairs, tables, and lamps was also a necessity, as was a library/conference room with multiple bookshelves, storage drawers, a conference table, and chairs. The library/conference room would be named the Terry Conference Room, and just down the inner hall, a new office would be built for Terry as well.

(4) New carpet was needed throughout the entire building in every faculty office, administrative suite, seminar room, classroom, and hallway. It stands to reason that a renovation project of this magnitude would call for the replacement and/or the reconfiguration of air conditioning and heating services, electrical and communication wiring outlets for

phones, computers and lighting, as well as plumbing in the refurbished kitchen and restroom areas.

The Fellers did not blink when Terry gave them the cost estimate for the building renovation. Instead, they sent Terry a check to see that all the work on Price Hall was done.

Who are Kenneth and Sue Fellers?

The Fellers are a fourth generation of farmers farming the land acquired by Kenny's great-grandfather in the land A run in 1893. He rode his horse from the Kansas border north of Burlington, Oklahoma, and staked his claim a few miles south of the Kansas border. Kenny, Sue, and the children have worked the "family ground" from a small plow to the larger modern tractors.

Kenny and Sue met at the BSU at Northwest University in Alva, Oklahoma. After graduation, they married and moved to the farm, forming a partnership with Kenny's father. Sue taught music in the local public school. Their farm operations included dairy farming, wheat, and alfalfa crops.

They have been members of First Baptist Church, Cherokee, Oklahoma, for 50 years. Sue has participated in the church's music ministry, serving for many years as the music director for the church as well as joining Kenny in other positions in the ministry of the church.

Kenny serves on the board of the local bank, and Sue serves as a member of the board of trustees for the Oklahoma Baptist Homes for Children. Sue and Kenny serve together on the Board of Visitors at Southwestern Seminary as well as on other university boards and foundations.

The Fellers considered it an honor to be able to be a part of the remodeling project for the Terry School of Church and Family Ministries honoring their friend Jack Terry for his many years of service to the Lord and to the many students who have walked these halls.[34] The Fellers provided all the resources for the complete renovation of Price Hall and committed to funding an endowment for the maintenance of the building into perpetuity (which they completed in 2016).

Commencement and MacGorman Chapel Perfect for Each Other

MacGorman Chapel makes commencement on the Southwestern Seminary campus so much more enjoyable because of the beauty of the campus for visiting parents, relatives, and friends who attend. The MacGorman Chapel, with its 3,500 seats and exceptional lighting and sound, provides the perfect venue for an exciting commencement exercise. Parents, relatives, friends, and church members of the graduates have the privilege of being on campus and visiting the various buildings where their children attended class, lived in residence halls or Student Village apartments, the library, the RAC, and the Student Center. All of these locations are important to the graduates, and they want their parents and relatives to see where they have been living and working for the past several years.

During the fall 2014 and spring 2015 commencements, over 350 students walked across the platform, receiving degrees for undergraduate, master's, and doctoral studies. The School of Theology had 92 graduates in the fall and 107 in the spring; the Roy Fish School of Evangelism and Missions graduated 20 in the fall and 14 in the spring; the Terry School of Church and Family Ministries graduated 43 in the fall and 51 in the spring; and the School of Church Music graduated two in the fall and 15 in the spring of 2015.[35]

Patterson, in his fall commissioning message, reminded the graduates of the model of Jesus' ministry, which is theirs also. He explained, "While other graduates from other institutions go forth in pursuit of a career to make money and a better life for themselves, Southwestern graduates have a different aim—going forth instead to make life better for everybody else, even if that means experiencing financial difficulties."[36]

Trustees Respond to SBC Recommendation

At the October 14-16, 2013, meeting, the trustees responded to a request made by the president of the Southern Baptist Convention, Ronnie Floyd, requesting SBC entities to report on past, present, and future efforts to assist churches in ministry with people who suffer with mental health challenges. The response read in part,

> The primary method by which we assist churches is in the training of future ministers and biblical counselors. Southwestern Baptist Theological Seminary has, on both graduate and post-graduate levels, a large counseling program that prepares people specifically for ministering to people undergoing acute mental and emotional difficulty as well as the endowed Hope for the Heart Chair of Biblical Counseling. Pastors are urged to take courses in the biblical counseling curriculum, which hopefully will prepare them for such a ministry. In addition, the school provides for the churches counseling workshops in which the laity comes to be trained in how to respond to the difficult problems that the people face. So, in this way, Southwestern not only trains its students but also reaches out to provide help for the churches. Further, our faculty in counseling spends a great portion of its time counseling the counselors from the churches who frequently call on us for help with various kinds of problems.
>
> Southwestern understands clearly that we are not equipped either by calling or by training to prescribe psychotropic medications or to work effectively with those who need a different level from what we can give. However, we also believe that the fact of conversion, the permanent indwelling of the Holy Spirit, and the writing of the infallible, inerrant, and sufficient text in the Bible is what the vast majority of suffering people need. That we can and do provide as part of our discipleship effort.[37]

In their meeting the following spring, April 8-9, 2014, trustees received the report of the conclusion of the strategic plan, 2009-2013, which included the recommendation that the center of the campus be moved from the north entrance of the B.H. Carroll Memorial Building and a new center of the campus established at the Naylor Student Center to the south. A vital part of the plan was the construction of additional two- and three-bedroom apartments in the J. Howard Williams Student Village; the removal of the 1958 flat-roofed apartments and the development of a common area with a pavilion, playground, picnic area, and green belt; the construction of a new chapel immediately to the east of Pecan Manor and to the west of the Ray I. Riley Conference Center for worship services, musical concerts, and large community usage; the renovation of several buildings on campus including Price Hall, Cowden Hall, and the Student Center; and the initial discussion and development of plans for a building to house the Roy Fish School of Evangelism and Missions and the College at Southwestern. These recommendations for the 2014-2019 strategic plan were approved by the trustees.[38]

The bylaws and policies committee recommended that the Board of Visitors (BOV) membership be approved and endorsed and that a "Statement of Purpose and Principles" be referred to the administration for editing and presentation and to be brought back to the bylaws and policies committee by the 2014 fall meeting.[39] The BOV consists of carefully selected pastors, denominational leaders, and laypeople who meet twice a year during the trustee meetings and can report to the president on the nature and condition of the seminary as they see and experience it while visiting on campus and in the classrooms. The organization was a mainstay on the major denominational campuses in the Eastern United States to help the school's administration have a better understanding of academic and spiritual activities on the campus that could affect the nature and condition of the institution.

A new faculty member was elected to the Terry School of Church and Family Ministries during the October 21-22, 2014, meeting. Kelly King was elected assistant professor of childhood education and executive assistant to the president. King graduated from Southwestern Seminary with both her M.A.C.E. (1992) and Ph.D. (2009). King had extensive experience serving in local churches, and she had also served as a teaching assistant at Southwestern Seminary and as adjunct professor of childhood education at Dallas Baptist University.

Two Major Conferences Bring Hundreds to the Campus

The Art of Homemaking Conference was held on the Southwestern Seminary campus October 25-26, 2013, with more than 1,000 women in attendance. President Patterson said of the conference, "The home is the first and most important institution, and if it fails, not far behind it will come the whole social order. Destroy the home and you will destroy the social backbone of any republic wherever it might be."[40]

Conference leaders included Michelle Duggar, the loving mother from TLC's hit cable reality show "19 Kids and Counting." Dorothy Patterson, first lady of Southwestern, also made a presentation. She said, "Are you just following the women in front of you, are you just following the culture ... or are you looking at the light that can be found in Scripture from God Himself?"[41] Another speaker was author Elizabeth George, who wrote *A Woman After God's Own Heart*. During her session, she said, "A woman after God's own heart is a woman of the Word."[42]

A surprise for the conference was the presentation of three wives of seminary presidents at the breakout sessions: Mary Mohler from Southern Seminary, Rhonda Kelly from New Orleans Seminary, and Ann Iorg from Golden Gate Seminary. A special treat for the group of women was the introduction of the new book *The Christian Homemaker's Handbook*, edited by Dorothy Patterson and Homemaking Professor Pat Ennis. Forty authors were on hand for a book signing including the Duggar family and other contributors to the Crossway publication. This conference had been in the heart of Dorothy Patterson, whose passion for the family and for training women to build healthy Christ-honoring homes came to fruition during this weekend in October 2013.

The 46th Youth Minister's Lab was held on April 4-5, 2014, featuring Ben Stuart as the inspirational speaker and Jeff Johnson as the worship leader. The Youth Ministry Lab bathed the conference in prayer for several weeks before the sessions began and once again brought together over 500 youth and youth leaders for the three-day conference from 175 churches from all over the United States and from as far away as Virginia, Wyoming, and Missouri.

Ben Stuart, executive director of Breakaway Ministries at Texas A&M University, called the youth leaders to be "All In" for the active, daily ministry of the Kingdom of God, preparing the next generation for leadership roles in that Kingdom. A breakout session of major importance for youth leaders and volunteer leaders was the rehearsal of the "9 Core Values That Shape Student Ministry" developed by Richard Ross, Johnny Derouen, and other colleagues in youth ministry to use as a guide to minister to students in local churches.

New School, New Faculty, New Construction

The trustees met in their two bi-annual meetings April 14-15 and October 21-22, 2015, approving the establishment of a new school, electing 10 new faculty members, and approving the construction of a facility to house the Roy Fish School of Evangelism and Missions and the College at Southwestern. The School of Preaching was unanimously approved as the seventh of Southwestern's academic schools. The School of Preaching is committed to training students in "text-driven preaching." David Allen, dean of the School of Theology, was elected as the founding dean of the School of Preaching. Some of the faculty joining Allen were Barry McCarty, chief parliamentarian for the SBC; Vern Charette, a specialist in evangelistic preaching; and Steven Smith, a recognized author in the discipline of preaching. The School of Preaching offers the Master of Theology, Doctor of Ministry, and the Ph.D. Additionally, certificates in preaching will be offered to supplement the Master of Divinity programs in the School of Theology.[43]

T. Dale Johnson Jr. was elected as assistant professor of biblical counseling in the Terry School of Church and Family Ministries. Johnson had just completed his Ph.D. in biblical counseling at Southwestern in December 2014 and was already serving as an instructor of biblical counseling in the Terry School. His previous ministry experience included serving as associate pastor of family life at Raiford Road Church in Macclenny, Florida.

In another action, the trustees recommended a reduction in the number of hours required to complete the Doctor of Educational Ministries in the Terry School of Church and Family Ministries, from 44 hours to 36 hours. The reduction had been previously approved by the faculty of that school, and final approval was given by the trustees at the April 14-15 meeting.[44]

The construction of Mathena Hall, to be located to the immediate west side of Pecan Manor, was approved unanimously by the trustees in the spring meeting. Mathena Hall is the new home for the Roy Fish School of Evangelism and Missions and the College at Southwestern. The building would house a memorial to Southern Baptist missionary Lottie Moon, whose home, furnishings, and personal effects will be found in the building.[45] Ground would be broken when funds reached 90 percent in cash and pledges.

Administration Professor Dies

Robert Mathis, professor of administration, died January 25, 2015, after a long struggle with ALS (Lou Gehrig's disease). Mathis was 67 years of age and had been on the faculty of the School of Educational Ministries (now the Terry School of Church and Family Ministries) since 1998. Mathis earned his Master of Religious Education in 1978 and his Ph.D. in 1984.

Mathis lived with ALS for over 10 years but never allowed the debilitating disease to stop him from doing ministry in God's Kingdom. Over the years, the faculty, administration, and students at Southwestern Seminary participated in ALS Walks in honor of Mathis to raise money for the ALS Foundation. In 2009, Southwestern organized a walk on the seminary campus in order to allow more students and faculty to participate.[46]

In 2009, there was a ribbon-cutting at Price Hall in honor of Mathis to mark the newest wheelchair accessibility ramp on the west side of the building where he worked. Because of the disease, Mathis used a wheelchair as his major source of mobility. The new ramp was constructed on the side of the Price Hall closest to the lot where Mathis parked. After a brief ceremony, he became the first person to ride up and down the new ramp in his wheelchair. He jokingly asked the ramp to be named the "Mathis Tollway," with charges for using the ramp going toward his retirement fund.

Mathis had an infectious smile, a gentle voice, and a loving heart for Christ and His Kingdom. Each time I use the "Mathis Tollway," I remember my former student, faculty colleague, and dear friend, and I say to myself, "Rest in peace, dear friend."

Art of Homemaking Teaches Biblical Principles

Women from across Texas and from out of state attended the second Art of Homemaking Conference on February 19-21, 2015. The special emphasis was to help Christian women learn how the Lord can use them in their homes, culture, and ministry. Featured speakers for the general sessions were Susan G. Baker, Devi Titus, Vicki Courtney, Candi Finch, and Dorothy Patterson.[47] There were over 24 breakout sessions available for those who attended dealing with subjects like house and home, marriage, parenting, engaging culture, life changes, and women's ministry, all led by Southwestern's Women's Programs leadership Terri Stovall, Katie McCoy, and Dorothy Patterson. Rhonda Kelly, first lady of the New Orleans Seminary, and Ann Iorg, first lady of the Golden Gate Seminary, also led conferences.

First Lady Dorothy Patterson used 1 Samuel 1, the story of Hannah, as the Scriptural background to impress the women of the necessity of being bold about the future of our children. Hannah's promise to God about her first child, Samuel, led her to see to it that he was placed in the very best environment for learning about the ministry he would have for God. Patterson reminded the women that "Hannah's journey is one that, as women, we must all eventually take if we want to protect our children."[48] In her conclusion, she gave important ways for women to leave an impact for the next generation by demonstrating to their children God's pattern for Christian marriage and teaching their children biblical truths.

Mathena Hall Groundbreaking

On October 21, 2015, several hundred people gathered on the parking lot across the street from the RAC and watched as 12 people, with bright stainless steel shovels, participated in the groundbreaking ceremony for Mathena Hall, the new home of the Roy Fish School of Evangelism and Missions and the College at Southwestern. Mathena Hall is named for Harold and Patricia Mathena, who gave the lead gift of $12 million toward the construction of the building.

During the groundbreaking, President Patterson said, "I want you to pray that the result of the construction of this building will be that tens of thousands of people come to know Christ as Savior. It's nothing but another brick and mortar structure unless it results in people coming to Christ. And so I want us to begin today, at groundbreaking, to pray that God will bring many to Christ."[49]

100 Years of Ministry at Southwestern

Over these 100 years, 89 professors have been elected by the board of trustees to serve in the various departments of the education school: administration, foundations of education, psychology and counseling (now biblical counseling), adult education, youth education, childhood education, recreation, women's ministry, and church and family ministries. Serving in an academic leadership role with these 89 faculty members over the years has been seven academic deans: J.M. Price served as founder and first director from 1915-1956 (named as dean upon his retirement in 1956); Joe Davis Heacock, professor of administration, served from 1956-1973; Jack Terry, professor of foundations of education, served from 1973-1996; Daryl Eldridge, professor of foundations of education, served from 1996-2004; Robert (Bob) Welch, professor of administration, served from 2005-2008; Wesley Black, professor of youth/student education, served as interim dean from 2008-2009; and Waylan Owens, professor of church and family ministries, has served as dean from 2010-present.

In 1921, the Department of Religious Education was named *The School of Religious Education*, although it was in the heart and mind of President L.R. Scarborough and J.M. Price as early as 1915. It was necessary to have more than one or two departments involved in an organization in order to name it a school. So, in 1921, there were five departments involved in the Department of Religious Education: administration (education and church), foundations of education (philosophy, history, psychology of education), counseling (psychology and counseling), age group ministries (children, youth, and adult), and church recreation.

The school was officially named *The School of Religious Education* in 1921. The name remained as such until 1998, when the faculty and dean felt the school needed a more inclusive name to better recognize the ministries involved. This was because, added to the five departments initially involved in 1921, were additional departments such as communications (radio/television, public relations, speech for Christian workers, drama and stage production, etc.), curriculum organization and development, online theological education, etc. The faculty felt a more inclusive name would be the *School of Educational Ministries*. The name was presented to the trustees and was officially changed in 1998.

Over the years since 1998, the emphasis of the education school has shifted yet another direction. In more recent years, the ministry of religious education has come to embrace an important spiritual movement in the educational leadership of the church that encompasses a more intense family ministry emphasis that intends to put the spiritual leadership of children, youth, and young adults back where God had intended it to be all along: in the home. Recognizing the importance of this needed spiritual emphasis in the lives of the members of the church, the School of Educational Ministries looked at the possibility of a new name that would identify the new church and family ministry shift and clearly spell out what the teaching philosophy of the school would be.

In 2009, the name chosen was *The Jack D. Terry, Jr. School of Church and Family Ministries*. The family ministry teaching philosophy was identified as "the process of intentionally and persistently realigning a congregation's proclamation and practice so that parents are acknowledged, trained, and held accountable as the persons primarily responsible for the discipleship of their children."[50] A family ministry concentration was added to the Master of Arts in Christian Education (M.A.C.E.) and was intended to permeate all disciplines in the school. Making the family responsible for the religious education of their children is in line with the commandment to parents in Deuteronomy 6:7-9:

> You shall teach [the words of the Lord] diligently to your sons and shall talk of them when you sit in your house and when you walk by the way and when you lie down and when you rise up. You shall bind them as a sign on your hand and they shall be as frontals on your forehead. You shall write them on the doorposts of your house and on your gates.

The evolution of the school over 100 years has come to a resting point in 2015. But with excitement and anticipation, the faculty and the school are looking into this new century, 2015-2115, with the same challenge to fulfill the charter given to the school in 1915: *to prepare men and women for educational ministry in the church.*

Notes
[1] *Southwestern News*, Summer, 2009, p. 10.
[2] Ibid.
[3] *Southwestern News*, Summer, 2010, p. 46.
[4] Trustee Meeting Minutes, April 6-8, 2010, p. 5.
[5] *Southwestern News*, Summer, 2010, p. 52.
[6] *Southwestern News*, Summer, 2010, p. 53.
[7] Ibid., p. 45.

8 Ibid.
9 *Southwestern News*, Spring, 2011, p. 45.
10 Ibid.
11 *Southwestern News*, Fall, 2011, p. 47.
12 *Southwestern News*, Winter, 2011, p. 37.
13 *Southwestern News*, Spring, 2011, p. 33.
14 Ibid.
15 Ibid.
16 *Southwestern News*, Fall, 2011, p. 44.
17 Terry, Jack D., Personal Reflection, 2011.
18 *Southwestern News*, Winter, 2012, p. 11,
19 Historic Enrollment Dates (1983-2015).
20 *Southwestern News*, Spring, 2012, p. 23.
21 Ibid., pp. 4-5.
22 *Southwestern News*, Summer, 2012, p. 46.
23 Ibid.
24 *Southwestern News*, Spring, 2012, pp. 13-14.
25 Historic Enrollment Dates (1983-2015).
26 *Southwestern News*, Summer, 2012, p. 51.
27 Historic Enrollment Dates (1983-2015).
28 Trustee Meeting Minutes, April 1-3 2013, pp. 4-5.
29 Trustee Meeting Minutes, October 14-16, 2013, p. 12.
30 *Southwestern News*, Fall, 2013, p. 43.
31 *Southwestern News*, Summer, 2013, p. 52.
32 *Southwestern News*, Spring, 2013, p. 44.
33 Ibid.
34 A plaque in the hallway of Price Hall in the Terry School of Church and Family Ministries, 2013.
35 Historic Enrollment Dates (1983-2015).
36 *Southwestern News*, Winter, 2014, p. 40, and Summer, 2015, p. 53.
37 Trustee Meeting Minutes, October, 2013, p. 4.
38 Trustee Meeting Minutes, April 6-8, 2014, p. 4.
39 Ibid., p. 5.
40 *Southwestern News*, Fall, 2014, p. 35.
41 Ibid.

42 Ibid.
43 Trustee Meeting Minutes, October, 2015, p. 4.
44 Trustee Meeting Minutes, April, 2015, p. 7.
45 *Southwestern News*, Spring, 2015, p. 56
46 Ibid., p. 54.
47 Ibid., p. 57
48 Ibid.
49 *Southwestern News*, Fall, 2015, p. 54.
50 Jones, Timothy Paul, p. 40.

Photos

Page 316 – Portrait of Waylan Owens.

Page 320 – Counseling professor Dale Johnson engages students in Bible study.

Page 325 – The graduation service of a biblical counseling certification program at a local church. From left, Ph.D. graduate Cheryl Bell, master's graduate Dale Allen, and professor John Babler congratulate one of the individuals who completed the program.

Page 351 – Professor Candi Finch addresses women at the Art of Homemaking Conference.

Afterword

Tracing the 100 years involved in the Price legacy of a Department of Religious Education to a School of Religious Education, the first of its kind anywhere in the world of educational academia, has been an interesting journey. I thank God for the administrators who led the charge for Southwestern Baptist Theological Seminary over the 100 years, for the faculties who have walked the hallowed halls of Price Hall, and for the thousands of students who blessed the hearts of the faculty and the churches and ministries where they have served. They prepared well and went into the fields "white to harvest" bearing the Gospel of the Lord Jesus Christ.

These memories have reminded me of my tremendous heritage as a part of this wonderful spiritual enterprise. I am honored to have been chosen to write this history and to have had the privilege of re-living once again the many years I have spent on a campus I dearly love and in the seminary to which I have given 48 years of my life. I have laughed at humorous events remembered, chaffed at stupid mistakes made, wept over dear friends who have gone to be with our blessed Lord—both faculty and students—and rejoiced that all our names are written in heaven with the glorious hope that one day we will all be in the Kingdom of our Lord and His Christ forever.

Index

A

Abu Abdallah, a Jordanian Bedouin 333
ACTS Network 148, 171, 194
Advanced Studies Council 35
Aerobics 107
Agee, Bob 226
Akin, Danny 295
Allen, Charles L. 139
Allen, David 271, 297, 321, 349
Allen, Jimmy R. 124, 143, 148
Allen, Wayne 179
American Association of Schools of Religious Education 28
Ashby, Charles 97, 106, 165, 329
Asociacion para la Educacion Theologica Hispana (AETH) 269
Association of Theological Schools (ATS 33, 49, 120, 136, 205, 324
Association of Youth Ministry Educators (AYME) 267
ATS 35
Austin, Lou Ella 15
Autrey, Denny 266, 271, 272, 281
A. Webb Roberts Library 135, 149

B

Babler, John E. 217, 241, 300, 301, 326, 338
Bachelor in Religious Education 15
Bachelor of Arts in Humanities 302, 338
Baergen, Darrel 127, 140, 144, 195
Baker, Dick 208
Baker, Jeroline 36, 37, 49, 61, 63, 69, 70,
    76, 101, 125, 134, 148, 151, 165, 203, 240, 256
Baker, Robert A. 43, 44, 68, 74, 114, 115, 135, 142, 240, 296, 313
Baker, Susan G. 351

Balducci, Paul 211
baptismal pool 318, 330
Baptist General Convention of Texas 12, 29, 104, 122, 141, 143,
    166, 178, 199, 235, 294, 310
Baptist Marriage and Family Counseling Center 127, 189
Baptist Religious Education Association of the Southwest (BREAS) 213
Baptist Religious Education of the Southwest (BREAS) 17, 214, 222, 226
Baptist World Alliance (BWA) 268
Barber, Bart 297, 338
Barnard, Floy 18, 19, 22, 36, 85, 149, 204
Barnes, W.W. 13
Barnett, Max 279
Barrett, Robby Wes 133
Baylor 11, 13, 123, 127, 130, 131, 136, 141, 151,
    161, 168, 182, 209, 213, 294, 323
Beargen, Darrell 194
Beaucamp. Harvey 13
Bell, A. Donald 22, 24, 36, 48, 49
Bessie M. Fleming Chair of Childhood Education 134, 151, 203
Bibelseminar in Bonn, Germany 279
Black, Jeff 300
Black, Wesley O. 20, 139, 144, 145, 162, 165, 173, 201,
    210, 226, 263, 264, 267, 268, 271, 289, 292, 293, 304, 306, 311, 334, 353
Blaising, Craig 275, 292, 294, 339
Board of Trustees 21, 50, 299, 337
Board of Visitors (BOV) 347
Bolet, Esther Diaz- 238, 251, 269
Bower, Debbie 101
Brackney, Bob 125, 149, 171, 201, 208, 215, 221, 232
Brackney, Bob Wayne 108
Bradford, Ann 22, 24, 25, 36, 44, 48, 187, 190, 203, 204, 256
Brandt, Matt 294
Bridges, Tommy 97, 192, 278
Briggs, Phil 58, 69, 76, 78, 88, 91, 93, 162, 166, 173, 177, 229, 230, 232, 277
Brooks, Jon 258

Brooks, Paula 93
Brumbley, Rosemary 202
BSU   106, 122, 212, 344
Building and Grounds committee 50
Burch, Robert.. 211
Burk, J. L. 50
Burleson, Rufus C. 11
Burns, Jim 198
Burroughs, Esther 162, 202, 207
BWA World Youth Congress.. 268

C

Caldwell, William G. 93, 147, 151, 161, 233, 255, 285, 286
Carroll, B. H. 11, 12, 13, 14, 21, 43, 107, 134, 142,
   149, 175, 188, 206, 261, 262, 264, 265, 266, 273, 278, 287, 291, 294, 295,
   296, 297, 298, 300, 309, 323, 324, 346
Catanzaro, Frank J. 324
Cauthen, Baker James 103, 116
Centennial Celebration 286, 294, 295, 297, 298, 302
Centennial Celebration Committee 286
Center of Christian Communications 126
Certification in Church Business Administration 286
Chair of Student Ministries.. 229, 277
Chandler, Matt 271
Chan, Francis.. 299
Charles D. Tandy Center for Archaeological Research...................... 150
Chicago Statement on Biblical Inerrancy... 273
Children's Building........................... 38, 50, 52, 58, 59, 60, 61, 63, 64, 69, 114
Childress, Chad 288
Chism, Tom... 206
Chrisman, Judge Oswin 94, 95, 100
Churchill, Ralph 22, 23, 36
Clements, Dan Earl 159, 176, 218
Clendinning, Monte 108, 109, 151, 154, 171, 202, 205
Coleman, Lucien E. 144, 154, 161, 162, 163, 209

College at Southwestern 279, 283, 291, 301, 302, 305, 338, 347, 349, 350, 352
Collins, L. L. 99
Collins, Olin 77, 78, 83, 201, 211, 224
Committee on Advanced Studies of the School of Religious Education 51
Conner, William T. 77, 272, 296
Conservative Resurgence 113
Cooke, Phil 251
Cooper, Davis 11, 96, 98, 107, 126, 129, 143, 161
Cooper, Dr. Kenneth 107
Cooper, Kenneth 208
Cooper, Lynn 211
Copass, Mrs. B. A. 28
Corts, Mark 216
Cotter, Sam 223
Couey, Richard B. 123, 161
Course Description Manual 94, 99, 100, 110, 152
Courtney, Vicki 351
Cowden Hall 35, 149, 180, 347
Creech, Marcie 154
Crews, William 198, 210
Crews, William L. 57
Criswell College 169, 218, 250, 273, 274
Crowder, Robert E. 101
Cunningham, Milton 158
Curriculum Council 35

D

Dallas Baptist College 82
Dana, H. L. 250, 296
Darby, James 271
David Gentiles Band 340
Davis, Bob 22, 31, 37, 39, 43, 47, 60, 68, 69, 70, 71,
    72, 76, 86, 91, 97, 109, 112, 115, 126, 164, 177, 178, 187, 188, 196, 201, 211,
    232, 233, 256, 352
Davis, C. T. 16

Davis, J. W. 15
Day-Higginbotham Lecture Series... 138
Dead Sea Scrolls 318, 319, 330, 331, 332, 333, 335
Dean, Clark Earl... 71
Dehoney, Wayne... 124
Department of Religious Education..................... 13, 22, 177, 230, 328, 353, 357
Department of Social Work and Ministry-Based Evangelism.................... 220
Derouen, Johnny 258, 276, 277, 293, 334, 349
DeVargas, Robert 235
DeYoung, Kevin 309
Dickerson, Ben 130, 136, 151, 209, 213
Diggs, Doug 225
Dilday, Betty 205
Dilday, Russel H. 96, 97, 102, 103, 104, 121, 126, 129, 135,
    136, 142, 145, 150, 153, 155, 156, 157, 159, 165, 166, 169, 173, 174, 175, 176,
    189, 191, 192, 198, 199, 200, 201, 206, 207, 210, 211, 257
Dilday, Russell H. 102, 124, 126
Dill, Harold 36, 37, 49, 75, 76, 78, 151, 203, 209, 293
Dockery, David... 295
Doctor of Educational Ministries... 228, 349
Doctor of Education (Ed. D.) 38, 51, 109, 204
Doctor of Religious Education 16, 17, 19, 38, 50
Documentary film on the CBS.. 137
Dottie Riley Prayer Tower 330
Dowell, Theodore (Ted) H. 69, 71, 127, 134, 224
Dozzier, Brooke 225
Drakeford, John.. 29, 37, 41, 88, 91, 95, 161, 197
Draper, Baily 169, 305
Draper, Jimmy 155, 157, 169, 176, 180, 196, 201, 216, 305
Driver, Barry 323
Drummond, N. R. 15
Drumwright, Huber L. 84, 104, 318, 319, 331
Duggar, Michelle 348

E

Eby, Frederick 12
"Eight by Eighty" Campaign 134
Elder, Lloyd 104
Elder, Wyona 119, 151, 162, 192, 201, 224
Eldridge, Daryl R. 151, 171, 192, 214, 218, 223, 228, 236,
    248, 251, 266, 267, 303, 304, 329, 353
Elkind, David 101
Engle, Joel 292
Equal Employment Opportunity Commission (EEOC) 120
Equipping U 251
Erickson, Millard 208
Esqueda, Octavo Javier 275
Evans, Wayne 102, 119, 152

F

Faculty Council 21, 235
faculty tenure 337
Fahringer, Dennis 253
Fant, Clyde 124
Feather, Othal 22, 23, 36, 38, 48, 87, 109
F. Howard Walsh Medical Center 35
Finch, Candy 351
Fish, Roy 265, 280, 283, 289, 331, 335, 336, 338, 345, 347, 349, 350, 352
Fite, David 241
Fleming Hall 149
Fleming Library 126, 134, 149
Fleming, William 33, 58, 63, 126, 134, 149, 151, 165, 203, 323
Flippin, Tan 226
Floyd, Ronnie 192, 220, 345
Fong, Gary 241
Ford, Le Roy 36, 54, 62, 67, 71, 74, 140
Fort Worth Hall 12, 93, 213, 300
Frierson, Eward C/ 101
Fuller, Charles 216

G

Gambrell, J. B. 13
Garman, Chuck 237
Garrett, James Leo 297
Garrett, Jenkins 120, 259
Garrison, Hillery Smith 241
Geisel, Paul 112
George W. Bottoms Chair of Missions 34
George W. Truett Chair of Ministry 34
George W. Truett chapel 27
Geren, Preston C. 58, 126
Giglio, Louie 282
Gonzalez, Justo 269, 283, 284, 311
Graduate Specialist in Religious Education 38, 56, 152
Graduate Specialist in Religious Education (GSRE) 152
Gresham, Felix 50, 104, 119
Griener, Jr., Max 265
Guffey, Paul 237
Guide Stone Financial Resources 296
Gulledge, John 161
Gulledge, Pat 163, 171
Guy, Cal 34

H

Hadden, Jeffery K. 124
Hallock Chair of Baptist Student Work 212, 279
Hallock, E. F. \ 176, 212, 229, 230, 232, 277, 279
Hardin, Joe 298
Hardin-Simmons University, Abilene, TX 73, 174, 273, 328, 329
Harris, Philip B. 22, 24, 143
Hatcher, Harvey B. 29, 35, 49, 109
Hawkins, O. S. 296
Heacock, Joe Davis 22, 31, 37, 39, 43, 47, 60, 68, 69, 70, 71, 72,
    76, 86, 91, 97, 109, 112, 164, 177, 178, 187, 188, 232, 233, 256, 352
Head, E. D. 28, 126, 206, 323

Headrick, James A. 224
Hell's Half Acre 309
Hemphill, Kenneth S. 215, 216, 217, 221, 222, 223, 225, 229,
    234, 237, 239, 248, 249, 250, 254, 259, 261, 262, 264, 265, 266, 296
Hemphill, Paula Moore 217, 261
Hendricks, Howard 222
Higgins, Caleb 301
Hime, Harold 209
Hispanic Baptist Theological Seminary 310
Holcomb, T. L. 28
Hong, Joshua 285
Hoover, Rosemary 226, 237
Hope for the Heart Chair of Biblical Counseling 304, 346
Horner, Andy and Joan 305, 330
Horner Homemaking House 290, 298, 305
Hospice Movement 131
Houf, Jeremy 339
Houston Baptist University 280
Howard, W. F. 97, 106, 109, 122
Howse, W. L. (Bill) 18, 19, 29, 48, 49
Hughes, Mike 284
Hull, Robert 124
Hunt, June 305

I

International Council on Biblical Inerrancy 273
Iorg, Ann 348, 351

J

Jack D. Terry, Jr. School of Church and Family Ministries 308, 317, 321,
    324, 325, 327, 331, 335, 336, 338, 341, 342, 344, 345, 347, 349, 350, 354, 355
Jane and John Justin Conference Center 149
J. Dalton Havard School for Theological Studies in Houston 281
Jerry Lambdin Memorial Scholarship 102
J. Howard Williams Student Village 35

Johnson, Robert K. 138, 160, 348, 349
Jones, Ian Fredrick 224, 238, 254, 338, 356
Jones, Orabelle Cross 25
J. Wesley Harrison Chair of New Testament 34

K

Keeshan, Bob (Captain Kangaroo) 148
Kellogg Lectures 209, 213
Kelly, Rhonda 348, 351
Kennedy, Tom 241
Kennemur, Jenni 285, 288, 327
Kennemur, Karen 285
Kennemur, Karen Lynn (Poteet) 306
Kimmer, Marinko 238
Kim, Paul 285, 322
Kim, Sung-Won 285
King, Clayton 340
King, Kelly 285, 327, 347
Kingry, Greg 283
Kiwiett, John J. 56
Klempnauer, Lawrence 109, 257
Knowlton, Gracie 22, 24, 25, 26, 37, 48

L

Lambdin, J. E. 102
Lawrence, Rick 109, 257
Lawson, Margaret 239, 267
Leadership Certificate in Women's Ministry 281, 302
Learning Center 53, 92
Learning Resource Center 64, 81, 107
Lee, E. E. 13
Leitch, J. R. 75
Library of Centennial Classics 296
Lim, Yunhee 285
Litton, Eward 211

Long, Jeff 295
Lottie Moon 322, 350
Lott, Jimi 254
Loveless, Gary 319, 330, 332
Lowery, Grady 109, 122, 129, 167
Lucille Freeman Glasscock World Mission and Evangelism Center 149
Luft, Bonnie 123
Lu, Louie 322

M

MacGorman, Jack 234, 259, 260, 287, 307, 329, 331, 332, 333, 335, 339, 345
Mahon, Judge Eldon 120
Maitland, David D 213
Marshall, William R. 283, 284, 310
Marsh, Leon 29, 38, 87, 91, 158, 178, 198, 328, 329
Martin, Hubert 213, 254, 261
Master of Arts in Biblical Counseling 320, 325, 327
Master of Arts in Christian Education (MACE) 286, 339, 354
Master of Religious Education 15, 16, 38, 39, 42, 55, 56, 73, 108, 110, 121, 122, 130, 135, 144, 204, 218, 221, 231, 350
Maston, T. B. 16, 17, 18, 19, 20, 22, 23, 25, 48, 91, 296
Mathena Hall 350, 352
Mathis, Robert R. 235, 350, 351
Matte, Greg 253, 258, 293
Mattingly, Don 203, 209, 237
McCarty, Barry 349
McClain, Van 290
McCoy, Bruce 286, 334, 351
McCoy, Lee H. 29, 36
McDonald, Patrick 285
McDonough, Reggie 155
McGill, Denise 253
McGuire, William Michael 250
McInnis, Gary and Shelia 55

McKinney, James C. 31
McLallen, Dan 156, 174
McMachon, Monte.. 29
McQuitty, Marcia....................................... 206, 240, 269, 270, 284, 285
Melton, Alpha 22, 24, 25, 37, 55, 209
Melton Social Ministry Institute Workshop.......................... 208, 215
Mendelsohn, Robyn.. 137
Mitchell, Bertha.. 15
Mohler, Al 210, 348
Moitinho, Elias 266, 305, 327
Moody, Chip 124
Moore, Cameron 261, 301
Morris, Hazel... 37, 58, 63, 69, 76, 165, 240, 256
Morris, Judy 58, 236, 256
Mower, O. Hobert 105
MRE/MSW 55
Murphy-Racey, Patrick... 253
Myers, Dennis..209
Myers, F. Marvin 147
Myers, Lewis A. 16

N

Nason, Patrica L. 324
National Association for the Education of Younger Children (NAEYC) . 239
National Association of Church Business Administrators 147, 161,
    168, 286, 303
National Association of Schools of Music (NASM).............................. 33, 324
National Autonomous University of Mexico.................................... 74
National Conference of Broadcast Ministries 139
National University of Mexico... 75
Naylor Children's Center ...25, 44, 69, 76, 77, 79, 119, 125, 149, 187, 191, 203, 239
Naylor, M.D., Rebekah 32
Naylor, Robert E. 32, 58, 61, 69, 76, 77, 94, 119, 126, 141, 200, 203
Newberry, Phil..258
Newman, Albert.. 49, 296

Newport, John 104, 119, 176, 191
Nickell, Tim 229
Northcutt, Jesse 75
Norton, Carl E. 212

O

Oakerson, Karen 135
O'Brien, Dellanna 124, 202
Office of Minister Relations 257
Oklahoma Center in Shawnee, OK 123
Olsen, Frank 124
O'Neal Prayer Garden 329
OnlineMaster of Arts in Christian Education 337
Online Master of Theological Studies (MTS) 337
Osborne, J. R. 82
Overton, Bob 242, 254
Owens, Waylan 306, 307, 321, 325, 327, 353

P

Palmer, Joe 203
Parks, Alva G. 58, 69, 71, 124, 177, 178, 187, 195
Patterson, Dorothy 272, 278, 299, 304, 348, 351, 352
Patterson, Dorothy Kelly 272
Patterson, Paige 169, 210, 271, 272, 273, 274, 275, 276, 278, 279, 280, 283, 286, 295, 296, 298, 299, 304, 306, 307, 308, 317, 319, 321, 324, 327, 329, 330, 331, 332, 336, 337, 338, 341, 345, 348, 352
Patterson, Roberta 272
Patterson, Thomas Armour 272
Pauker, Mollie 139
Paul Stevens Chair of Christian Communication 159
Pecan Manor 278, 290, 329, 330, 347, 350, 352
Penley, David 236, 326
Phillips, Carliss 278, 291, 330
Photojournalism Conference 240, 253
Piland, Harry 106, 109, 143, 154, 233

Pillow, David J. 129, 130
Platt, David 308
Presidential Review Committee 159
Presidential Search Committee 95, 211, 215, 266, 271, 272
Price Chair of Religious Education 180, 189, 230, 231, 279
Price Hall 27, 28, 35, 36, 50, 52, 53, 59, 60, 63, 64, 68, 75, 77, 79, 81, 91, 93, 119, 178, 187, 219, 341, 342, 343, 344, 347, 350, 355, 357
Price, J. M. 14, 15, 16, 17, 18, 19, 22, 23, 25, 27, 28, 29, 31, 35, 36, 37, 40, 43, 44, 48, 50, 52, 53, 59, 60, 63, 64, 68, 75, 76, 77, 79, 81, 82, 89, 90, 91, 92, 93, 101, 112, 115, 119, 177, 178, 180, 187, 188, 189, 190, 191, 207, 213, 219, 230, 231, 232, 233, 244, 279, 296, 328, 341, 342, 343, 344, 347, 350, 352, 353, 355, 357
Privette, Jerry 101, 165, 212
Programmed Instruction 54
Pulley, Dorothy 79
Pulley, Ralph 211

R

Raikes, Robert 124
Raus, Robert P. 121, 176
Ray I. Riley Alumni Center 287
Ray I. Riley Center 318
Ray, Jeff D. 31
Recreation/Aerobics Center 107, 111, 122, 134
Relief and Annuity Board of the Southern Baptist Convention
  (now Guidestone) 32
Richards, Jim 330
Rich, Windy 231, 232
Riley, Harold 259
Riley Leadership Development Center 238
Robert E. and Goldia Naylor Student Center 35
Rodabough, Tilman 136
Rogers, Adrian 113, 155, 201
Ross, Richard 139, 162, 166, 199, 203, 237, 250, 258, 263, 268, 271, 279, 282, 320, 334, 340, 341, 349

Roy Fish School of Evangelism and Missions 280, 283, 345, 347, 349, 350, 352

S

SACS   33, 35, 49, 120, 136, 205, 324
Sandlin, Mark 241
Sarah Walton Miller Drama Festival 139
SBC's Empowering Kingdom Growth 266
SBC's Hundred Thousand Club Campaign 21
Scarborough, L. R. 11, 12, 13, 14, 15, 21, 28, 33, 35, 43, 76, 77, 126, 134, 189, 273, 287, 296, 309, 323, 353
Scarborough Memorial Building 27
School of Church Music 83, 85, 92, 104, 105
School of Educational Ministries 228, 232, 234, 235, 236, 238, 239, 247, 250, 251, 255, 261, 266, 267, 269, 275, 276, 277, 278, 279, 283, 284, 285, 287, 289, 290, 292, 294, 300, 302, 303, 304, 306, 308, 317, 350, 353
School of Preaching 349
School of Religious Education 12, 16, 17, 19, 20, 21, 22, 23, 24, 25, 27, 28, 29, 30, 31, 35, 37, 38, 39, 40, 41, 42, 43, 47, 48, 50, 51, 52, 54, 55, 56, 57, 58, 59, 60, 61, 62, 63, 64, 65, 68, 69, 70, 71, 72, 73, 74, 76, 78, 82, 83, 85, 86, 87, 89, 90, 91, 92, 93, 95, 97, 98, 99, 100, 102, 104, 105, 106, 108, 109, 110, 115, 116, 121, 123, 124, 125, 128, 129, 131, 139, 140, 142, 144, 145, 146, 149, 151, 152, 153, 154, 157, 158, 159, 160, 162, 164, 165, 168, 169, 170, 173, 174, 176, 177, 178, 180, 181, 187, 188, 189, 191, 192, 193, 194, 195, 197, 198, 201, 203, 204, 206, 208, 209, 212, 213, 217, 219, 220, 222, 223, 224, 227, 230, 232, 257, 280, 286, 287, 293, 308, 353, 357
School of Sacred Music 31
School of Theology 11, 20, 22, 31, 35, 43, 57, 70, 77, 79, 83, 84, 86, 92, 99, 104, 105, 109, 123, 128, 134, 146, 147, 152, 164, 168, 169, 173, 174, 181, 193, 194, 197, 198, 201, 222, 224, 236, 239, 250, 254, 255, 261, 266, 275, 276, 283, 297, 302, 306, 318, 331, 335, 336, 338, 345, 349
Seaborn, Miles 211
Seelig, John 75, 104, 119, 140, 191
Self, Gregory 260
Seltmann, Lyle 201

Shahid, Samuel 260, 261
Shin, Heuikwang 285
Shirley, Nathan Chsristian (Chris) 290
Shoemake, Earl L. and Vivian Gray 131, 132
Shook, Damon 211
Sid Richardson Foundation 149
Skaggs, Ricky 217
Slay, Lamar 162
Slover, J. Roy 98, 119, 134, 149
Smith, Andy 296
Smith, Bailey 155, 157
Smith, Cameron 262, 263
Smith, Ralph 234, 254, 259, 261
Smith, R. E. 271
Smith, Stephen 349
Smith, William (Budd) A 97, 176, 212, 223, 231, 241, 267, 329
Solomon, Marti 199, 270
Southeast Texas in Houston 123
Southern Baptist Association of Ministries with the Aging (SBAMA) 137
Southern Baptist Convention ... 11, 17, 25, 28, 31, 34, 39, 60, 73, 75, 85, 86, 89, 97,
    103, 108, 113, 121, 134, 136, 139, 140, 141, 142, 150, 151, 155, 162, 169, 175,
    177, 178, 179, 182, 187, 199, 201, 202, 207, 208, 210, 215, 226, 233, 251, 273,
    274, 295, 296, 307, 317, 318, 321, 345
Southern Baptist Home Mission Board (now NAMB) 139
Southern Baptist Radio and Television Commission 124, 127, 139, 171
Southern Baptist Sunday School Board 29, 34, 48, 49, 54, 97,
    100, 101, 102, 106, 107, 109, 122, 123, 131, 143, 144, 145, 151, 162, 166, 179,
    199, 203, 213, 216, 226, 233, 237, 286, 292
South, Rheubin 158
Southwestern Advisory Council 107, 291
Southwestern Baptist Religious Education Association (SWBREA) 16
Southwestern Baptist Theological College 276, 277, 279
Southwestern News 23, 28, 36, 52, 71, 74, 113, 114, 115, 116,
    178, 183, 184, 185, 242, 243, 244, 311, 312, 313, 314, 354, 355, 356
Southwestern Religious Education Association (SWBREA) 101, 187

Southwestern Seminary Advisory Council 103
Southwest Texas in San Antonio 123
Spring Evangelism Practicum 241
State Sunday School Convention of Texas 16, 24
Stone, Ted 280
Stovall, Teresa 262, 281, 282, 289, 290, 304, 336, 351
Stuart, Ben 87, 348, 349
Student Missions Conference 124
Student Wives Certificate 302
Stutz, Paul 290

T

Take the Hill 300
Tarrant Baptist Good Will Center 25
Tell the Generations Following 43, 44, 74, 114, 115, 135, 142, 313
Terry, Jack D. Jr. 36, 40, 44, 49, 52, 62, 63,
    71, 72, 73, 75, 82, 85, 87, 99, 104, 107, 110, 112, 140, 160, 177, 178, 188, 189,
    191, 201, 206, 207, 208, 211, 212, 217, 218, 223, 233, 244, 249, 254, 262, 265,
    278, 280, 286, 287, 291, 292, 304, 308, 317, 321, 324, 325, 326, 327, 328, 331,
    335, 336, 338, 341, 342, 343, 344, 345, 347, 349, 350, 352, 354, 355
Texas Alliance Raceway Ministries (TxARM) 300
Texas Baptist Association of Ministries with the Aging (SBAMA) 213
Texas Baptist Religious Education Association 16
Thames, Trey 335
The Company 171, 226, 270
The J. Dalton Havard School for Theological Studies,
    Park Place Campus, Houston, TX 276
Theological Education by Extension (TEE) 67, 152
The School of Church Music 33, 35, 43, 57, 70, 78, 84, 99, 105,
    109, 110, 128, 146, 164, 168, 169, 173, 174, 181, 187, 193, 194, 198, 201, 224,
    236, 239, 250, 255, 261, 265, 297, 318, 331, 335, 336, 338, 342, 345
The School of Evangelism and Missions 276
Thomas, Clay 19, 272, 300
Tidwell, Charles A 34, 36, 49, 54, 61, 88, 95, 97, 101, 177, 219
Titus, Devi 351

Tolar, William B. 96, 104, 123, 191, 211, 224
Tomlin, Greg...287
Touch the World, Impact Eternity\" Campaign..234
Travis Avenue Baptist Church 32, 109, 167, 173, 192, 198, 206,
    216, 217, 257, 258, 307, 331
Truett Auditorium 79, 103, 119, 134, 141, 142, 143, 266,
    270, 292, 295, 297, 307, 331
Trustee Meeting 13, 51, 52, 75, 76, 108,
    109, 119, 150, 157, 158, 159, 169, 170, 176, 192, 205, 206, 215, 217, 224, 234,
    235, 261, 275, 276, 278, 280, 283, 286, 290, 298, 304

U
Unified Southwestern Counseling Program Model 319
Upward 90 – 1985-1990 150

V
Vassar, J. R. 263, 321
Vaughan, Robert 284
Vision for Excellence 199, 200

W
Waller, Gary W. 109, 151, 192, 201, 285, 286
Walsh Counseling Center..326
Walsh, F. Howard...52
Walter, Jim Woodrow... 159, 251, 311
Watkins, Derrel 71, 86, 125, 163, 165, 208
Webb Roberts Library 149
Welch, Robert 192, 224, 276, 277, 303, 304, 353
Westerhoff, John...285
West, Shelia 90, 202, 309
White, David 28, 125, 226, 260
Wicker, Dana Abernathy 250, 338
William R. Marshall Center for Theological Studies 283, 310
Williams, C. B. 13
Williams, James D. 36, 49, 56, 71, 131, 151

Williams, J. Howard 28, 29, 31, 32, 102, 126, 205, 225, 264, 299, 323, 335, 347
Wills, Keith C. 126, 152
Wilson, George R. 71
Winburn, Sarah 339
Winter Olympic Games in Salt Lake City on February 8-24, 2002 262
Woman's Leadership Consultation 202, 207
Woman's Missionary Training School 13, 16, 21
Woman's Missionary Union of Texas 28
Women's Studies Program 281, 289, 304
World Mission Center 293
Wyrtzen, Don 297, 336

Y

Yount, William R. 127, 151, 159, 160, 223, 224, 329
Youth Lab 37, 66, 88, 111, 124, 139, 151, 166,
 167, 195, 199, 202, 209, 225, 252, 258, 264, 268, 270, 271, 282, 283, 287,
 288, 292, 293, 299, 308, 334, 339
Youth Ministry Lab 37, 162, 182, 209, 214, 237, 263, 270,
 282, 293, 308, 321, 334, 339, 348

Z

Zettler, Laura 304

Numbers

21st Century Committee 239, 248
21st Century Task Force 227
58 Million Master Plan 254
75th Anniversary Celebration Year 135, 191
1963 Baptist Faith and Message 33, 266